Introduction

We are in the middle — or possibly at the beginning —— —— ecological crisis: how are we to respond? The usual reply to this question is to list a series of behavioural changes alongside a number of technological innovations which, combined, will "fix" the problem. This mirrors our culture's mechanistic approach to most problems: it externalizes wherever possible.

But suppose our real problem is not with externals, but within ourselves? That the external world is merely reflecting a flawed internal condition, just as a body in the grip of a disease signals its ill-health by displaying a range of external symptoms? Among ecologists there is an emerging group called "deep ecologists" who claim that a resolution to the crisis before us will only be found by a fundamental change in humankind's *understanding* of its relation to the natural world. They argue that without that change we will simply move from one particular problem to another in a never-ending round of sticking plasters over ulcers mysteriously appearing before us and demanding our urgent attention. In other words, if the disease arises from our false beliefs about our relation to the natural world, we must address the disease itself and not merely its symptoms.

Deep ecology — a term coined by Arne Naess in the early 1970's — is attracting an increasing number of supporters as the immensity of the ecological crisis becomes apparent and this book starts from an acceptance of its general veracity. But it also seeks to go at least one step further: it explores the possibility that the erroneous assumptions concerning our relation to the natural world are symptomatic of a more wide-ranging and deeper failure of philosophic understanding — and that we need to see the failure of our dealings with the natural world in a wider context. This is, perhaps, a difficult position to argue — not because the philosophical consensus (such as it is) of our society is beyond reproach, but because the very idea that philosophy is the problem is one that is likely to be viewed with profound scepticism. It was with this in mind that when the Prometheus Trust organized its 2017 conference, "Deep Philosophy, Deep Ecology"; its initial invitation started with these words:

> Philosophy in the west — especially in its English-speaking part — has been considered an isolated and private venture, with little influence upon the way in

which societies conduct themselves: like Earth itself in Douglas Adam's *Hitchhikers Guide to the Galaxy*, its description hovers between "harmless" and "mostly harmless". But is this really the case? Can we trace today's ecological crisis to the philosophy (or philosophies) adopted consciously or unconsciously in recent centuries? Perhaps the errors embedded within it are now revealed as very far from harmless – in fact a flawed philosophy may be the most toxic thing known to humankind.

Why is it that we humans behave the way we do? The short answer is *because of what we believe*. No other species on Earth has such a widely differing range of behaviours than humankind, and this is because so much of our activity arises from a set of beliefs which overrides or at least significantly modifies our instinctive behaviour. Beliefs arise through a mixture of careful thinking, occasional revelations, emotional and instinctive reactions to experiences, and unexamined assumptions largely inherited from previous generations as they coalesce in the present age. The thought, runs the old adage, is father to the deed – and we might add that the worldview which frames the thought is grandmother to the deed.

Philosophy is the means *par excellence* by which we bring the best of our thoughts to bear upon the activities of life, whether those activities are inner or outer ones: it allows revelations, experiences, assumptions, and the fruits of others' thinking to be built into a coherent whole by each philosophical individual. The misconception that philosophy is the reserve of specialists in university departments and not an integral part of every human being's life runs counter to the affirmation of Socrates in the *Apology* – "the unexamined life is not lived". If we are to change our behaviour for the better, collectively and individually, we all need to philosophize, and this is especially the case in an age of rapid change in which repeating the patterns of our grandparents' way of life is not an option.

This is not a conventional academic book. What you have in your hands are the transcribed voices of thinkers applying their minds to the question of the relationship between humankind and the planet and its wider philosophical context. But their words come to you direct, not filtered through the lens of other experts and this immediacy challenges you to respond in kind, honestly and from the

Deep Philosophy, Deep Ecology

PAPERS FROM THE PROMETHEUS TRUST CONFERENCE, 2017

Editor
Mary-Ann Crumplin

Contributors
Etain Addey
Tim Addey
Robert Bolton
Kevin Corrigan
Mary-Ann Crumplin
Stuart Dunbar
Paul Fagan
Sally Jeanrenaud & Jean-Paul Jeanrenaud
Eccy de Jonge
Marilynn Lawrence
Freya Mathews
Ann van Ryn
Valeria Zanon

The Prometheus Trust

The Prometheus Trust
7 Pine Crest Way,
Bream, Lydney,
Gloucestershire, GL15 6HG, UK

A registered charity, number 299648

Deep Philosophy, Deep Ecology

ISBN 978 1 898910 701

The front cover is a picture of Ardmair Bay, Scotland, by
Andrew Tobin – reproduced with his kind permission.

British Library Cataloguing-in-Publication Data. A catalogue
record for this book is available from the British Library.
Printed in the UK by

Printed in the UK by 4edge Limited, Hockley

Contents

Connection

Anthropocene

Thinking: Western, Eastern, Ancient

heart. Underlying that challenge is the affirmation that you are a philosopher with a right – and a responsibility – to claim philosophy as your own and to shape your activities in accord with it. The ecological crisis serves to illustrate in the starkest of terms what is at stake if we fail to embrace good philosophy.

The anthology began life as an interdisciplinary conference held over several days and organised by The Prometheus Trust in summer 2017. It was apparent from the start that the theme of 'Deep Philosophy, Deep Ecology' is one which has the potential to draw a response from almost all of us. Perhaps not every reader will respond to every single voice here because, being different, we all focus our attention differently – but there will undoubtedly be several chapters in this collection that engage and provoke you to further thought. The chapters that make up the anthology differ in content and style; some are presented in a more or less academic way, while others are much less slanted in that direction. The book as a whole is not offering a single diagnosis of the ecological crisis or a single solution to it: but this is not a weakness – quite the reverse, it is a strength because it requires the reader to weigh up for him or herself the complimentary or even conflicting views of the main issues. The anthology invites you in to join in a dialogue of real importance centred around the questions, "what are we?" and "what are we to do?" The ecological crisis has revealed how much depends upon the wisdom of humankind's response.

The original conference opened with a keynote address from Tim Addey, *Delphic Ecology*, and so it is that we begin the anthology with this contribution. It explores the relevance of the famed exhortation, "Know Thyself", which was said to be written at the entrance of the Delphic sanctuary of Apollo – the oracular centre to which so many of the Hellenistic world would go to seek guidance to the pressing questions of life. At the heart of the chapter is the view that we need to understand human life in the larger context of an overflowing of goodness which links all things in the universe to each other and, ultimately, to a unifying first principle which cannot be named but which Plato gave the title "the Good".

The theme of oracular wisdom is continued in the next chapter, *The Ibis Omen*, from Etain Addey: here we have a story drawn from life in which we see how the inner reality of the physical manifest universe speaks to those human communities who know how to listen in a language composed of the world's bodies. The ancient narratives which all human cultures have woven out of the rocks, trees, rivers and living creatures of their own particular place reach out towards the One, offering a human framework of meaning for this living dialogue.

Valeria Zanon's chapter, *Brotherhood as the Relation between Man and Nature: a comparison between St. Francis of Assisi & the Spiritual Wheel*, explores an important and largely overlooked strand of medieval Christianity and its connection to Native American thinking. The Franciscan embrace of the All – our fellow creatures, the Sun and Moon, the Elements and even Death – has much to teach us and sits easily alongside cultures with roots established before and beyond modern materialism.

Plato's Conscious Universe and the Unity of Things from Stuart Dunbar considers consciousness implicit in the living cosmos of Plato's *Timaeus*. He asks about the effects of our movement away from natural life towards artificial lifelessness: does our construction of a manmade world dim our recognition of other forms of internal experience participated in by other kinds of creatures? Does this, in turn, undo our relations with others? And can we rekindle our sensitivity to the "dance of daffodils" and the whole pulse of the living cosmos that held Wordsworth's inner eye?

Ann van Ryn's chapter, *The Intelligible Intricacy of the Natural World*, is the first of two pieces that centre on the philosophy of Plotinus. In this chapter we see how the principles articulated by a third century Platonist are developed by a series of more recent thinkers – David Bohm, James Lovelock, Eyjolfur Emilsson, Rene Guenon amongst others – to show how the whole of reality can be understood as a unitive vision embraced by the contemplative intellect and the moving soul.

In *An Ecstatic Naturalist Approach to the Anthropocene*, Marilynn Lawrence offers us the possibilities enshrined in Ecstatic Naturalism (in its various forms) which understands the natural world as the primary locus of enquiry, and which therefore includes within itself anything which other philosophies claim lies above or beyond it. From this viewpoint we must see that nature is not only an ordered whole, but also it is simultaneously an ordering whole – both nature nurtured and nature nurturing. It thus provides a profound challenge to the commonly accepted worldview which requires nature to be a patient to our agency.

In *Navigating the Anthropocene: Insights from the Wisdom of the Corpus Hermeticum*, jointly authored by Sally and Jean-Paul Jeanrenaud, the reader is invited to consider the Hermetic "three heads of knowledge" – God, Cosmos and Man – as a way of understanding and integrating the (apparently) competing narratives of reality which humankind tell to each other. Such an integration, it is argued, serves as a basis for a spiritual life which would benefit rather than harm the world in which we find ourselves.

Paul Fagan, in exploring the philosophy of John Locke in his *How Lockean Influence May Contribute to an Ecological Ethos,* takes on what he openly admits is a surprising and difficult task: can he find within Locke's philosophy an answer to the problems which many attribute to the attitudes arising from the so-called "age of enlightenment" philosophers? Locke, the "father of liberalism", does have principles of moderation, sharing and charity – can these be widened to the point where true sustainability is achieved?

The next chapter moves us in a radically different direction: Eccy de Jonge in her *Thinking Ecologically: a post-Enlightenment perspective* explores what a philosophy might yield if it rejected entirely any suggestion of anthropomorphism and any denigration of the body. Setting off from the position that the body is the essential being that connects us to others (including non-human nature) the chapter suggests that such an affirmation moves us into the now.

In *Returning to Wonder,* Mary-Ann Crumplin tackles the philosophical groundwork upon which our contemporary approach to environmental ethics founders. She links Emmanuel Levinas's ethics of alterity to the spirit of our ancient Common Law approach to questions of law and responsibility, an approach that still stands in jurisprudence today. And from here, argues that recognising justice as a question of response-ability rather than accountability signals the change of heart that leaves room for a return to a more sympathetic relationship with the living world around us.

During the conference a paper was given from Australia via video – Freya Mathews' *Do the Deepest Roots of a Future Ecological Civilization Lie in Chinese Soil?* In it we find a challenge to the direction that philosophy has taken in the West insofar as it treats its truths as primarily abstract constructs produced by logical operations: this is in contrast to those approaches to life which seek to become sensitive to, and aligned with, an already existing reality. The way of Tao rooted in the soil of China, as an example of this second approach, is offered as an alternative to the present destructive course of our civilization.

The Relation of Crisis to Constant Order from Robert Bolton examines what has been lost by modernity's embrace of exclusively empirical and materialist philosophies – in particular our collective loss of confidence in purpose (both our own, and that of creation as a whole). The chapter asks us to reassess our understanding of cyclical crises within the framework of an underlying and constant order: the resulting mindset would, it is suggested, allow us to respond intelligently to the present crisis.

The last chapter returns again to Plotinus: Kevin Corrigan's *Graveyard, incubator or something much stranger? Blind World or Multiworlds versus Deep Ecology and Neoplatonism* also returns to the theme of a living and all-embracing cosmos. It explores neoplatonism (the last phase of the development of Platonism in the ancient world) as a comprehensive philosophy – a meeting point for other-worldliness and this-worldliness. This final chapter ends with the same theme with which our first one opened – the mystery of what Plato calls the Good – here described as "the source and refuge of all things, living and non-living . . ."

In our attempts to live sustainably, we have to move past the idea that one's own habit of recycling or avoidance of harmful consumption of resources makes so little difference as to be hardly worth the effort. So it is with the thought-life: what difference will it make if I as an individual alter my philosophical outlook - surely the momentum of the present consensus will carry on regardless of my own change of thinking? Such a doubt is, perhaps, at once both an over estimation and an under estimation of the self: each one of us has a place to cultivate – the garden of the inner self in which seeds grow into full bloom solely according to how we tend it. In a world of seven billion people, it may seem that that single inner life has no power to bring about the desired change – but the words of Lao Tsu are worth recalling: "The weakest thing in the world may overcome the strongest. The inner life is all-pervading . . ." Tend your garden, and who knows where the gentle breeze may take its perfume.

Delphic Ecology

Tim Addey

Abstract: This essay argues that the foundation of the whole of reality is, insofar as it can be named, what the Platonic tradition calls the Good – a principle that is beyond language and thought, but which can be understood as distributing to all things its own inexhaustible nature, or goodness, through an overflowing of itself. That as this overflowing establishes succeeding levels of reality, from the most powerful and enduring to the lowest reaches where things are the most transient and least powerful, the harmony of the whole depends on each thing receiving and then giving its own measure of goodness – acting, so to speak, as links in the great chain of goodness. That for humankind the most pressing task is to discover what kind of creature we are: for without this knowledge, we cannot play our full part in the great chain of goodness because we will not know what good we should be receiving, nor what good we should be passing on. Lacking self-knowledge we are liable not only to harm ourselves, but also that corner of the universe with which we have an intimate relation and influence. The Delphic exhortation "know thyself" is, then, the key to ecological justice and friendship.

* * *

What kind of reality do we humans find ourselves in? What part do we play in this reality? Does the way we play that part make any difference to the unfolding of things? These are some of the fundamental questions which the sages and philosophers of all times and lands have pondered: indeed one might claim that every man and woman who has ever lived has had to give consideration to them, for no human life can be lived without some kind of response to them – as Socrates said, the unexamined life is not lived.[1] The difference between the wise and the foolish is only a matter of how easily satisfied the individual is with a superficial response to these

---

[1] The *Apology*, 38a.

questions before getting on with the business of shaping his or her life in the light of that response.

Very well: if we are going to pose such basic questions, let us return to the most foundational level of reality. The foundation and principle of all particular things cannot itself be conditioned by any quality or measure: it must be beyond all things which allow speech or thought to be true. It cannot be *being itself* because, if the foundation is being, non-being could play no part in the drama of the all — as it certainly does. Nor can it be any of the particular forms or characteristics which appear in the world of being: it cannot even be *form itself*, because an integral part of reality is the formless substratum of infinite receptivity[2] in which forms appear in the never-ending parade of things that "come to be". The foundation embraces being and non-being, form and formlessness, as the simply transcendent. We attempt to conceive it in some way, but at every turn we must reject as too constricting all those things which allow us to think — identity and otherness, change and permanence, whole and part, number, and so on. It seems we are defeated before we begin.

And yet we act and think and all the distinctions we dismissed from the foundation play their busy parts in our experience of reality. Whatever the nature of the foundation is, it cannot be withdrawn from any particular thing without that thing immediately becoming true non-entity; nor can it be withdrawn from any particular quality without causing that quality to become utterly powerless in shaping things and experiences. Our most important task is, I suggest, to find some way of understanding that which is beyond all understanding in such a way as to ensure that our thoughts and actions draw most directly upon its ineffable power — and that the boundaries we seem to place upon that which is boundless are in harmony with it and with all other forms which it allows to manifest.

So many of the world's religions and philosophies have attempted this task, each using its own terms, in order to draw the individual into the mystery of the foundation. Here, for example, is Lao Tzu:

---

[2] Plato, in the *Timaeus* (48e-51d) speaks about this as the *chora*, the "nurse and mother of all", saying that it "never departs from its own proper power, but perpetually receives all things, and [itself] never contracts any form in any respect similar to one of the impressing forms [which it receives]": so elusive is this formless "something" that Timaeus claims it cannot be spoken of without deception.

All-pervading is the Great Tao. It extends at once to the right and to the left. All beings live by receiving it, and all are in its care. It accomplishes its works, but claims no title of merit. It cherishes and nurtures all, but does not assume their lordship. It ever seeks the innermost, and its name is in the smallest. All things return to it – Tao their final root. But Tao is not increased thereby, nor claims to be their ruler; and its name is in the greatest . . . Before Heaven and Earth existed there was already something undefined but already perfect. How calm it was and formless; all-forereaching without effort – the universal Mother. I do not know its name but for title call it Tao.[3]

Now for a westerner, to hear that title – Tao – may lead him or her to understand how mysterious, how immanent and at the same time how transcendent it is. We are unlikely to misrepresent it as something particular, but neither are we likely to misrepresent it as something altogether removed from each particular thing. We understand that to remove Tao from anything will immediately mean that it is transferred to non-entity; that the whole of reality – both material and immaterial – is sustained by Tao and yet the whole taken as one is still not Tao.

The ecological crisis we face today is truly global and distinctions of East and West are likely to be lost in the coming shared conflagration: nevertheless there is one important way in which the crisis is western – in the sense that the underlying worldview developed especially over the last 3 or 4 centuries in the western world is being adopted by everyone.[4] The madness of the pursuit of infinite growth, of boundless consumption, in which all nature is dedicated to the gratification of human desires without regard for justice has taken hold like an incurable fever: every government promises annual growth *for ever*, and no politician ever suggests that we have enough, let alone the possibility that we already have too much. Like separated parents competing for the affections of their children, they seek to pile their citizens with useless toy upon useless

---

[3] *Tao Teh King*, verses 34 and 25. The Shrine of Wisdom translation, slightly adapted.

[4] For a brief overview of the philosophical roots of this dominant worldview, see Brendan O'Byrne's essay, 'The Urgency of Platonism: the Philosophical Background to the World Crisis' in *Platonism and the World Crisis*, 2010, Westbury, The Prometheus Trust.

toy while ignoring the true gift of cultivating temperance and justice within their own sphere. Has any politician ever said that he or she thought that their country was wealthy enough? That while there are questions of the distribution of wealth to be sorted out, there is no longer any reason to grow the economy?

Perhaps then we must address the crisis in terms which underlie western thought since, I would claim, while the great truths of existence are shared by all great philosophies and cultures, it is the corruption of western philosophy that has been the accelerator of the crises we now find ourselves facing.

The great tap-root of western thought is Platonism – and what has allowed the flowering of our technological culture is what might be termed Platonic realism. Those who hold a superficial view of Plato and his tradition criticize it because, it is claimed, it has a dualistic understanding of reality, in which the external world is held in varying degrees of contempt. But this is very far from the actual case: it is Plato's insistence that the temporal world is the best reflection of the eternal world and that there is an unbreakable, living and intelligible connection between the two states that marks the Platonic tradition. All western science rests, firstly, upon the axiom that material reality is governed by immaterial laws; and secondly, upon the optimistic affirmation that the human mind can discover these laws.[5] You will note that the laws are to be discovered, not invented: recently, of course, an anti-realist stance has raised its venomous head which has somewhat obscured the realist position of western science[6] – but for the present, we should be quite clear that when Plato offers us the instrument of dialectic in order to better understand the nature of reality he insists that dialectical distinctions are to be made where there are *natural* branches or joints in things and that, therefore, truth is not projected from our human conceptions but is rather something already existing and with which we must align ourselves and our thoughts. As Socrates says in the *Phaedrus* (265e), when practising

[5] As Socrates says, "we ought to suppose and to search for some one idea in everything around us; for that, since it is there, we shall, on searching, be sure to find it". *Philebus*, 16d. The translations of Plato throughout this article are Thomas Taylor's (occasionally slightly adapted) except where explicitly stated.

[6] For a detailed examination of the Platonic "realist" basis of western science, and its challenge to the antirealist position which denies the reality of immaterial laws see John Spencer's *The Eternal Law*, 2012, Param Media Publishing, Vancouver.

dialectic, things "should be cut into species according to members, naturally; not by breaking any member, like an unskilful cook".[7]

But let us return to the question of the foundation. Where in the Platonic tradition is Tao? Plato himself uses two names – or perhaps, to be more accurate, two titles – for this truly ineffable root of all things: he calls it the One (especially when discussing metaphysics) and he also calls it the Good (usually when he is discussing ethics and cosmology). Compare the Taoist quote on page 3 with Thomas Taylor's opening to his summary of Platonic theology[8] drawn from his long and profound study of the wisdom of the Platonic tradition, which he called "a synopsis of the pagan creed" –

1 That there is one first cause of all things, whose nature is so immensely transcendent, that it is even super-essential; and that in consequence of this it cannot properly either be

---

[7] The same view prevails in the *Statesman* (262d), where the main speaker says – "In this respect, that if anyone should attempt to give a twofold division to the human genus, he would divide just as many [thinkers] of the present day divide. For these separate the Grecian genus apart from all others, as one thing; and denominate all other kinds of men, which are innumerable, unmixt, and discordant with each other, by one appellation, that of Barbarians; and through this one appellation, the genus itself appears to them to be one. But this is just as if someone, thinking that number should be divided into two species, should cut off ten thousand from all numbers, as one species, and, giving one name to all the rest, should think that this genus will become separate and different from the other through the appellation. He however will divide in a more beautiful manner, and more according to species, and a two-fold division, who cuts number into the even and odd, and the human species into male and female; and who then separates the Lydians or Phrygians, or certain other nations, from all others, when he is incapable of finding the genus and at the same time part of each of the divided members." Interestingly, Chuang Tsu (a Taoist of the fourth century BC) in the third of his *Inner Chapters*, uses a similar image as Socrates in the *Phaedrus*: when a cook is asked why his knife if always sharp, without it ever being sharpened, he replies, "I work with my spirit not my eyes . . . I follow the natural grain, letting the knife find its way through the many hidden openings *taking advantage of what is there.*" Chuang Tsu (1974) *Inner Chapters*, Gia-Fu Feng and Jane English, (trans.) Wildwood House, London.

[8] Thomas Taylor, the great English Platonist wrote an article for the *Classical Journal* in 1820, 'The Theology of the Greeks', towards the end of which he attempted to summarize the primary teachings of the tradition. He called his 24 point summary "a Synopsis of the Pagan Creed" – the article is reprinted in the fourth volume of the Thomas Taylor Series – *Collected Writings on the Gods and the World* (1994) Frome, The Prometheus Trust.

named or spoken of, or conceived by opinion, or be known, or perceived by any being.

2   That if it be lawful to give a name to that which is truly ineffable, the appellations of *The One* and *The Good* are of all others the most adapted to it; the former of these names indicating that it is the principle of all things, and the latter that it is the ultimate object of desire to all things.

That the two words are addressing a single first principle is clear – all the great Platonists of antiquity accept this and, for example, Proclus thinks it worth proving in the thirteenth proposition of his *Elements of Theology.*[9] In the *Parmenides* (in the first hypothesis), Plato has Parmenides himself strip the One of all qualities which allow particular things to exist and which also allow us to think about them. Thomas Taylor in his introduction to the dialogue says,

> But our intention in pursuing these mysteries is no other than by the logical energies of our reason to arrive at the simple intellection of beings, and by these to excite the divine one resident in the depths of our essence, or rather which presides over our essence, that we may perceive the simple and incomprehensible one. For after, through discursive energies and intellections, we have properly denied of the first principle all conditions peculiar to beings, there will be some danger, lest, deceived by imagination after numerous negations, we should think that we have arrived either at nothing, or at something slender and vain, indeterminate, formless, and confused; unless we are careful in proportion as we advance in negations to excite by a certain amatorial affection the divine vigour of our unity – trusting that by this means we may enjoy divine unity, when we have dismissed the motion of reason and the multiplicity of intelligence, and tend through unity alone to *The One Itself,* and through love to *the supreme and ineffable Good.*[10]

Since our conference is especially concerned with ethics I'm going to use the second of the tradition's titles, the Good, as the basis of

---

[9] Taylor's translation of this is the first volume of the Thomas Taylor Series (*Elements of Theology*, 1994, Frome, The Prometheus Trust); the standard scholarly edition is by E R Dodds, 1933, Oxford, Clarendon Press.

[10] Thomas Taylor (1996) *Works of Plato III*, Frome, The Prometheus Trust, p. 32.

this address – nevertheless, we should not forget that the Good is as mysterious and as elusive as the One of the *Parmenides*. I think it is for this reason, rather than issues of how far his companions have progressed in philosophy, that Socrates in the *Republic* (506d) is unable to speak about the Good, when pressed by Glaucon to describe the Good itself –

> Do not, by Zeus, Socrates, said Glaucon, desist at the end; for it will suffice us, if in the same way as you have spoken of justice and temperance, and those other virtues, you likewise discourse concerning the good.
>
> And I too shall be very well satisfied, my friend, said I; but I am afraid I shall not be able; and, by appearing readily disposed, I shall incur the ridicule of the unmannerly. But, O blessed man! let us at present dismiss this inquiry, what the good is; (for it appears to me a greater thing than we can arrive at, according to our present impulse,) . . . I could wish both that I were able to give that explanation, and you to receive it, and not as now the offspring only . . .

In fact, when we look closely at what Socrates does say about the Good we will see that he is forced into using either negative terms or, at best, emphasizing its transcendence and otherness

> And as both these two, knowledge and truth, are so beautiful, when you think that *The Good* is something different, and still more beautiful than these, you shall think aright. . . . (509a)
>
> We may say, therefore, that things which are known have not only this from *The Good*, that they are known, but likewise that their being and essence are thence derived, whilst *The Good* itself is not essence, but beyond essence, transcending it both in dignity and in power . . . (509b)

And the later Platonists, especially, are keen to emphasize this: "For The Good indeed, is exempt from all silence, and all language." says Proclus.[11] Plotinus, in his treatise *On Nature, Contemplation and the One* explores it with these words:

> What is it, then? The productive power of all things; if it did not exist, neither would all things, nor would Intellect be the

---

[11] Proclus (1999) *Theology of Plato*, V, 28, p. 366, Frome, The Prometheus Trust.

first and universal life. But what is above life is cause of life; for the activity of life, which is all things, is not first, but itself flows out, so to speak, as if from a spring. For think of a spring which has no other origin, but gives the whole of itself to rivers, and is not used up by the rivers but remains itself at rest, but the rivers that rise from it, before each of them flows in a different direction, remain for a while all together, though each of them knows, in a way, the direction in which it is going to let its stream flow . . . other things have their activity about the Good and because of the Good, but the Good needs nothing; therefore it has nothing but itself. Therefore, when you have said "The Good" do not add anything to it in your mind, for if you add anything, you will make it deficient by whatever you have added . . . But The Good Itself is without desire; for what should it desire? Nor does it pursue any thing; for it has never desired: it is not therefore intellect, for in this there is desire, and a movement to converge with its form . . . Intellect, however, possesses true plenitude and intelligence, because it possesses the first of all things; but that which is prior to intellect, neither needs or has; or it would not be *The Good*. [12]

If all this indicates the profound difficulties in recognizing, thinking and speaking about the Good, the other side of the coin is that since it pervades all things we are all very much concerned with it, and there is nothing alien about the good: it is for this very reason that I am suggesting that a more or less universal renovation of philosophy and the radical revisioning of our world and our place in it should be based on the recognition of its place throughout the universe. This curious situation, in which we are both very familiar with the good, and yet unable to grasp it is noted by Socrates in the *Republic* (505e): "This then is that which every soul pursues, *and for the sake of this it does everything*, sensing that it is something, but being doubtful, and unable to comprehend sufficiently what it is, and to possess the same stable belief respecting it as of other things . . ."

We are familiar with the good because we are creatures that are forever making choices: how many choices does each one of us make every day? Almost too many to count – and although most are very

---

[12] Plotinus (1967) *Ennead III*, viii, 10-11, Armstrong, slightly amended. Harvard University Press.

minor, and many made so easily that we hardly notice we are doing so – yet every option before us is ultimately judged upon its inherent goodness: whether we eat or not, what we eat; whether to marry, and to whom; whether to consciously philosophize or not; whether to go to war, or make peace; whether to turn left or right; to move or stand still; to act justly or unjustly; to speak or keep silent – everything we do or refrain from doing is measured against the goodness that it is expected to yield, and even when faced with two evils, the one with more goodness attached is selected. Let me repeat the words of Socrates, "This then is that which every soul pursues, *and for the sake of this it does everything . . .*"

The usefulness of all our possessions, whether they are external or internal resources, is entirely dependent upon whether or not we turn them towards the good: again Socrates:

> This I rather think, since you have often heard at least, that the idea of the good is the most important thing to learn: which idea when justice and the other virtues employ, they become useful and beneficial. You now know more or less that this is what I mean to say, and besides this, that we do not sufficiently know that idea, and that without this knowledge, though we understood everything else in the highest degree, you know that it is of no advantage to us: in the same manner as it would avail us nothing though we possessed anything whatever without the possession of the good: or do you think there is any greater profit in possessing all things without the possession of the good, than in knowing all things without the knowledge of the good, knowing nothing at all that is beautiful and good?[13]

Just as Lao Tzu exhorts the Taoist to cultivate Tao within and without, so Socrates exhorts us to cultivate the Good – not that the thing itself is changed or increased by such cultivation, but that we ourselves are entirely transformed by that act.

My view is that the crisis that lies before us is one that has arisen because of a shared worldview embraced by more or less the entire population of the world – around 7 billion of us – and that if there is a solution to the crisis it must be one to which everyone can give consent. The great advantage of considering the starting point of the all as the Good, and the underlying nature of the universe as an

---

[13] *Republic*, 505a

unfolding goodness, is that everyone should be able to agree that whatever name anyone customarily gives the first cause, it must in some transcendent way be good, and that we all have an inborn desire to share in that goodness – again, no matter what particular terms and practices we adopt.

* * *

At this point let me take a step back and attempt to outline what kind of universe is brought about by the Good: I'm going to frame my description in Platonic terms, because that's my own background and I happen to think that it is the most accurate.   However, the important thing here is the broad principle rather than the particular details – looking at the other contributions to this project, it is clear that its authors are coming from several different backgrounds and I'm sure that other terms and other concepts can be used to colour in the details of this universe.

The beginning, then, is the Good:[14] it is just what it is and transcends all states – strictly speaking we cannot even call it a cause since it must transcend even causality – nevertheless, viewed from within a world of causes and effects it can be seen as the first cause, producing everything by its own overflowing goodness.

Its first recipients, immediately rooted in the Good, can be considered as the primary agents of providence – that is to say, they begin the process whereby the simply good is passed on as particular goodnesses so that Being can be brought into the scheme, along with the possibility of different kinds of beings. These primary agents are, for the Platonic tradition, the Gods[15] – which Plato insists are authors only of good unmixed with evil.

---

[14] Let me emphasize one final time, that as the first principle and foundation of things it cannot be named, and that the title "The Good" is the closest approximation we can give to it – it is not the good which has an opposite, but something towards which even things we call evil are ultimately made to turn. As Proclus says in his treatise *On the Existence of Evil* (61,6), "It is not possible that evil exists without taking on the appearance of its contrary, the good, since everything is for the sake of the good, *even evil itself*." Opsomer and Steel (trans.) 2003, Duckworth, London.

[15] There is no space to go into detail here concerning ancient Greek theology – nevertheless it is important that those unfamiliar with those profound teachings avoid mistaking the highly symbolic language of myth for the literal truth – something which Socrates in the second and third books of the *Republic* is at pains to condemn.

From the distribution of particular kinds of goodness arises the whole eternal world of real being and intellect: within this world is an entire hierarchy of beings passing from the most monadic beings unfolding into a multiplicity – at each stage reducing in power but growing in number. In this eternal world, of course, are to be found the forms which will shape what succeeds: for eventually the power of the eternal world brings forth the temporal world.

Again, the first temporal recipients of this eternal power are the simplest and most stable of time-bound beings, filled as they are, with the stable knowledge which flows from eternal intellect; these Plato calls divine souls. Then follow daemonic souls,[16] followed by rational human souls, irrational[17] animal and vegetative souls. After souls come bodies of various types, and finally below the informed bodies is a substratum of matter upon which forms are impressed – a pool of "almost nothing" being constantly moulded into particular forms, flowing from *this* to *that*, from *that* to *this*, to and fro without end.

Whether this is an accurate description of the hierarchy is less important than the actuality of it: that it is a *great chain of goodness* with distinct classes of things each with their appropriate part to play as links in that chain. Some of its basic principles should be articulated.

Firstly, it is a systematic unity. This unity arises both from the fact that the Good never departs from itself and therefore is unbroken by its infinite reach into effects; and also from the binding power of love – that is to say the desire of all things for the Good ensures that every effect is itself and by its own power drawn to the centre of things.

Secondly, the hierarchy coheres through the power of similarity – effects attempt, as far as possible, to be like their causes, and causes attempt to produce things as much as possible like themselves. Goodness is passed onwards and downwards because things wish to imitate the first cause, and because the goodness they possess is a power so to act. Goodness is received from above because all things

---

[16] In the Platonic tradition daemons were considered to be the intermediaries between the Gods and mortals, constant participants of the goodness of the Gods and, therefore, always bestowing what is good to mortal-kind: a very different doctrine to the later Christian view of them. See especially the speech of Socrates in the *Symposium*.

[17] By 'irrational' the reader should not understand something as being against reason, but rather the characteristic of something which does not hold pure immaterial ideas before its inner eye.

wish for their own well-being and goodness is the key to well-being; the power to receive is itself an intrinsic goodness.

Thirdly, every entity within the hierarchy exists for the sake of the whole: its function within it is the cause of its existence.

The whole scheme is thus a finely graded hierarchy which unfolds goodness through the power of similarity – each level holding as far as it is able the goodness of its immediate cause and passing on to the next level down what goodness it possesses and is capable of being received. The higher in the hierarchy the more power each thing possesses – that is to say the more power to manifest goodness – so the movement downwards is marked by a diminution of power but an increase in multiplicity.

So here is the vision of reality as an unfolding of the Good. Everything begins with the absolute unqualified good, which is both transcendent and yet the underlying immanence within all things; as it overflows everything comes into existence – that which first arises being the primary agents of providential good, and as each successive and distinct class of goodness takes its place in the great scheme of things, so it receives all the goodness it is capable of receiving, and then passes on the measure of goodness it is capable of giving. Thus, everything except the first and last of things has a twofold power – that which actively gives and that which passively receives.

As the good is distributed throughout the universe in this hierarchy of good, we can see the procession of the Good itself into the all: and while the Good itself is undiminished by this procession, since it is the very thing which allows each particular to be, so it provides the inextinguishable connection between all things.

But this is only half the story: the Good is also the most desirable of all things – indeed we might call it the only desirable thing. And as each thing is brought into existence – whether as something eternal, something perpetual, or something purely temporal – so it is drawn into a dance of desire as it attempts to return to the Good, through whatever intervening principles which have passed downwards and outwards the underlying good of that thing.

What I think we must do is hold two views of how reality is: the first is the simultaneous procession downwards from, and reversion upwards towards, the Good, of the living power of goodness. This is the hierarchical viewpoint which rests on the distinction of particular things at particular levels. The second is the underlying simplicity of the good which pervades the all. This is non-hierarchical – everything in existence (of whatever kind) is a presentation of goodness and is therefore one, because the boundaries and distinctions within the hierarchical viewpoint are of a lesser order than the Good itself.

As the force of the present ecological crisis has imposed itself upon thinkers in recent decades the question of the place of the rational human soul in the unfolding of the scheme of reality has been raised: I think there are two extremes that we need to avoid under these circumstances. The first is to remove all distinctions and claim that human beings are no different from other physical animals – if we adopt this position we are unlikely to play our distinctive part in the passing on of goodness and, in reality, likely to worsen the situation: for good people to pretend that our powers of reason are not distinct is to invite others of less good motives to do as they like with their own powers of reason. The other extreme is one that we have strayed towards in the present era, which is to overplay our place in the scheme: when the monotheistic religions attempted to sweep away the panoply of powers above us in the hierarchy and teach that humanity was second only to God, the seeds of our present crisis were sown – this view, so contrary to the understanding of the ancient cultures of the West has profoundly distorted our thinking and, once modernism did away with God, made us the tyrants of the world. But, in line with Socrates' estimation of the tyrant,[18] we find that we are able to do as we please, but unable to obtain what we truly desire: we have emptied the universe of meaning and purpose, beauty and intelligence, and exiled ourselves from our own good. We need to look anew at our surroundings with a clearer, deeper eye for, in the words of the *Tempest*, the world

> "is full of noises,
> Sounds, and sweet airs that give delight and hurt not.
> Sometimes a thousand twangling instruments
> Will hum about mine ears."   (Act 3, Scene 2)

The universe and the great chain of goodness is greater than we can possibly imagine. Everything in this scheme is in a state of well-being and happiness insofar as its nature gives and receives the

---

[18] Plato's *Gorgias*, 466e: "despots have the least power in their cities as I stated just now; since they do nothing they wish to do, practically speaking, though they do whatever they think to be best." (trans. Lamb)

appropriate goodness: our first problem, then, is to discover what our appropriate good is, both in terms of giving and receiving.

The universe, it seems, is full of different kinds of beings with different powers and therefore acting differently: since activities naturally arise from the powers possessed, and powers arise naturally from the essence of each being, the key to our understanding our appropriate exchange of goodness is understanding our particular essence. Once this is known, we can then explore how that essence unfolds itself into activity – or, in other words how that essence plays its part in the community of goodness which is our universe.

It is for this fundamental reason that so much of Plato's philosophic path is firmly affixed to the Delphic exhortation, "know thyself". So, to take just one example, faced with speculations concerning the physical interpretation of myths, Socrates says,

> With respect to myself indeed, I have not leisure for such an undertaking; and this because I am not yet able, according to the Delphic precept, to know myself. But it appears to me to be ridiculous, while I am yet ignorant of this, to speculate things foreign from the knowledge of myself. Hence, bidding farewell to these, and being persuaded in the opinion which I have just now mentioned respecting them, I do not contemplate these, but myself, considering whether I am not a wild beast, possessing more folds than Typhon, and far more raging and fierce; or whether I am a more mild and simple animal, naturally participating of a certain divine and modest condition. [19]

Of course, to know one's self in the connected universe cannot be a disconnected understanding of one's self: context is everything. The more we study the structures of the universe, the more we are impressed by the intrinsic interactions between what on the surface seem to be quite disparate things: and this is especially the case when we study things from the point of view of life. In the physical universe nothing is more concerned with communication than life – the very survival of the individual as a living thing, as well as the survival of each species is totally dependent upon communication. In the immaterial world life is the great connector between being itself

---

[19] *Phaedrus*, 230a.   But see also the *First Alcibiades* 129a, *Philebus* 48c, and the *Protagoras* 343b.

and intellect: in the *Timaeus* the eternal paradigm towards which the Demiurge [20] looked in order to bring into being the manifested universe is called *autozoon* – "animal itself", or the living thing. In other words, the eternal universe is profoundly connected to the temporal universe because of the power of life to communicate across an otherwise unbridgeable gap. And, of course, since it is a living and intelligible paradigm that is before the Demiurge's contemplating and creative eye, the resulting manifested universe is not only good, but also alive and intelligent.

What we are, and how we cultivate our inherent excellences – that is to say our inborn virtues – must be understood in terms of the continuum of good: each individual human being as well as humankind as a whole is at once both a single entity and a part of the All. The unfolding of good is central to the idea of *eudaimonia* – well-being, happiness, living well – and as Aristotle says, [21] "But if happiness (eudaimonia) consists in activity in accordance with virtue, it is reasonable that it should be activity in accordance with the highest virtue; and this will be the virtue of the best part of us."

But here is our problem: what is our virtue? and what our highest virtue? These are difficult questions because we appear to have a mixed nature: we seem to be both incorporeal and corporeal – in Platonic terms we seem to have both a soul and a body. At its simplest, we have something which governs and something which is governed – this seems to me to be incontrovertible, even though we can certainly argue for and against the separability and independence of the governing part, and whether it has arisen because of the unfolding of intellect from some immaterial world, or from the complexity of the material living body. The unseen governing part thinks, looks ahead, directs, makes choices; the visible part necessarily follows: if the governing part decides that there is good reason for the body to be sacrificed for some greater end, or that it must undergo some painful experience, then it has the power to make this happen. When such a decision is made, and we then waver between doing what seems to be good albeit painful or what is less good but

---

[20] The Demiurge (in Platonic theology) is the creator God, who creates the physical and temporal universe after other Gods have unfolded the eternal world – the never-ceasing act of creation is therefore understood as an outcome of an eternal contemplation.

[21] Aristotle, *Nicomachean Ethics* X, 1177a11

preservative of body, it is not the governing part clashing with the governed part, but rather one wish of the governing part clashing with a different wish of the same governing part. Given this relationship, we must look to the governing part as the seat of the highest virtue – in other words, we are in the best state of well-being when we are manifesting the excellences of the soul, for virtue is perfect power and the greater the power the greater the possible virtue. It is for this reason that Plato prioritizes the care and cultivation of the soul above that of the body, and the care of the body above that of our possessions. *Eudaimonia* is ours insofar as we exercise soul virtues: and when in a *eudaimonic* state, we are most aligned with the Good, which certainly means we are receiving and giving goodness in the best possible way.

The virtues of the soul are those which allow it to bring its essential nature into activity – to direct itself and its life towards the good through its engagement with Eros;[22] to understand and know itself and the universe in which it moves through its engagement with wisdom; and to bring these two impulses together, so that to live and to know are one act. And, to summarize, to imitate the Good by becoming god-like – for as Plotinus tells us in his treatise on Virtue,[23] the person who unfolds his or her highest virtues will "choose a life of the gods" – "for the aim is not to be without sin but to be a god."

Whether we want to see virtue in these terms or through the lens of some other tradition it is important that we recognize that a key element within every virtue is that of establishing right measure: things dissipate when boundaries are lost, but become truly themselves when they give and receive within their essential limits; powers, too, are at their most effective when focussed but fail when focus is lost.

If we are right – that the human being is part of a continuum of good, receiving and giving goodness in appropriate ways when embracing his or her virtue – then there should be connections both upwards and downwards in the hierarchy of reality. The primary

---

[22] The universal desire for the Good – especially as it shines forth as the Beautiful – is the subject of Plato's *Symposium*, and the profound connection between the intellectual vision of the soul and Eros (Love, or Desire) is explored at length in his *Phaedrus*: here he calls the inspiration of Eros of all inspirations "the best, and composed from the best."

[23] Plotinus, *Ennead I*, ii, 6.

channels of goodness – being, life, consciousness – must have their paths through human nature and the more we understand ourselves the more we will understand other manifestations of these three great gifts. Now here is the problem we face: if we only recognize being, life and consciousness in our own terms then we will fail to see their extension both above and below our own level. If, for example, we cannot see consciousness within the tree or insect, we are, by a curious law of balance, unlikely to see consciousness in entities above ourselves. As our worldview shrinks and flattens our perception of depth in one direction, so we begin to flatten our understanding in the other direction. To my mind the point in Western history where we stopped looking towards and seeking to involve ourselves with the plenary hierarchy above the human level was also the point at which we began to assume that nature was devoid of divinity and intelligence: no longer could we say with the sages of the ancient west[24] that "all things are full of the Gods".

Worse was to follow: once we had denied the reality, the life and the intelligence above and below, it was not long before we stripped ourselves of these things and began the long crawl towards the position we now find ourselves in which we believe – despite the interior experiences we all have – that we are merely machines. We now worry that we will become superseded by the computers and machines which we are designing. Such an anxiety would, of course, be perfectly justified if we are the soulless entities we conceive ourselves to be – calculators without the anchor of self-rooted consciousness. As we suffer a loss of perception of elements of the hierarchy above and below us, so the equivalent elements within ourselves begin to fade from our self-consciousness and we flatten ourselves. Our understanding of ourselves, of wisdom and of life's joys become two-dimensional for we cannot escape the determining law of consciousness – that what we *know* we *are*. Or as Kathleen Raine so beautifully puts it:

> Little children have known always
> What Plotinus taught the wise,

---

[24] A phrase used throughout the long history of the Platonic tradition: Aristotle says (*De Anima* 411 a7-8) that Thales made this assertion in the 6th century BCE; Plato repeats this in his Laws, 899b; and Proclus some 1100 years after Thales constantly reminds his readers of this – see, for example, *Ten Doubts concerning Providence* 16,10 and proposition 145 of his *Elements of Theology*.

> That the world we see, we are:
> Soul's country beyond time and place
> Her bright self-image in a glass,
> Tree, leaf and flower,
> Sun, moon and farthest star.

In a gregarious universe in which the exchange of goodnesses is fundamental, the harmonizing virtue of justice requires each individual and each species to play its part. For that to happen in a species whose form of life is especially centred on intelligent choices, each of us individually, and the whole collectively must be able to prioritize differing aspects of life. Here is Plato, in his *Laws* (697b):

> Proper distribution, therefore, is this, to establish the goods pertaining to the soul, as the most excellent and first in rank, temperance at the same time being present with the soul: but as second in rank, things beautiful and good pertaining to the body; and in the third place, things pertaining to possessions and riches. If any legislator or city proceeds without these, and either causes riches to be honoured, or through honours renders something which is posterior, prior, they will act neither in a holy nor in a political manner.

Is this how we think? And is this how we act? Clearly not: at present the vast majority of human beings are acting as if the gaining of material wealth were the primary path to the good – although if you stop and ask anyone if this is their actual understanding of material wealth, and bring the question into focus, quite a few will hesitate to say that this is their view. But the proof of deeply held views is action – and virtually everyone behaves as if increasing wealth is the key to *eudamonia*. Every politician promises to introduce measures to increase the flow of wealth – they may argue about its distribution but rarely its intrinsic desirability – and austerity is held up as something to be avoided if possible, or at best a temporary means to long-term growth and prosperity.

The aim in a mature economy is, for almost all politicians, an annual increase in *incomes* of around 2-3% per annum: but what does this mean? It means an increase in *spending* of 2-3%, because apart from minor variations in savings rates, what comes in must go out. Are we really saying that our happiness depends upon our ability in 25 years time to spend 50% more than we do at present? Because that is the implication of the almost universal consensus regarding economic growth. Here is a graph showing the average individual income growth over the last 25 years in the UK (adjusted for inflation) which is very much in line with other mature world economies:

UK GDP PER CAPITA PPP

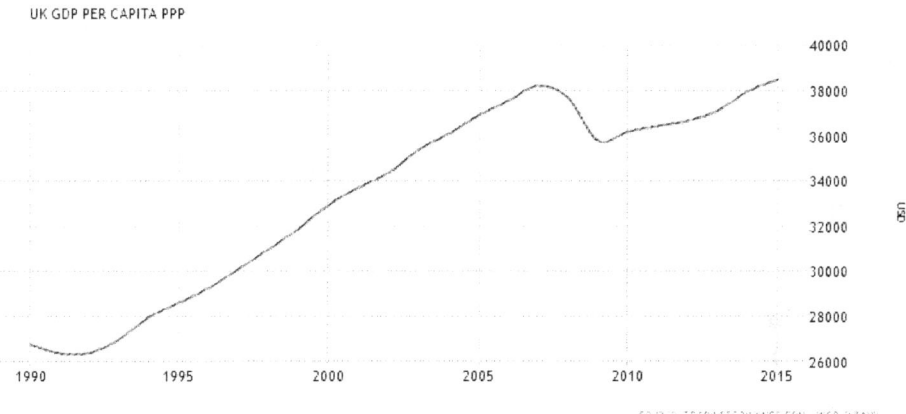

You will see that the average annual income for each one of us has risen from $26,000 to $38,000 over the last generation, despite the 2008 crash. Were we unhappy in 1990? Did we feel oppressed by poverty? Do we now feel 50% happier? Do we now think we have enough? Where is the politician who says that we should actually shrink our economy by 2-3% per year until we return to the level of, say, 1995 in terms of income and spending?

I am not going to go into the question of the rising economies – they are starting from a much lower base, but just to note that in the same period of our graph, the average per capita income of everyone in India tripled and in China rose sixfold.

We have a collective psychological problem here: we are in a curious state in which the human race knows it cannot continue to ignore the consequences of its behaviour but seems incapable of changing. So what kind of knowledge is this that does not manifest itself in activity? It is not, of course, a recent phenomenon: individuals and societies have frequently detached their thinking from their actions – nevertheless, I think that the ideals we have set before ourselves over the last three or four centuries have played their part. The primary ideal of so-called intellectuals from the time of the self-declared Age of Reason has been that of the objectification of knowledge which can only be relied upon insofar as the thinker detaches him- or herself from what is known. We hold everything at arm's length: truth is peered at through the glass of microscope, telescope and test tube. Knowledge is one thing, what we are is another, and what we do is yet another thing. Fragmentation rules. This is very far from the position held by Socrates in the *Protagoras*, the *Gorgias* and the *Meno* – here the ideal is that we pursue knowledge that is so completely part of ourselves, so profoundly united to virtue, that what we *know*, we *are*, and what we *are* we *do*.

The thoughtless race to the cliff edge must be arrested: individually and collectively we are reaching for an ideal which is unobtainable: an "end of the rainbow" which will bring ruin to many of the species we share the planet with, and which will bring about the growth of the greatest disease within our souls – that of injustice. It is an injustice that many of the most complex and beautiful species of animals which Nature has brought forth and nurtured over millions of years through her instruments of evolution should be thoughtlessly removed from existence, in order that humankind can enjoy a surfeit of material pleasures and comforts for a few short years; an injustice that across the world, in both sea and land, we steal the spaces which are rightfully the range of other species; an injustice that around the world in so many areas we impose ugliness where once resided beauty.

It is better that rust consumes all our possessions than for the body to become diseased; and it is better for our bodies to be assaulted by a thousand diseases than for our souls to become so corrupted that we are unable to direct our lives towards the Good. We think of ourselves in the midst of the accomplishments of modernism as more knowledgeable and more powerful than past generations, yet still the words of Socrates when on trial for his life are ignored:

> O best of men, since you are an Athenian, of a city the greatest and the most celebrated for wisdom and strength, are you not ashamed of being attentive to the means of acquiring riches, glory and honour, in great abundance, but to bestow no care nor any consideration upon prudence and truth, nor how your soul may subsist in the most excellent condition?[25]

---

[25] *Apology*, 29d.

Plato's greatest work, the *Republic*, is a meditation on justice for this very reason: he takes 300 pages to show that the rewards of justice are to be highly valued, and that even if there were no external benefits to living justly, justice itself is to be cultivated for its own sake. Several hundred pages or not, Plato is able to reduce his description of justice to a single line – justice arises when each thing practises one thing only, the thing to which its nature is best adapted. Justice, after all, allows a complex thing to act as one – whether that thing is an individual human with all his or her powers and energies, a city-state with its varied population, a planet with its inhabitants, or a universe with its almost infinite manifestations of goodness. Only the individual who considers himself or herself as entirely disconnected from everyone else, or the species that thinks it is the only one worthy of the name, would attempt to live without justice – and it is likely that the goodness of the universe would, in the face of that attempt, offer a lesson or two to expose the error of that viewpoint. The simple fact is, *there is no good life which is not just.*

* * *

So where is the path out of this dilemma? How are we to change the course of 7 billion individuals who seem to be running full tilt towards the cliff edge?

The best cures are those that give the least medicine but draw upon the very nature of the patient to reassert the healthy state.[26] The momentum we are dealing with in this crisis is a drive towards what is considered to be goodness: let that stand – in truth we cannot do otherwise – but the small nudge we need to redirect the drive is to be found in self-knowledge. To lecture somebody and claim that the pleasures of the senses, the comforts of the material life, and the luxuries of wealth are unfulfilling is, of itself, unlikely to be believed or have any great effect: something better must be put in their place. And this cannot be a mere abstraction – it must be experienced, or it is nothing – but our experiences are centred in the self, and if we are to stop our individual and collective selfishness, we must regain our

---

[26] Thus Olympiodorus in his *Commentary on the First Alcibiades* (54.17, 55, 9) says, "There are three methods of purification, the Pythagorean, the Socratic and the Stoic . . . the Socratic method converts likes to likes: by saying to someone who loves possessions, 'learn what true self-sufficiency is', or to someone who loves pleasure, '[learn] what divine ease is' . . ." (trans. Michael Griffin, 2015, Bloomsbury, London)

true self-centredness. Because we neglect the care of philosophy, we ignore the proper order of inquiry in self-discovery, rushing to the question "who am I" before asking "what am I?" We must discover *what* we truly are, rather than what we seem to be — the self, rather than the instrument — because our connection to the Good is necessarily centred in our essence.

What has emerged in modern thought as regards what our nature is, and what in consequence our good is, is a profound misunderstanding of the self: the body is seen as the basis of selfhood; the soul — if it exists at all — is merely a by-product of the body-based self. The signal to a body of the presence of goodness is pleasure (and, of course, the signal that goodness is absent is pain): if we are just body, or even primarily body, then the pursuit of the pleasure arising from the exploitation of nature would, perhaps, be justified. While this modernist assumption goes largely unquestioned we cannot expect the general pursuit of material wealth to be checked: utilitarian self-interest is no answer because it will merely drive us towards more hidden methods of exploiting nature. Pleasure and pain are experiences of the present moment: this is why the addict finds it hard to resist what he or she knows will do damage at some point in the future. The rational soul — the thing that can really think ahead of experience — is the only bulwark against the over-exploitation of nature and her present and future resources; but what we *think* we are we more or less *become*, and so as we imagine we are body, so we diminish the power to act as soul, and its impulses are quieted. Modern man and woman thus fall into a profound sleep of the soul — and just like the Sleeping Beauty story, a forest of thorns grows up around the long-forgotten palace. That which lies within the soul is neglected: we become what Pythagoras called the "people of the dream". Only the kiss of self-knowledge will awaken us to our own inner resources.

What lies within? What treasures are held in the depths of the self? Proclus, in his *Theology of Plato* writes,

> For the soul, when looking at things posterior to herself [that is, material objects], beholds the shadows and images of beings; but when she turns to herself, she unfolds her own essence, and the reasons which she contains. And at first indeed, she only, as it were, beholds herself; but, when she penetrates more profoundly into the knowledge of herself,

she finds in herself both intellect, and the orders of beings. But when she proceeds into her interior recesses, and into the inner sanctum, as it were, of the soul, she perceives with her eye closed, the genus of the Gods, and the unities of beings. For all things reside in us according to the peculiarity of the soul, and through this we are naturally capable of knowing all things, by exciting the powers and the images of wholes which we contain. [27]

The soul is intrinsically able to receive a greater good than the body – but only if it is active at its proper level, and, if it is filled with its proper goodness it, in turn, is more able to give goodness to those that depend upon it. If one could convince the general population that an inward turning is profoundly rewarding (whether in arts, sciences or philosophy) then the next step would be to talk bluntly about our actions in relation to our world and, indeed, towards each other.

Here, I think, is some of the things which need to be said:

Most individuals in the advanced economies of the world are too wealthy, and working too many hours; there are, of course, periods of life when one needs to set oneself up on a firm financial footing but we all need to be looking to reduce the time we spend servicing our material needs. For every advance in productivity through mechanisation and technological advances, we need to cut back on hours worked for money. The cultivation of wisdom – whether through formal philosophy, or the arts and sciences, through charitable works, or simply through a more contemplative way of life – is a truly human activity which should take precedence over the pursuit of material wealth once the basic needs of life are met.

Most advanced economies need to shrink – a difficult task to handle because of the corner into which we have painted ourselves with debt. It needs to be said clearly that sovereign debt – that is to say debt held by governments on behalf of their population – is a way of locking future generations into a level of economic activity which may well be detrimental in human and ecological terms.

The general education system needs to switch over to a more cultural and philosophic based approach: at present far too much

---

[27] Proclus (1999) *Theology of Plato*, I, 3, Frome, The Prometheus Trust, p. 58.

emphasis is given to education as a preparation for earning a living (and, by implication, consuming material resources). A liberal education liberates the soul; other forms enslave. It is not surprising that at present when someone finds themselves with leisure time more often than not, it is filled by the consumption of material goods and trivial occupations; this is nothing short of a scandal when almost everyone has had at least 15 years in our educational system – the opportunity to build on our inborn love of learning is consistently squandered.

The most academic students in our system are at present encouraged to embrace a post-enlightenment view of knowledge as ideally being purely objective and detached from the self. This is deeply damaging for all, but especially for the brightest minds because they are most likely to construct the strongest barriers for themselves and thereby cut themselves off from that living truth which is at once within and without, objective and subjective. Of course there are levels of thought which demand objectivity, but, as I have said, the ideal is to pass onto the state in which what we know we are, and in which activities naturally follow this unified state of being and knowledge. If we do not, individuals and humankind as a whole will be trapped in a cave of cleverness, far removed from the light of wisdom.

The more inclined anyone is to move up the political ladder (and I'm using the word politics in the widest sense) the more frugal needs to be their way of life: it is quite clear that there is deep suspicion amongst the general population of the so-called "liberal elite" – and in large part this is because such an elite enjoys material rewards well beyond the average, and moves in circles of great wealth. In Plato's ideal state the governors were required to live entirely without money and free of all luxuries – and this for the very good reason that those whose thoughts are taken up by material concerns are less able to give proper attention to their cultivation of wisdom, which is the basis of good governance. In truth, a liberal elite that is busy pursuing wealth may be an elite, but it is certainly not liberal: it is just as much enslaved as anyone living in poverty. Stable government requires the general consent of the people which is best brought about by a genuine sense of community, which can never arise if the governors are seen as unwilling to share the lives of the governed. Nor can we expect the general population to consider the pursuit of material wealth and ease of secondary importance if those who are – or claim to be – the wisest and most educated put it first in their own lives.

Above all the joys which arise from the cultivation of wisdom, beauty and interior goodness should be the inheritance of all: such gifts of the spirit are not consumed and exhausted like material goods; the more we cultivate these gifts the better our children's inheritance, in contrast to the results of our present over-exploitation of material (and exhaustible) resources. What we gain from a life of inner wealth is, by its very nature, unlikely to be enviously withheld from others, nor be the subject of greed or fear by a dispossessed class. Its treasures are not robbed from other species – quite the contrary, if anything our deepened understanding of life is likely to benefit our fellow inhabitants of earth and – if we are to believe the ancient teachings regarding the existence of an intelligent hierarchy above and below the human level – bring us into deeper communion with those intelligences.

Envy, greed, fear – all drivers of war (and high spending on arms to "prevent" wars) – thrive where there is injustice and grossly unequal distribution of wealth between individuals and between nations: we need to be part of a movement to address this because it is unlikely that we can act justly towards other species if we cannot act justly within our own.

* * *

There are many extremely difficult ecological, social, economic and political problems to be faced because of the thoughtless way we have slipped into our present condition. One is reminded of the countryman who, when stopped by a motorist asking the way to a particular village – "If I were you," he replied, "I wouldn't start from here."

But we do start from here. I hope that in this and the other articles which make up this book directions to that elusive village will be found.

Bibliography

Aristotle (2002) *Nichomachean Ethics, The Works of Aristotle IV*, Thomas Taylor (trans.) Frome: The Prometheus Trust.

Armstrong, A. H. (1966-1988) *Plotinus*, Volumes 1-7, Cambridge, Mass. and London: Loeb Classical Library.

Chuang Tsu (1974) *Inner Chapters*, Gia-Fu Feng and Jane English (trans.) London: Wildwood House.

Lao Tzu (1924) *Tao Teh King*, (published under the title *The Simple Way of Lao Tsze*), Godalming: The Shrine of Wisdom.

O'Byrne, Brendan (2010) 'The Urgency of Platonism: the Philosophical Background to the World Crisis' in *Platonism and the World Crisis*, The Prometheus Trust, Westbury.

Olympiodorus (2015) *Commentary on the First Alcibiades*, Michael Griffin (trans.) London: Bloomsbury.

Plato (1995-1996) *The Works of Plato* volumes 1-5, Thomas Taylor (trans.) Frome: The Prometheus Trust.

Proclus (1994) *Elements of Theology*, Thomas Taylor (trans.) Frome: The Prometheus Trust.

— (1999) *Theology of Plato*, Thomas Taylor (trans.) Frome: The Prometheus Trust.

— (2003) *On the Existence of Evil*, Opsomer and Steel (trans.) London: Duckworth.

Spencer, John (2012) *The Eternal Law*, Vancouver: Param Media Publishing.

Taylor, Thomas (1994) *Collected Writings on the Gods and the World*, Frome: The Prometheus Trust.

Connection

The Ibis Omen

Etain Addey

Parfa dersua cornaco dersuo, peico mersto peica mersta, mersta avief,
merstaf anglaf

Gubbio, the nearest town to our farm, has seven bronze tablets, dug up in 1444 and known as the *tavole eugubine*. They date from between the first and third centuries BC and they set out, in ancient Osco-Umbrian (a language which stands as a parent to Latin), the instructions for the ceremonial rituals for the gods. Scholars assume that these instructions antedate by several centuries the moment when they were cast in bronze. Ancient Ikuvium (the name comes from the proto-indo-european root word for oak, *aigo,* thus "the place of oaks") had a rich pantheon of gods and goddesses and oak is an attribute of many of them: sure enough, 87% of the trees in this area still consists of diverse species of oak.

Many of the ceremonial instructions begin thus: *"This ceremony shall commence with the observation of the birds",* and even in present-day Gubbio many surnames are bird names and one name, Uccellani, seems to imply "bird man". The ancient Bird Man sat high above the town on a rocky spur, outlined against the sky. His seat, carved out of the rock, still exists. As he looked down, he had the plain of Gubbio lying on his right, and the sacred mountain Fisio on his left - still a holy place for the Gubbio people, whose 12th century saint, Sant'Ubaldo, lies embalmed on the hilltop.

The Bird Man, sitting high above the priest and the people, was watching for the appearance four particular oracular birds. A great ritual silence reigned while he watched his "celestial temple"- a airy space delimited by specific points on the ground (the bend in the river, the roof of Salius, the roof of the gens Nonia, the cave of the god Hoius) where he waited for Hoopoe and Crow to fly in from his right and Woodpecker and Magpie from his left. Below, in the town, on a large, elliptical stone, stood the priest, waiting for the omens which would enable him to start the ceremony.

Only when the Bird Man called down "I have perceived Hoopoe from the right-hand, Crow from the right hand, Woodpecker from the left-hand, Magpie from the left-hand, the right birds, the right calls according to the divine wish, for me, for the Town of Gubbio" (*Parfa dersua cornaco dersuo, peico mersto peica mersta, mersta avief, merstaf anglaf esona mehe tote iiouine*) could the priest set in motion the long litany of incantations and sacrifices.

What was the understanding here? The implication seems to be that *if all were not well with the community of Gubbio*, the augural birds would simply fail to appear and any ceremony and all the expensive sacrifices (many oxen, bull-calves, heifer-calves, sows, boars and sheep as well as spelt loaves) would be null. If this were not so, why go to all the trouble of observing the birds, possibly a lengthy operation?

* * *

I am the first person to give credence to the efficacy of the traditional rituals. On a rational level, the sensation of sacrificing something tangible and precious for the sake of deserving an intangible good (health, prosperity, protection from enemies) is an understandable human act. I can even believe the extraordinary idea, suggested by the Italian ethnographer Ernesto De Martino, that there is a "cultural conditioning of nature" so that where a deep belief in the miraculous exists, miracles do in fact happen: in other words, there are different concepts of what constitutes reality. Many centuries of communities and individuals consulting the oracles and watching for omens cannot be dismissed as just childish superstition or clever political manipulation.

"Intelligence is the swiftest of birds" says the Rig Veda. The Gubbio augural birds themselves are very specific: crow, hoopoe, woodpecker, magpie. The Corvid family has a long and widespread tradition as harbingers of fate, divine messengers and prophets of things to come. The archeologist Maria Gimbutas finds many instances of birds of prey representing the Death aspect of the European Neolithic Goddess: the megalithic tomb at Isbister in Orkney contained sacrificed crows and ravens. The Vulture/Owl/Crow Goddess is a death-dealer but also a promise of regeneration. It was Crow who brought news of a lover's betrayal to Apollo, who scorched Crow's feathers black in his rage. Irish Morrigan, goddess of bloody battle with her premonitions of death sometimes appears as Crow. The two Ravens who ranged over the whole world and flew back to sit on the shoulders of the Norse god Odin and murmur their gathered knowledge into his ears were *Huginn*, Thought, and *Muninn*, Memory. In several North American mythologies, Raven is a demiurge and a Trickster god, crafty and knowledgeable. In Japan, holy crows are messengers of the deities.

It is interesting that a review of research in 2004 has found both Crow and Magpie to have a brain-to-body mass ratio equal to most great apes and whales and to possess high levels of intelligence in terms of social cognition, causal reasoning, flexibility, imagination and prospection.

Hoopoe is mentioned in the Quran as the bringer of distant knowledge to King Solomon, as a finder of water, sharp-sighted, a guide to truth, the only bird which cares for its elderly and thus a symbol of kindness.

Woodpecker is a prophetic bird with magic power, a guardian of trees; sacred to Jupiter, Mars and Silvanus, he guarded Romulus and Remus; in the German tradition he was a rain bird and a weather prophet. The legendary figure Picus who led the Italic peoples to new colonies, was the son of Mars. Circe, whom he rebuffed, turned him into a Woodpecker and his lover Pomona, the goddess of fruitful abundance, into a Magpie: so Woodpecker and Magpie are a pair of lovers, *peico* and *peica*.

Magpie is sacred to Bacchus, intelligent and cunning, and known as a thief. She is ambiguous as representing both good luck and ill-luck. Cornish folklore associates magpies with death and the Otherworld and says they must be greeted respectfully. In the Chinese tradition, Magpie is "the bird of joy" and represents good news.

And the Bird Man stands as Shaman, he "flies", he is the Hero who understands the language of the birds and interprets their divine messages for the community.

* * *

But we live in disenchanted times and nowadays no Bird Man stands above us on the high rock: we are left to work out the nature of reality for ourselves and it is a slow job. Daily life on the farm is full of hard work and our glimpses of the celestial come from those times when we pause to watch the oaks on the opposite hill heaving in the wind or to catch the swift passage of deer as they leap away from our line of sight or the winter flocks of finches wheeling across the sky.

* * *

For several days past, there had been small birds in great numbers swooping over the farmyard in the early evening, making a soft, babbling noise like baby ducklings. Noa came to look at the bees and she frowned and said, "Those are bee-eaters!" I looked them up in the bird book and she was right, but the illustration showed their exquisite plumage - blue, green, yellow, red and white (perhaps to bees they look like flying flowers?) and their companionable calling to each other sounded liquid and innocuous rather than predatory.

So late one afternoon that July, Martin and I went and sat on the field with the binoculars and tried to see this display of colour. The birds were flitting by so fast that they just looked like a blur in the sky, and from below their bodies seemed transparent. "If only they'd sit down for a second or two!" I said, but they never stopped their joyful weaving backwards and forwards over our heads.

In the end, we lay back in the grass and stared up at the sky and suddenly, right over our heads, like a scene from a dream, a whole flock of white birds appeared, flying very high up in a silent V formation: there must have been about forty of them. I had the binoculars in my hand. "Quick, look what they are!" said Martin.

I was just in time to see that they were ibis – cattle egret – heading down the valley. It felt like a vision from another time, as if we were suddenly back in the Neolithic with the skies full of a great abundance of water birds. How strange that we had looked in their direction just in those few seconds that it took the ibis to appear and disappear over the treetops towards the river Chiascio.

I remember when I had seen the first of them, the year before. I had been watching the sheep in the early morning when I saw a white bird circling the valley. At first I thought it must be one of our white doves, but it seemed too big. Then it came towards the hillside where I stood and flew in three wide circles around the sheep, lower and lower – until suddenly it landed on the back of one of the ewes, who stood quite still and unafraid. The bird was an elegant, upright figure and the word "ibis" came into my head - from who knows where? I am no expert on birds.

Later that morning, I realized the word came from an Egyptian hieroglyph and in fact reminded me of the ibis-headed god, Thoth: he was the God of Writing and Memory, because the tracks of the ibis in the wet sand looked to the ancients like writing.

We shared the morning shepherding turn, Martin, Dave, me and various visitors to the farm and slowly over that summer, we all saw the cattle egret - which is a small heron - and sometimes as many as six of them, landing on the sheep and watching for the grasshoppers that jump out of the way of the pasturing sheep.

In the late summer, just one affecionado stayed with the flock every evening down in the olive grove, as if he had elected himself their friendly attendant, until the weather turned autumnal and even he disappeared.

* * *

Now this sudden vision of a huge flock of white birds was amazing to me. We are so used to the idea that the world's wildlife is disappearing, that to catch sight of that abundance was almost magic.

It seemed as if, now that we had seen the whole flock, they had become visible to all of us who were sharing the early morning tasks. Dave or Martin would come down from shepherding and say, "I saw all the ibis flying up the valley this morning" and I would look up from watering the summer garden before the sun rose and catch sight of them as they flew over the ridge. And in the evening, I would come out of the sheep shed after the milking and look up – and there they would be, flying back down towards the river. I never lost the feeling that they were a vision from another time, they were so fleeting and so silent. It felt like a kind of privilege.

Then Martin and I had a terrible argument.

It was hot and there were a lot of us: ten members of my family, several visitors, and then . . . there was the film crew.

Two women had written to ask if they could come and make a film. This happens to us often and we are always torn between the uneasy feeling that they will romanticize this way of life and a desire to cooperate with people who want to "spread the word". So, hesitant, not knowing how to reply, I had let a whole month go by. In the end, the film-makers caught up with us and we invited them to come and talk it over.

As usual, Martin shuffled his feet and appeared reluctant in the extreme during our discussion with Ornella and Donata, while I was more forthcoming. It is an old contrast between us: getting on with it and staying below radar, or opening up towards other people, who may need inspiration, just as we did at the beginning? The two women were enthusiastic, energetic and persuasive and promised to come and work alongside us for a few days before they started filming. In our mind's eye, we saw the two of them following the daily work with a small video-camera, being as non-intrusive as possible, and we said yes.

Thus when they arrived with their two husbands and all their children it was a shock when they announced, "The cameraman will arrive with the audio guy and all the equipment on Saturday". Martin looked daggers at me. However, they were good-hearted people and everyone got on well, the old Pratale magic was working. I waited for Saturday with great foreboding.

The cameraman was a cynical old Roman and his audio guy was, as the profession perhaps demands, absolutely silent. I could tell the cameraman thought we were a bunch of old hippies and it wasn't until he tasted the homemade pecorino cheese that I watched his opinion of us rise vertiginously: skillful cheese-making is a high on the Roman list of cardinal virtues. His audio sidekick was amiable and truly invisible until, horror of horrors, they unpacked their equipment.

Martin was down in the vineyard when this unpacking began so he got the full effect as he came up for lunch. There, piled in the farmyard, stood enough film-maker's technology for a serious Hollywood blockbuster. I had seen it glittering in the sun, looking extraordinarily inappropriate as it stood towering over the woodstack, the donkeys standing round it in amazement and the sheep, ruminating on the flat place, looking on with expressions of ovine amusement. I would have liked to magic it away: hide it behind the house, move it into the deep shadow under the oak trees, mulch it over with bales of straw before Martin the Luddite saw it all.

During lunch, Martin set about Ornella and Donata with loud complaints about the level of technology, but they replied that to get true poetry in motion, all this equipment was vital. Martin, returning guiltily to his role as host, retreated into a grim silence and it was lucky the numbers at the table prevented it from becoming too noticeable. The spaghetti with cherry tomatoes and basil and the voices of small children were a grateful distraction and I wondered if we might get through the next few days without a major crisis.

Next morning, half asleep, I set off for the vegetable garden with my little grandson Seth leaping in front of me, longing to pick ripe tomatoes. Out of the corner of my eye I was shocked to see a battery of film cameras set up in front of the gate I'd come out of. Only my youthful experience as a pauper-cum-film extra prevented me from looking straight at the camera in horror. I took Seth by the hand and picked up the hose pipe and set off towards the bottom of the garden to get the water flowing. Seth immediately homed in on the tomatoes. '*Nonna!* Here's a ripe tomato!' "Well, love, that's a bit green ... here, look at that big red one. Pick that instead!" I turned round to go up the path again so as to start watering at the top of the garden, but my path was cut off by the cameraman with a great deal of technology on his shoulder creeping through the tomato canes at me.

Caught between Seth's picking frenzy and this piece of true poetry-making, I stayed where I was and re-watered the plants I had already done the day before. I knew I would bear quietly with this whole operation and I knew Martin would not.

So for two days, the filming went on and Martin growled in more and more audible tones. "Oh, Martin," called one of the women at dawn, "Are you going to let the sheep out now? Could you put on the same shirt you had yesterday please?"

Meanwhile I tried to enjoy having both daughters home with their partners and Seth and Isabelle running about the farm, as well as the film crew children and a very nice group of visitors, including two Roman lads who were pulling dead trees out of the wood and sawing them up. These lads took it on the chin when the cameraman mysteriously had them saw logs on camera for several hours. That was the day I had to go to town, so I wasn't home when things came to a head.

I only heard the story when I came home and Melissa explained that the film people had sent up a drone to take aerial shots and Martin had finally exploded and insisted that they would freak the sheep out and must stop. When he got me on my own, we had the Mother of all Arguments. My view was that we had misunderstood how this film would be made and this was nobody's fault: "Now we are at the ball and we just have to dance until it's over" as they say here. The film people were also our guests and I couldn't bear to have them upset. His view was that we are trying to live simply and it is ridiculous to go to such techno-lengths to portray it. We were both hot with rage and indignation.

I went down to milk the sheep and wipe my tears. The sheep shed is always a place of great peace. Nothing is as soothing as the sound of sheep ruminating and once I had finished milking, I stayed to enjoy the calm of their evening quietude.

When I had filtered the milk and left it to cool, I came out and gazed up the valley. No ibis that evening. The sun set and I went to join the others.

* * *

The fact is that I never saw the ibis again as long as the argument was unresolved. At first I hardly noticed. I had never deliberately looked for them, they had just appeared morning and evening, always a vision of delight. After a day or two, I began to feel left out. The others continued to see the flock fly overhead at dawn and dusk. I got a little desperate and began to ask exactly what time had they passed. I began to search for them: but no, they had just disappeared from my world.

Then I remembered the bird omens in ancient Gubbio. Was it possible that those bird omens were a real expression of the inner life? Here and now, in this ordinary, everyday world? I felt uneasy and incredulous: surely this was just a coincidence? And yet, what *were* those people noticing, millennia after millennia, about the nature of reality?

Apart from anything else, I felt *I was in the right.*

If I were in the right, why would *my* ibis disappear? How about *Martin's*? I couldn't ask him if he still saw them, obviously, because we were not on speaking terms.

It took several days to make the peace. Those deep differences which occasionally explode into the open are hard to get over. Eventually, grudgingly, we picked up where we had left off.

The next morning, without thinking, I looked up from the watering and the flock was flying over my head.

* * *

Now I imagine being a small child in the middle of a crowd, the entire population of Gubbio standing in complete silence behind the priest as he waits on the huge, elliptical stone gazing up at the Bird Man silhouetted against the sky.   This little girl knows they are all watching for Crow to fly in from the plain: an ordinary, everyday bird she has thrown stones at to keep him off the corn. But the deep, ritual silence is telling this child that Crow has another aspect: he is also a form of the great Mystery. This teaching is silent. But the reverent attitude of her elders tells her that the outer forms of the world are profoundly connected with the inner life of the whole community.

" *You should not ask but understand, you too, in silence, as I am silent and not accustomed to speak"*: thus would Nature reply to those who would question her, says Plotinus.

Etain Addey, Gubbio June 2017

Bibliography

Corrigan, Kevin (2005) *Reading Plotinus: A Practical Introduction to Neoplatonism,* Purdue University Press

de Martino, E. (1948) *Il mondo magico,* Torino:, Einaudi

Devoto, Giacomo (1977) *Le tavole di Gubbio,* Sansoni Studio

Emery, Nathan J. and Clayton, Nicola S. (2004) 'The Mentality of Crows: Convergent Evolution of Intelligence in Corvids and Apes' in *Science,* vol. 306, 10 Dec. 2004

Gimbutas, Marija (1989) *The Language of the Goddess,* Thames and Hudson

Brotherhood as the Relation between Man and Nature: a comparison between St. Francis of Assisi & the Spiritual Wheel

Valeria Zanon

1. Introduction. A Dysfunctional Conception of Man

In this writing I started from the quite obvious consideration that the world we live in is shaped by our actions: everything we do impacts – more or less evidently – on our context and can improve our lives or make them worse. In turn, our actions are guided and defined by our education, by our culture and by our deepest beliefs, even if unconsciously. The way we live and relate with our surroundings is indeed deeply influenced by the conception we have of ourselves.

Thus, the problems we are now facing may derive from a dysfunctional conception of the man-nature relation, based on the separation between them and on the predominance of one element (mankind) over the other. The predominant Western tradition has indeed turned the objective diversity of mankind into a constitutive superiority that allowed him to use (and abuse) all the resources offered by nature. Using Rachel Carson's words,

> as man proceeds toward his announced goal of the conquest
> of nature, he has written a depressing record of destruction,
> directed not only against the earth he inhabits but against the
> life that shares it with him.[1]

The mainstream tradition had so exalted the uniqueness and superiority of mankind that it lost contact with the very elements that allowed mankind to live and prosper: animals, plants, and the earth itself. Consequently, in order to achieve a radically and effective shift in our behaviours, we need to change first of all our deepest beliefs[2]:

---

[1] Rachel Carson (1962) *Silent Spring*, Crest Books, p. 52.

[2] This is a consideration that emerges clearly since the beginning of the environmental movement: referring to Aldo Leopold, Bill Shaw highlights that "(Leopold) does not invite us into a world of deep ecology. He does, however, urge upon us *a different way of thinking*, a different mind-set or paradigm" (my italics). For

the key question to which we need to answer is "what is the role and the place of man in a natural world which, at the same time, he needs for its own survival and yet pretends to dominate?"

In the last thirty years many authors have tried to challenge the predominant anthropocentric approach that stated the undisputed supremacy of the human race in the natural world; in this operation the starting point consisted of the recognition that other things, in nature, can have a value and a meaning independent of the values and meanings that men have attributed to them.

This was what emerged from the writings of Rachel Carson[3] or Aldo Leopold: they both[4] stated that we have to recognize that nature is more than just a "free-use" reserve of goods and resources, and that it provides us with goods that cannot simply be quantified in economic terms. Their texts are imbued with two main concepts: the first one is that of respect, from which it derives that we need to change our role as humans from conqueror to plain member of a land community, in which we live as citizens among other; the recognition of our place and role in this community should led, to Leopold, to the development of an attitude of respect towards other members of the community and towards the community itself.[5]

The second concept is the recognition of the interdependence between every being and its environment, from which it derives that the wellbeing and the development of every single part rely on a balanced relationship with the whole. This bond emerges through statements such as

> all ethics so far evolved rest upon a single premise: that the individual is a member of a community of interdependent parts. His instincts prompt him to compete for his place in

---

more about the analysis of Shaw on Leopold's work, see Bill Shaw (2005) 'Aldo Leopold's Land Ethic' in *Environmental Virtue Ethics*, Rowman & Littlefield Publishers Inc., p. 102.

[3] Her book *Silent Spring* is largely recognized as one of the "milestones" in the development of the environmental movement.

[4] I decided to mention just these two authors because of their relevance in the birth of environmentalism, relevance that has been recognized also by *Nature Study* in the article by Sean Duffy (1991) '"Silent Spring" and "Sand County Almanac": the Two Most Significant Environmental Books of the 20th Century' *Nature Study* 44, pp. 6-8.

[5] Aldo Leopold (1949) *A Sand County Almanac*, Oxford University Press.

that community, but his ethics prompt him also to cooperate.[6]

From this and similar affirmations also transpires the recognition of how delicate the balance between every part of the system is and how low our knowledge of every relationship taking place in so complex an ecosystem.

The words of Carson and Leopold (in recent times) were just the first on a long trail that reaches to this day: since then many other authors have deepened the reflection on these themes, some developing new perspectives, some widening their initial considerations. Just to mention one of them, we can find similar remarks in the words of Holmes Rolston III, when he points out that

> if we are to be human, then we have to distinguish ourselves from nature . . . We inhabit culture within nature, bracketing ourselves off from wild nature with an insulating culture. In doing this we demonstrate our excellences. But this anthropocentric account of the nature-culture encounter is *too one-sided*. Evolution and ecology have taught us that *every kind of life is what it is environmentally*, in its surroundings, not autonomously. Humans too are environmental reciprocals, indebted to our environment for what we have become in ways that are as complementary as they are oppositional. Dialectically, the character is achieved within us, but *the context is relational*.[7]

The recognition of the (quite obvious) fact that everything on earth – and so also man – needs a favourable context to grow and prosper leads to the awareness that this is not a one-way relationship, but that everything is bound in a network of reciprocal influences; consequently, Rolston says, if mankind wants to live a good life and prosper, we have to rethink our concept of ethics, widening it.

> Ethics is not merely about what the humans love, enjoy, and find rewarding or about what they find wonderful, find ennobling, or want as souvenirs. It is sometimes a matter of what humans *ought* to do, like it or not, and these *oughts* may

---

[6] Aldo Leopold (1949) 'The Land Ethic' in *A Sand County Almanac and Sketches Here and There*, Oxford University Press, pp. 203-204.
[7] Holmes Rolston III (2005) 'Environmental Virtue Ethics' in *Environmental Virtue Ethics*, Rowman & Littlefield Publishers Inc., p. 62 (emphasis added).

not always rest on the likes of other humans or on what ennobles character. *Sometimes we ought to consider worth beyond that within ourselves* . . . The real concern is for the other benefited.[8]

In the words of Rolston we can find the same appeal to a different kind of ethics that Carson and Leopold expressed in their works: the thread that winds through their texts is the recognition that the development and the application of ethical concepts cannot stop at the limit of the human horizon but, if we want to really fulfil our potential as humans, we have to consider and take care also of beings different from us.

Finally, this link between the wellbeing of the natural world and the wellbeing of mankind is also mentioned in the last encyclical of Pope Francis "Laudato si' – On Care for Our Common Home", when he states that

> Authentic human development has a moral character. It presumes full respect for the human person, but it must also be concerned for the world around us and "take into account the nature of each being and of its mutual connection in an ordered system.[9]

This encyclical emphasizes once more the inseparable bond that links our lives with our environment: first of all because our behaviours influence the places we live in and, vice versa, our environment's health effects the possibility of our having a good and healthy life. Moreover, and maybe more importantly, because the way we act with respect to our environment also tells something about the kind of person we are: an attitude of disrespect and neglect towards nature, treating the world we live in as a mere reservoir from which we get all that is useful for us without worrying or caring about the consequences are symptoms of a deep misunderstanding of our place and role in nature and can easily lead to the adoption of the same attitudes in different aspects of our lives.

All the authors I have mentioned briefly expressed some similar thoughts: (a) that we have to recognize that mankind is not independent from its environment, (b) that developing the wellbeing

---

[8] Ibid., p. 72 (emphasis added).

[9] Pope Francis (2015) *Laudato Si' – Lettera Enciclica sulla Cura della Casa Comune*, Libreria Editrice Vaticana, p. 8 (my translation).

of one can also lead to the wellbeing of the other, and (c) that if we really want to protect nature and to reach a stable and real state of wellbeing, we need to reconsider our relationship with nature, including in our ethical consideration also these elements (animals, plants, earth itself) that the main philosophical tradition has left aside.

This concept, although developed in relatively recent times, is just the rediscovery of something that has been said in other times and from other cultures.

In the following pages I will consider two different perspectives that, I believe, show some interesting similarities; and, in the final section, I will try to underline some aspects that, in my opinion, emerge from the analysis of these perspectives and that can be useful to shape a different concept of - and attitude towards - nature.

2. Our Tradition. Saint Francis's Theocentric Approach

The first perspective I am going to present is the one offered by Saint Francis of Assisi; the saint's attitude towards nature and creature has been recently mentioned by the Pope in the aforementioned encyclical, when he referred to Saint Francis as a "beautiful and inspiring model", underlining that

> Saint Francis is the example *par excellence* of care for the vulnerable and of an integral ecology lived out joyfully and authentically . . . He shows us just how inseparable the bond is between concern for nature, justice for the poor, commitment to society and interior peace.[10]

I will focus on what we can consider as the "spiritual will" of the Saint, the praise that expresses in words what Saint Francis expresses through his life: the "Canticle of Creatures".

2.1 The Canticle

This is a praise to God to thank Him for the beauty of creation, which is conceived as a visible expression of God's power, grace and love for man. The prayer is divided in three sections, each praising God for a different gift: the first praises Him for all of his creatures,

---

[10] Ibid. p. 12.

the second for those who forgive for the love of God, and the third for "sister bodily death".

It should be noticed that each section was written in a different moment of the saint's life: Saint Francis wrote the first at the church of Saint Damiano (a church in Assisi that played a really important role in the life of Saint Francis) in the spring of 1225, when he was sick; the second was written a few months later, in September 1226, and the third just few weeks before the saint's death, in October of 1226.

These are the saint's words:

> *Most High, all-powerful, good Lord,*
> *Yours are the praises, the glory, and the honour, and all blessing,*
> *To You alone, Most High, do they belong,*
> *and no human is worthy to mention Your name.*

> (1) *Praised be You, my Lord, with all Your creatures,*
> *especially Sir Brother Sun,*
> *Who is the day and through whom You give us light.*
> *And he is beautiful and radiant with great splendour;*
> *and bears a likeness of You, Most High One.*
> *Praised be You, my Lord, through Sister Moon and the stars,*
> *in heaven You formed them clear and precious and beautiful.*
> *Praised be You, my Lord, through Brother Wind,*
> *and through the air, cloudy and serene, and every kind of weather,*
> *through whom You give sustenance to Your creatures.*
> *Praised be You, my Lord, through Sister Water,*
> *who is very useful and humble and precious and chaste.*
> *Praised be You, my Lord, through Brother Fire,*
> *through whom You light the night,*
> *and he is beautiful and playful and robust and strong.*
> *Praised be You, my Lord, through our Sister Mother Earth,*
> *who sustains and governs us,*
> *and who produces various fruit with coloured flowers and herbs.*

> (2) *Praised be You, my Lord, through those who give pardon for Your love,*
> *and bear infirmity and tribulation.*
> *Blessed are those who endure in peace*
> *for by You, Most High, shall they be crowned.*

(3) *Praised be You, my Lord, through our Sister Bodily Death,*
from whom no one living can escape.
Woe to those who die in mortal sin.
Blessed are those whom death will find in Your most holy will,
for the second death shall do them no harm.

Praise and bless my Lord and give Him thanks
and serve Him with great humility.

Starting from this brief introduction, I will now try to underline three aspects of this praise that I found peculiar and interesting for our subject.

2.2 Experiencing Human Limits

The first aspect is that the praise to God originates from an experience of sickness and fragility, an experience that puts man face to face with his limits and weaknesses; disease drops all the masks of superiority with which we protect ourselves, and brings us to the awareness of our vulnerability, since we can no longer consider ourselves as the rational and invincible rulers of the world but become aware of our corporal and mortal status.

Pain and illness are certainly painful and destabilizing experiences but can also be of great potential to those who are able to welcome them in the "right" way, as the example of the "Canticle of the Creatures" shows us: the loss of our superior state due to sickness can indeed bring us closer to the rest of the world and helps us to feel the bond that binds us to every other being. Thus, such an experience of weakness and suffering can be transformed through an attitude of humble acceptance, thanks to which we are able to recognize our place in the world and our relation both with other creatures and the One from which we all derive.

This vision is reinforced in the last part of the Canticle, when Saint Francis praises God through "our sister bodily Death": this can be seen as the greater acceptance of the fact that we are not the master of the world, since we can't even control our life.

This expression of complete acceptance and the praise even for elements that are commonly feared by ordinary men (pain, illness, death) reveals a peculiar aspect of Saint Francis' point of view: his thought is not anthropocentric – and so he does not glorify or exalt man as the creature that has been created "in the image and likeness of God". He instead adopts a *theocentric* point of view:[11] all that exists in the world glorifies God, and the fact that the saint is able to recognize its greatness and its presence even in the extreme experience of death (that is, in the most radical annihilation of the individual) shows how the consciousness of his role as a mere creature is deeply rooted.

2.3 A Double Origin for "Brotherhood"

This theocentric approach is really important since it helps us to comprehend the real perspective from which Saint Francis considered the world, and the real meaning of terms as "brother" or "sister". This approach constitutes the second element of interest I found in this praise.

Saint Francis, as his biographers depicted him, always had a special relationship with every creature and had the ability to talk to them and to be heard: we can consider, as example, the episode of the wolf of Gubbio when Saint Francis by only speaking managed to tame the wolf that terrorized the Umbrian town; or when he preached to the birds that were listening to him with devoted attention.

This closeness with every creature also emerges in the Canticle we are considering: here, the feeling of brotherhood - not just with animals - extends to all beings, animate and inanimate, and even to abstract concepts such as death. The list of "brothers" and "sisters" stated by the saint ideally comprehends the whole creation: he first refers to the sun, the moon and the stars – as representative of the higher sphere that, in the cosmology of his time, was the closest to the divine sphere. He then descends to our world and, referring to fire, wind, water and earth, ideally encloses the whole of what constitutes our daily experience: the four traditional elements become the symbols of every creature that lives in our world, both animate or

---

[11] This theocentric approach has a really great importance in Saint Francis's thought, and it is the element that gives meaning and order to all his reflections. The saint's view is not anthropocentric but neither pantheistic, nor does it perfectly equate man to other creatures: the real centre around which everything revolves is God, that gives birth and meaning to every creature. This emerges well in the analysis of the Canticle in its entirety. For more about this theocentric approach, see Martin Carbajo Núñez (2017) *Sorella Madre Terra – Radici Francescane della Laudato sì*, Messaggero di Sant'Antonio Editrice, pp 86-87.

inanimate.[12] The last part of the canticle, as we have seen, even welcomes death, calling it "sister" and recognizing it as the necessary passage that can lead us to the presence of God and to His beatitude.

So, for Saint Francis the source of the link binding all animate and inanimate beings lies in the fact that they all share the same status of "creature", since they all derive their own existence from God. This would already be sufficient to provide the basis for the recognition of a universal brotherhood, which connects everything that exists.

But the bond lies further and deeper, in the very essence of every being: all that exists is in fact deeply intertwined by weaving the praises of God with his very existence.

Thus, for Saint Francis the source of the brotherhood between man, animals, plants and all that lies under this sky is *double*: on the one hand, all the creatures are connected by sharing the same origin and the same condition of having been created by God – and this is from the perspective of the *cause*. On the other hand, all the creatures are united by sharing the same activity, the same meaning, by sending the same message to the eyes of those who can watch: to praise God with their very existence, to be visible traces of his presence and power, and to witness his glory - and this is from the perspective of the *purpose*.

This is the very essence of the theocentric perspective expressed by Saint Francis in his Canticle: we are all brothers and sisters because (a) we have the same Father (and so we share the same status as creatures in front of the Creator) and because (b) we find our common meaning and signification in praising God and testify His magnificence. Thus, we can speak of a "theocentric interdependence", in which everything assumes its very sense in function of God: God that is at the same time the source, the guardian and the recipient of the universal harmony that transpires from his creation.

2.4. The Value of the Individual

However, such a perspective could have easily led to the devaluation of creatures, to the loss of significance of the single being that can be considered nothing more than one among a billion other

---

[12] Martìn Carbajo Núñez (2017) *Sorella Madre Terra – Radici Francescane della Laudato sì*, Messaggero di Sant'Antonio Editrice, p. 91.

creatures: if every being has meaning and is important only because he is a visible manifestation of the power of God, then his value is just external to him. It can be considered as just a means, only of value thanks to something else.

But the originality and importance of Saint Francis lies right here: obviously he believes that the reference to God is the ultimate source of the significance and the importance of every being, but he also recognizes the intrinsic value that every creature has for his own sake. When he praises God through his creatures he is able to see both the reflection of God in the single being *and* the unique and unrepeatable creature in front of him, that is worthy of respect in his own sake.

So the great contribution Saint Francis can offer us is exactly this ability to see everything through a "double" perspective: on the one hand, he emphasizes the brotherhood between every being thanks to their common origin and purpose, and in this sense all that exists derives its value and significance from God; on the other hand, he is also capable of recognizing the other in his singularity and can value it for its uniqueness. When he looks at a bird, a star, a tree, a man, Saint Francis can see at the same time the unique being in front of him *and* the trace of God in this single creature: this generates a double nearness with the being he's facing, a proximity that invites us to feel brothers with the single being in front of us thanks to the recognition of a bond that goes beyond what we can see and binds us, first and foremost, to a single Father.

The emphasis put by the Saint on the relationships (a) between creatures and their Creator and (b) between the creatures themselves is so relevant that it is possible to talk about a relational concept of identity, in which the bonds that link every creature are what deeply constitute the individual: without these bonds we cannot exist, nor prosper.[13]

3. Other Traditions. Native American Spirituality

This perspective is particularly close to the native American's one: I believe we can find some analogies that emerge when considering the native spirituality expressed through the concept of the "spiritual wheel", or "medicine wheel" in other translations.

---

[13] For another analysis of the Canticle and its composition, see also Jacques Dalarun (2015) *Il Cantico di Frate Sole - Francesco d'Assisi Riconciliato*, Biblioteca Francescana Edizioni.

3.1. The Meaning [14]

The concept of the spiritual wheel is not only an abstract one: it is a way of conceiving the world and a practical ritual that helps the believer to find his place in the world. The wheel has indeed an *ethical value* since it shows man his essence and his role in the universe, and so must be primarily understood as a practical tool to orientate beliefs and behaviours. It conveys various other meanings, as we can see.

It is the symbol representing *the universe and the relation* binding everything that exists: it represents the universal harmony, the perpetual movement that constitutes life and all the possibilities that are still not real but could become so.

It is the *tangible manifestation* of the abstract idea that everything is interconnected and that, if balance is lost in any of the parts, the whole system is broken. This awareness and the profound responsibility resulting from it are the basis for the development of a deeply respectful attitude towards all animate and inanimate beings, and for the practice of a behaviour devoted to maintaining this

---

[14] For other considerations on this concept and on the native American spirituality, see Giulio Fanin (2014) *La Visione Sacra degli Indiani d'America*, Area51 Publishing; and Giulio Fanin (2014) *Il Legame con la Natura degli Indiani d'America*, Area51 Publishing.

harmony through the recognition of a *"responsible limit"*[15], which we should observe in every daily activity.

The wheel also has the purpose of *moving the point of view out of us*: it helps us to abandon our limited singular perspective and to consider everything from a more comprehensive point of view. Through this experience the believer is able to recognize his own place in the world and, above all, to understand his responsibility towards other beings.

In the spiritual wheel the individual *understands his essence as a fragment*, a singular manifestation among all other possibilities: consequently, he is able to develop his full potential only if he recognizes his limited nature and comprehends that his own life is deeply intertwined with thousands of other existences, in a system where the flourishing of every part depends on the realization of a harmonious relationship between it and every other part. Moreover, this symbol makes us aware that life is always changing and reminds us that with every thought, every decision, every act we are building our life and the world around us.

3.2. The Ritual and its Purpose

We can easily say that the very design of the wheel conveys this message of interdependence and relationship, and the passages of its representation communicate to us a really clear message. The ritual is carried out following a very accurate sequence of gestures, each with a recognized meaning that every member of the community knows. The symbol is represented by placing stones on the ground, to remind our bond with mother earth who gives birth to every creature and sustains them. Each stone represents one of the things that we experience in nature: it could be a bird, a plant, a deer, another man, and so reminds us of the bond we have with every other creature.

The first rock to be put on the ground is the one that represents the *centre* of the wheel, the pin around which everything revolves; this

---

[15] This notion of "responsible limit" is very similar, in my opinion, to the one of moderation typical of ancient Greece: the Aristotelian notion of *mesotes* (μεσότης) and the emphasis put on the importance of self-knowledge and moderation are expressions of a conscious attitude towards the world, an attitude aware of the limits of our surroundings and of the importance of not exceeding the right measure. It could be interesting to develop this analysis further, showing how this notion of moderation was widespread in the ancient world and how it got lost in modern and contemporary times; the loss of such a consciously moderate attitude could be recognized as one of the sources of our contemporary environmental crisis.

represents the common origin from which everything derives, the Unity that precedes the multiplicity and remains present in all its manifestation.

The centre is the principle from which the *circumference* originates; this circle represents the world around us, that is at the same time (a) originated by and (b) the manifestation of the Unique perfect source of existence.

After the centre and the circumference, the third element is the subdivision of the circle in four parts, thanks to two perpendicular *lines*: this, after the radiant movement from the centre to the circumference that originates all the existing beings, is the introduction of a circular movement. This circularity is the very essence of life, as the native American philosophy conceived it: the passage through the four seasons, the four lunar phases, the four parts of the day, is a movement from a start to an end and back again to the start.

Thus, the two lines that divide the circle in four parts represent exactly the becoming of the world and the cycles of Life: this circularity binds everything that exists and expresses the harmonious movement of the universe. In this last step, the centre becomes the symbol of Eternity, and the circumference the expression of Time: through the central cross Eternity and Time are united, and so are all the visible and transitory manifestations of the principle with their origin.

The cross also represents "coming-to-be" since birth is the proceeding from the centre to the circumference (from the undifferentiated whole to the particular individual), and death is the return back to the common origin.

It is really important to notice that in this cosmological representation *man does not occupy the centre* of the wheel: he is a creature among other creatures and depends on them in the same way that they depend on him, and all of them equally relies on the centre. He does not have a special superior status nor does he perform a special role in this world: his place is the same as every other creature, and so the wheel also teaches man to be humble towards a power greater than him, and to be kind to all other living beings.

Furthermore, the structure of the wheel and the message it conveys remind us that all we see is the visible manifestation of a *power beyond us*, of a force that has shaped this universe and has given birth to every creature: the experience of the wheel emphasizes our connection with other living beings and with the Creator, reminding us our place in the world and the balance that subtends every relation.

4. Conclusions. Seeds for a Different Way of Thinking

At the end of this analysis I would like to underline some central aspects that, in my opinion, emerge from St. Francis's view and from the symbolism of the spiritual wheel; I believe that rediscovering these elements can help us to develop a different approach to the environmental problems we are facing nowadays, even if one doesn't share the religious assumptions from which they derive.

The first aspect that emerges particularly from the vision of St. Francis, is the ability to really *see* others, to comprehend their intrinsic value and to recognize them as worthy of consideration. Is the ability to enlarge one's perspective and to develop a different point of view, no more focused on the self but comprehensive of what is different from me; this attitude allows us to consider plants, animals, even inanimate beings *per se*, not simply valuing their possible uses and utility for us.

This ability to recognize the intrinsic existence and value of other beings consequentially leads to the second element I wish to underline: this is the dimension of *respect*[16], understood in its deepest sense. To respect another being does not simply mean "do not harm" or "do not interfere with"; to respect something I should have previously recognized it as something worthy of attention, as something that has his own life, meanings and rights; the respect I can show is proportional to how much I am aware of the intrinsic value of the other being, and to how I conceive the relationship between me and this being.

---

[16] The same notion of respect is defined by Shaw as the recognition of the fact that "respect for biotic communities (...) equates with a respect for things with a *telos*. The human community is not isolated from the environment but a part of it – part of a greater whole that functions in very complex and dynamic, if not fully understood, ways. (...) After all, things with a telos are, literally, things with a purpose, things with intrinsic value. Respect for this intrinsic value cautions us that they are not merely for our play but are placed here by nature for purposes we may not even fully understand". See Bill Shaw, "Aldo Leopold's Land Ethic", p. 100.
The same point is underlined by C. M. Núñez when he says that "to love nature is to want every creature to be herself. (...) that is to say, to observe the magnitude of all that exists, without regarding the utility that can be derived from it". See Martín Carbajo Núñez, *Sorella Madre Terra*, p. 170 (my translation).

Thus, the more I am able to really see other beings and I am aware of my role and place in this world, the more I will be able to show respect for every other existing being, both animate or inanimate. This respect concretizes in the consideration of other's well-being and in the consciousness of the effects of my actions.

Respecting other beings also means feeling *grateful* for what I receive that allows me to live, and to show gratitude towards every being because my own life depends on a chain of relationships. This gratitude is what emerges from the Canticle of Creatures, when St. Francis praises God even through death and suffering and is the attitude that subtends the Indian ritual of praising the Great Spirit and the spirit of the killed animal when they went hunting.

The last passage is the assumption of a *responsibility*, deriving from our ability to internalize the previous steps: when I recognize the value of other beings and I am grateful for what they give to me I begin to take care of them and I become responsible for them, because I have the power and the knowledge to do so.

In the end, what harmonises the abilities to see, to respect, to be grateful and to become responsible is an attitude of real *humility*: this does not mean I need to humiliate myself, but it is simply the recognition of the fact that we are not the masters of the world and that there is Something (we can call it God, the Good, the One, the Principle, Nature or Life itself, but I believe that the name doesn't really matter) that exceeds our capacity to comprehend and control it, Something that constitutes the very origin of every existence and that, for these reasons, deserves our respect.

Mankind is now in a truly unique situation; we face problems that our race has never seen before, problems so complex that it is difficult event to understand them in their entirety: we are not able to foresee all the consequences deriving from our environmental choices, and maybe we don't even have an ethical reference framework to guide us and tell us what the best course of action is.[17]

---

[17] A really interesting analysis of the complexity of the contemporary environmental crisis is offered by Stephen M. Gardiner in his book *A Perfect Moral Storm*. In his text Gardiner shows very effectively why it is so difficult to act resolutely with regards to climate change (in his book, climate change is used as an example representative of the deep structure of other environmental problems, which share some specific underlying characteristics). In a nutshell, Gardiner recognizes the roots of this crisis in the intersection of three serious "storms": the global storm (characterized by the global scale of environmental problems' origins and effects), the intergenerational storm (due to which there is a problematic distinction between the authors and the

But we bear still the responsibility to act on the basis of what we believe to be right and true, and to try to rectify the mistakes we have made, due to ignorance or indifference to the effects of our actions. Man is capable, with his technology and knowledge, of having the biggest impact ever on this world: it is up to us to decide whether to use this tremendous power to protect and preserve our world, or to lead to the exploitation and destruction of it.

Bibliography

Carbajo Núñez, Martìn (2017) *Sorella Madre Terra – Radici Francescane della Laudato sì*, Messaggero di Sant'Antonio Editrice.

Carson, Rachel (1962) *Silent Spring*, Crest Books.

Shaw, Bill (2005) "Aldo Leopold's Land Ethic", in *Environmental Virtue Ethics*, Rowman & Littlefield Publishers Inc.

Dalarun, Jacques (2015) *Il Cantico di Frate Sole - Francesco d'Assisi Riconciliato*, Biblioteca Francescana Edizioni.

Duffy, Sean (1991) '"Silent Spring" and "Sand County Almanac": the Two Most Significant Environmental Books of the 20th Century' in *Nature Study* vol. 44.

Fanin, Giulio (2014) *Il Legame con la Natura degli Indiani d'America*, Area51 Publishing.

— (2014) *La Visione Sacra degli Indiani d'America*, Area51 Publishing.

Gardiner, Stephen M. (2011) *A Perfect Moral Storm – The Ethical Tragedy of Climate Change*, Oxford University Press.

Leopold, Aldo (1949) *A Sand County Almanac*, Oxford University Press.

— (1949) 'The Land Ethic' in *A Sand County Almanac and Sketches Here and There*, Oxford University Press.

Pope Francis (2015) *Laudato Si' – Lettera Enciclica sulla Cura della Casa Comune*, Libreria Editrice Vaticana.

Rolston III, Holmes (2005) 'Environmental Virtue Ethics' in *Environmental Virtue Ethics*, Rowman & Littlefield Publishers Inc.

---

victims of climate change), and the ethical storm (originated by the fact that traditional ethics doesn't have the conceptual tools to deal with such a complex situation). The complexity of the relationship between these elements constitutes the obstacle we have to overcome, if we want be able to seriously undertake actions that are really effective to resolve this situation. For more about Gardiner's analysis, see Gardiner, Stephen M (2011) *A Perfect Moral Storm – The Ethical Tragedy of Climate Change*, Oxford University Press.

Plato's Conscious Universe and the Unity of Things

Stuart Dunbar

If you look around right now, chances are you see four dead walls and a ceiling, some furniture, a lamp and a bookcase, probably a computer. You might see the inside of some vehicle you're riding in, an automobile, a subway or an airplane. Wherever you are, it's very likely to be a manmade environment created to keep you inside and safe with all your stuff. If you're fortunate, you can look out a window and see something alive out there. You might have a purring creature or some other furry friend sleeping next to you. You might have some flowers or potted plants around the room. But for the most part these are tiny lights against the backdrop of a totally manmade and artificial environment.

Even the "natural" world outside your window is engineered, like the roads and buildings, to work with the rest of the things that we've created and surrounded ourselves with. The parks in the city, the garden out back, the little patch of protected forest, they're not concrete and pavement, but these too are essentially artefacts of society. Everything around us is constructed to cater to our needs. The "room" that keeps you inside, safe, productive, and preferably consuming things, is now effectively the whole world we operate in, a world of manmade artefacts, constructed from materials we've collected and refined: concrete, plastic, glass, metal, asphalt, vinyl, ceramics. Even natural wood and stone are slowly disappearing from our environment.

All these clever things, constructed and artificial, make our homes and cities more efficient and safe, our lives easier and more comfortable, but they come with a big price, which we've been more than willing to pay. They're all dead. The living world has receded from our view and we've effectively surrounded ourselves with dead stuff. We're completely preoccupied with this stuff, getting more of it, putting it in order, keeping track of it, trying to get rid of it. Even animals, plants, and trees, have become objects to own, trade and manage. In fact, we can barely relate to a living world out there beyond our control. We live cut off and uninterested in it. This is the modern predicament: we moderns float like lonely clouds over a world we perceive to be essentially dead. The world we have chosen to live in is fast becoming our worst nightmare, a kind of a cruise ship planet with all the lifeless amenities to meet our every material desire, drifting through open dead space.

It's as if our materialist convictions have a life of their own. We're convinced that everything around us is made of dead matter, and as a result we've surrounded ourselves with dead stuff. We've created this world for ourselves, immersed ourselves in it, and now assume that things just are this way and can be no other. We ignore and disrespect the life that is still present around us, because our deepest metaphysical assumptions about reality have been projected onto the world.

Ralph Waldo Emerson describes this process beautifully,

> Every nation and every man instantly surround themselves with a material apparatus which exactly corresponds to . . . their state of thought. Observe how every truth and every error, each a thought of some man's mind, clothes itself with societies, houses, cities, language, ceremonies, newspapers. Observe the ideas of the present day . . . see how timber, brick, lime, and stone have flown into convenient shape, obedient to the master idea reigning in the minds of many persons . . . It follows, of course, that the least enlargement of ideas . . . would cause the most striking changes of external things.[1]

The current ecological crisis is not about recycling and land trusts and animal rights and rain forest protection, it's about our whole relationship to life. *We actually believe that we live in a dead universe.* That's the problem. Nothing's going to change until that changes.

No wonder it sounds ridiculous to us when we come across someone like Plato, who says in the *Timaeus* that the universe is not dead; it's actually alive, not just the various flora and fauna in it, but the whole universe, a living intelligent creature. And not just theoretically "alive". Alive in every sense of the word. Much more sensitive, perceptive, and intelligent than we are, created in the most

---

[1] Emerson, Ralph Waldo as quoted in Meadows, Donella H. (2008) *Thinking in Systems: A Primer*, White River Junction, VT: Chelsea Green Publishing, p. 163.

perfect way, whole and good, through and through. In fact, a most "happy God".[2]

The English romantic poet, William Wordsworth, captures the spirit of Plato's living world in his well-known poem:

> I wandered lonely as a cloud
> That floats on high o'er vales and hills,
> When all at once I saw a crowd,
> A host, of golden daffodils;
> Beside the lake, beneath the trees,
> Fluttering and dancing in the breeze.

This is a real stretch for us, isn't it? A *living universe!* It's much too fantastic for most people to take seriously, much less take in. We're more comfortable approaching it as a kind of thought experiment. How wonderful to think such a thing, we might say, the whole Universe, alive and conscious in some extraordinary way, and we are part of it. Our lives are part of its life. Our hopes and fears, thoughts and feelings, trials and tribulations, all part of what is, ultimately *one experience*. There's an incredible redemption in this thought. Nothing about my life is wasted, nothing is lost. All of me is gathered with everything that has ever happened into a kind of ultimately conscious event which is experiencing itself, through its experience of my experience. It's a stunning thought.

> Continuous as the stars that shine
> And twinkle on the milky way,
> They stretched in never-ending line
> Along the margin of the bay:
> Ten thousand saw I at a glance,
> Tossing their heads in spritely dance.

But to us moderns this beautiful thought is "just a thought", and thought like everything around us, is dead too. The problem with Plato's description of a living universe in the *Timaeus*, as inspired as it may be, is that even though it starts from the premise that the whole universe is alive, it leaves room for a whole lot in the world that is *not* alive. It's not clear from Plato's description of creation, for example, whether the original elements, the stuff this living universe is *made* of, actually participate in the life that they support.

---

[2] Plato, *Timaeus, 34b*, in *The Works of Plato, Vol II*, Thomas Taylor and Floyer Sydenham (trans.), The Prometheus Trust, p. 435.

Aristotle picks up on this ambiguity and wagers that they do not. He presents us with a picture where only human beings, animals and plants have souls. Soul is alive and sentient. The rest of the world is not.[3] In maintaining that Soul played this role in the movement and life of certain things, Aristotle was responding to the early atomists, particularly Democritus, who attempted to explain everything as the interactions of passive particulate matter. (He was also responding to his own teacher, Plato, who gave credence to atomism when he presented his own version of the theory in the *Timaeus*, representing the fundamental elements as particulate solids with specific shape and form.) [4] Plotinus took this position to its logical conclusion, characterising matter as "evil" because it was furthest removed from the purity of the Good[5], and while he probably did not mean to *separate* matter from the Good[6], this is effectively what happened. This probably has more to do with Augustine than with Plotinus. Augustine presented several arguments to prove Plotinus' notion of the immateriality of the soul.[7] His efforts effectively cemented the dichotomy between immaterial soul and material body, mind and

---

[3] *Aristotle in 23 Volumes*, Vol. VIII, (1986) *On the Soul, Parva Naturalia, On Breath*, W.S Hett (trans.) Harvard University Press. pp 79-81 ". . . those are right in their view who maintain that the soul cannot exist without the body, but is not itself in any sense a body. It is not a body, it is associated with a body, and therefore resides in a body, and in a body of a particular kind; not at all as our predecessors supposed, who fitted it to any body, without adding any limitations as to what body or what kind of body. . ."

[4] Berryman, Sylvia (2016) 'Ancient Atomism' in *The Stanford Encyclopaedia of Philosophy* (Winter 2016 Edition), Edward N. Zalta (ed.), URL = <https://plato.stanford.edu/archives/win2016/entries/atomism-ancient/>

[5] Plotinus, III.6.11, *Collected Writings of Plotinus*, translated by Thomas Taylor, Prometheus Trust, 2017, p.210: 'But that which possesses nothing, as being in poverty, or rather being poverty itself, is necessarily evil. For this is not the want of wealth or of strength, but it is the want of wisdom, and the want of virtue, of beauty, strength, morphe, form, and quality. How is it possible it should not be deformed? How is it possible it should not be perfectly base? How is it possible it should not be perfectly evil?'

[6] It should be noted that Plotinus also wrote a treatise which Porphry called, "Against those who say that the Universe and its Maker are Evil" otherwise known as *Treatise Against the Gnostics* (Enneads II.9) in which he argues that the cosmos is not "disjointed" but rather "a clear and noble image of the intelligible gods." II.9.8.

[7] Hannegan, Brother Justin, "How Augustine Made Us More than Matter – and Immortal" in *Homelitic and Pastoral Review*, 9th Aug 2015, URL = <http://www.hprweb.com/2015/08/how-augustine-made-us-more-than-matter-and-immortal/>

matter, into Christian theology. By the time we get to Descartes, the dualistic split between mind and matter is complete. Mind is where we reside, alive and indivisible but separate from the world. Matter is divisible and dead.[8]

As modern materialists, most of us are particularly attached to this conception of matter as inert stuff out of which everything is made. But does it actually hold up under scrutiny? When physicists look deeply into what matter actually is, it starts to look like a whole lot of empty space and some very strangely behaving bits that appear and disappear for no apparent reason. For some strange reason, we moderns don't seem to have a conceptual problem with this. What we *do* struggle with, however, is Descartes' notion of "mind", or what we call "consciousness" today. How does Wordsworth's internal experience of a host of daffodils dancing by the lakeside come out of the interactions of a whole lot of dead matter? One thing doesn't follow from the other. That's a problem for us.

Contemporary philosopher and cognitive scientist, David Chalmers, calls this the "hard problem" of consciousness. He distinguishes between the psychological and phenomenal properties of consciousness. Psychological properties have to do with the functions of the mind and nervous system which generate sensations, emotions and behaviours. These properties are associated with mental activities like introspection, self-consciousness, attention, wakefulness, voluntary control, and knowledge. Even awareness, Chalmers says, is "a state wherein we have access to some information, and can use that information in the control of behaviour".[9] As such it too is

---

[8] Descartes, Rene (1998) *Meditations on First Philosophy*, Donald A. Cress (trans.) Hackett Publishing Co., p.56: "Now my first observation here is that there is a great difference between a mind and a body in that a body, by its very nature, is always divisible. On the other hand, the mind is utterly indivisible. For when I consider the mind, that is, myself insofar as I am only a thinking thing, I cannot distinguish any parts within me; rather, I understand myself to be manifestly one complete thing. Although the entire mind seems to be united to the entire body, nevertheless, were a foot or an arm or any other bodily part to be amputated, I know that nothing has been taken away from the mind on that account. Nor can the faculties of willing, sensing, understanding, and so on be called "parts" of the mind, since it is one and the same mind that wills, senses, and understands. On the other hand, there is no corporeal or extended thing I can think of that I may not in my thought easily divide into parts; and in this way, I understand that it is divisible. This consideration alone would suffice to teach me that the mind is wholly diverse from the body."

[9] Chalmers, David (1996) *The Conscious Mind: In Search of a Fundamental Theory*, Oxford University Press, pp 26-27.

considered a psychological property of consciousness. Neurobiology and cognitive science are making great progress in understanding how the mind and body support these functions.

Phenomenal properties of consciousness have to do with our experience of the world. The yellowness of a daffodil, the sense of awe we feel when gazing at the milky way, the satisfaction of a well composed poem. These are experiential events that defy precise description, and yet they are so real to us; we long to communicate them. The science of consciousness is currently at a loss to explain how and why we have any experience at all. Science doesn't even know how to approach this problem. Chalmers considers this a failure of materialism itself. It's one thing to explain how the brain focuses on and processes signals coming from your optic nerve. It's another to explain why your experience of the colour red arises from these signals. That's the hard part. The phenomenal experience may have physical correlates, but it doesn't seem to have any obvious physical *explanation*.

Plato was not a materialist. He didn't have a problem with consciousness. He conceived of a universe structured by Ideas, filled with things that naturally desired the Good through their experience of form. Plato's whole philosophy is a kind of theory of consciousness. He didn't have a problem with consciousness; he had a problem with matter. What is this stuff, he asked, that seems to be receptive to any form that is given it? How can we even think of something that has no form?[10]

Plato was looking all the way to the bottom of the metaphysical ladder. Today we might ask the same questions. What is the stuff that

---

[10] Plato, *Timaeus*, Thomas Taylor (trans.) 52a: "we must confess that the form which subsists according to same, is unbegotten and without decay; neither receiving anything into itself externally, nor itself proceeding into any other nature. That it is invisible, and imperceptible, by sense; and that this is the proper object of intellectual speculation. But the form which is synonymous and similar to this, must be considered as sensible, generated, always in agitation, and generated in a certain place, from which it again recedes, hastening to dissolution; and which is apprehended by opinion in conjunction with sense. But the third nature is that of place (Chora); which never receives corruption, but affords a seat to all generated forms. This indeed is tangible without tangent perception; and is scarcely by a certain spurious reasoning the object of belief. Besides, when we attempt to behold this nature, we perceive nothing but the delusions of dreams, and assert that every being must necessarily be somewhere, and be situated in a certain place."

subatomic particles are made of? It has no form until it miraculously gives birth to a quark or a lepton. There doesn't appear to be anything there at all, certainly nothing we can measure. Plato thought there *must* be something there; things can't just arise out of nothing, but whatever it is, it defies our ability to conceptualize it, much less measure it. Matter must "be" in a way that is hardly in fact "being". It seems to borrow its being when it takes form.[11] It's remarkable how aligned Plato's thinking was with the observations of particle physics.

Plotinus struggled with Plato's notion of matter. He observes that a matter that does not have qualities in the way that Plato describes must be completely inert and "entirely impassive".[12] In fact, it could be argued that Plotinus contributes to our modern conception of matter by concluding that matter must be in fact "perfectly evil".[13]

Proclus takes a different approach. He speculates that this "receptive substratum" must in fact want to be "enformed". It doesn't make sense, he thought, that form imposes itself on matter, in the way Plotinus describes, without matter somehow responding to the call.[14] Participation in form requires that matter *desire* form in

---

[11] Plato, *Timaeus*, Peter Kalkavage (trans.) 52c: "Since it is always swept along as a phantasm of something other, for these reasons it is appropriate that it come to be in some other thing, holding fast to Being in some way or other, or else be nothing at all."

[12] Plotinus, III.6.11, *Collected Writings of Plotinus*, Thomas Taylor (trans.) Prometheus Trust, p. 252: "If, therefore, matter being deformed is rendered beautiful, it is no longer that base thing which it was before; so that in being thus adorned, it loses its subsistence as matter, and especially if its deformity is not accidental. But if it is so deformed as to be deformity itself, it will not participate of ornament. And if it is so evil, as to be evil itself, it will not participate of good. Hence it does not participate in such a way as some fancy it does, *viz.* by being passive, but after another manner, which is that of appearing to participate."

[13] See footnotes 5 and 6

[14] Proclus (1987) *Commentary on Plato's Timaeus*, Glenn R. Morrow and John M. Dillon, (trans.) Princeton University Press, p. 214 "we must affirm that the cause of this participation is, on the one hand, the efficacious power of the primordial divine Forms themselves, and on the other hand the appetency of the beings that are shaped in accordance with them and that participate in the formative activity that proceeds from them. For the creative action of the Forms is not alone sufficient to bring about participation; at all events, though these Forms are everywhere to the same degree, not all things participate alike in them; nor is the appetency of the beings that participate adequate without their creative activity. For desire by itself is imperfect; it is the perfect generating factors that lead in the form-giving process."

some way.[15] In saying this, Proclus seems to be committed to the notion that matter must desire the good of form more intensely than any particular instance of form. Matter doesn't just desire the good of one particular form; it desires them all.

> For since it is potentially everything, but actually nothing, and since it is filled with the indefiniteness of the more-or less, it accepts different reason-principles at different times, for although it desires to enjoy them all, it is not able to partake of them all at the same time.[16]

Hence, for Proclus, matter must be a kind of pure desire. That's about as far from dead stuff as you can get. If we take Proclus' interpretation seriously, the Platonic metaphysical model is not dualist in the end, it's one thing through and through and that one thing is something like what we would call consciousness today.

What difference does it make if the Platonists thought this way? Doesn't evidence based science answer questions about the nature of the universe better than any speculative philosophy ever could? Well, yes . . . and maybe that's not the issue. We as a species have clearly hit an impasse in our relationship to the planet, one that science might be capable of explaining to us, if we cared to let in what it has to say about the subject. But that's the point. *We're not letting it in.* We know what to do, but we don't do it. It's as if we don't really care that the world is falling apart at the seams. Why is that? What's missing from the picture? We look back at earlier traditions like Platonism to understand how we ended up where we are today. We also look to

---

[15] *Ibid*, p. 214. ". . . all things would be alike if each thing came to be according to the divine creativity alone. For since that creativity is always the same and present to all things, unless there were a difference in the aptitudes of the subjects how could we explain their variety and the fact that some things always participate in the same way and others sometimes in one way, sometimes in another? It must be that some things possess a substratum such that it always holds the Forms and is susceptible to its creative action, and others sometimes an aptitude for participating in the Form and at other times for participating in its contrary. For since it is potentially everything, but actually nothing, and since it is filled with the indefiniteness of the more-or-less, it accepts different reason-principles at different times, for although it desires to enjoy them all, it is not able to partake of them all at the same time. Consequently, we must affirm that the cause of the form-giving activity is not only the generating power of the demiurgic intellect, but also the appetency of its substrata and their varying aptitudes."

[16] *Ibid*, p. 214.

history for other paradigms in order to gain a vantage point from which we can see our own unquestioned assumptions. Front and centre in the Platonic conception of physical reality is this notion that the universe is alive. Less obvious is this notion that matter plays an *active* role in creation. For all kinds of reasons history rejected these ideas and yet it seems we are being forced to rethink them.

Even if we don't accept Proclus' interpretation of Plato's notion of "Chora", this perfectly receptive substrate, there's enough in Plato's own metaphysics that suggests he himself didn't think the living Universe was made of dead stuff. For example, Plato is very careful to depict Soul as pervasive throughout the manifest universe.[17] Every sensible thing in Plato's world exists within Soul. Contrary to Aristotle, Plato thought Soul must affect everything, and since Soul affects things by enlivening them, it follows that everything is in some sense, for Plato, alive. Moreover, if all things exist within Soul, all things are connected through Soul.[18] Iamblichus, the fourth century Neoplatonist, is particularly inspired by what this implies. "All things are full of the gods", he says, quoting the great pre-Socratic, Thales. It is the light of the gods which "holds together all things . . . causes lasts to be joined to first, as for example, earth to heaven, and produces a single continuity and harmony of all with all".[19]

---

[17] Plato, *Timaeus, 35b,* Thomas Taylor (trans.) "But placing soul in the middle of the world, he extended it through the whole; and besides this, he externally invested the body of the universe with soul."

[18] Note, this notion of Soul as pervasive throughout the Universe is not unlike the eastern notion of Chi as the mediating substance between Shen (consciousness) and Jing (physical being). Consciousness does not affect physical matter directly; it does so through Chi. Chi brings life to physical things. Without it, physical things become corrupted, diseased and die. Because all things contain Chi, Chi connects all things. Plato's notion of Soul seems similar in this sense. Because all things are contained in Soul, all things participate in Soul to some degree and are connected through it.

[19] Iamblichus, On the Mysteries 1.9, translated by E.C. Clarke, J.M. Dillon and J.P. Hershbell, 2003, with slight emendations by Crystal Addey: "This light [of the gods] is one and the same in its entirety everywhere, is present indivisibly in all things . . . and has filled everything with its perfect power; by virtue of its unlimited causal superiority it brings to completion all things within itself. . . It is, indeed, in imitation of it that the whole heaven and cosmos performs its circular revolution, is united with itself, and leads the elements round in their cyclic dance, holds together all things...causes lasts to be joined to first, as for example earth to heaven, and produces a single continuity and harmony of all with all."

Also important for understanding the Platonic notion of matter, is Plato's concept of the eternal Dyad, presented in the *Philebus*, which represents the first differentiation of the highest principle, the One, and consists of two derivative principles, the Bound and the Infinite, present in every Idea that gives form to matter.[20] The Infinite is what allows an Idea to multiply into endless variation. The Bound is what gives an Idea it's unity, it's definiteness. However general or universal it is, an Idea is this and not that because it participates in some way in the Bound. Because all things desire the good of the One, all things desire the fundamental unity of the Bound as well, the primary principle of agency in the unfolding of reality. Our desire for the Good, our desire for the One, and for this fundamental unity of the Bound, are one and the same movement.

This is important, because Plato depicts Chora as existing *prior* to the creation of the universe.[21] As such it would have been brought into being as the direct production of the highest principle, either by the agency of the Bound or by the One itself. Chora exists, then, "prior" to form (if we can use a temporal term in regard to eternal causes), even "prior" to the intellectual creative act of the Demiurge. In other words, there is no intervening principle in Plato's metaphysics between the unity of the One and this perfectly receptive substrate, the "nurse" and "mother" of all that is. Whatever matter is, Plato thought it must be more intimate with the unity of the One than anything else in the universe. This notion contains a jewel of wisdom that I think sheds some light on our contemporary questions about the nature of matter, life and consciousness and how they interact in the development of the cosmos. It's worth drawing this out a bit.

In brief, Plato is saying that everything in the universe is somehow in touch with and *desires* the unity of the One in an intimate way. This is a powerful conception of reality. It suggests not only that there is some degree of unity in all things, but that this unity is *internal*. Desire

---

[20] Plato *Philebus 16c*, Dorthea Frede (trans.) in *Plato: Complete Works (1997)* John M Cooper (ed.), Hackett, p. 404.
[21] Plato, *Timaeus 52d*, Thomas Taylor (trans.) "This, then, is summarily my opinion; - that, prior to the generation of the universe, these three things subsisted in a triple respect, *viz*: being, place (chora), and generation. And the nurse of generation, fiery and moist, receiving the forms of earth and air, and suffering such other passions as are the attendants of these, appeared of an all-various nature to the view."

is an internal event, an 'experience' of some kind. Something cannot 'desire' unity without having a degree of unity already. The presence of desire implies the existence of something that is already unified enough to have an experience.

Can this really be what Plato is saying? The word 'experience' sounds inappropriate. It is reserved for human beings. How could a beetle, a thistle, much less a piece of rock or a river have an 'experience'? But if we pull it apart like this, isn't this what Plato's philosophy, his theory of consciousness, is pointing to?

As Thomas Nagel puts it, when we talk about an internal experience of this kind, we're talking about some form of subjectivity. We're saying it must be "like something" to be that thing. In his famous essay[22], Nagel uses the example of a flying bat. It must be like something to be a bat, he says, something for the bat itself. Having an internal "experience" doesn't necessarily mean having thoughts and feelings and a sense of the passing of time which are characteristic of *human* experience. We have no idea what the internal experience of a bat is like, but it must have one.

Any living creature must have enough integrity in its sensory experience of the world to respond to its environment as a unified whole and not as a collection of parts. Sensations are psychological properties, functions of consciousness that come from a well-organized nervous system. But the unified *experience* arising from those sensations is something different. If what Plato is suggesting is true and there is an internal dimension to *all* things, then this unified experience must arise wherever some degree of unity becomes manifest, whether or not a nervous system exists to generate sensations. Sensations give rise to a specific kind of internal experience, but presumably there are other ways for it to manifest. In other words, it must be like something for a thing, anything, to have its own kind of unity. Again, Wordsworth:

> The waves beside them danced; but they
> Out-did the sparkling waves in glee:
> A poet could not but be gay,
> In such a jocund company:
> I gazed - and gazed - but little thought
> What wealth to me the scene had brought:

---

[22] Nagel, Thomas (1974) 'What's it Like to Be a Bat?' in *The Philosophical Review* 83 (4) pp 435-450

What is this unity actually? What holds something together and makes it a thing instead of an amorphous set of relationships that fade into causal obscurity? When we ask, what makes a thing real, we typically point to its causal effects. If a thing causes something to happen in the world, we consider it real. But, notice this is not how we look at *ourselves*. What makes *us* real is not our ability to cause things to happen in the world. Most of us would say that we exist as long as we have some experience of the world, whether or not that experience has any effect on things around us.

Notice, a unified experience is not the same as a specific experience of unity. We don't have to have an idea of "self" or "I" in order to have an experience of the world, but our experience of the world has to hold together in some way in order for it to be an experience at all. In other words, it has to have some degree of Platonic unity. It must participate in the Bound in some way.

There is a certain delicacy in this internal unity. We're especially aware of it when we start to lose it, when it feels like all our parts are going in different directions. We can become confused and even panicked when for whatever reason all our senses are firing at once without a way to filter what's important and what's not. One feature of autism is this scattering of experience. The autistic child is desperate to hold onto some order in the world. It's conceivable that neurobiology and cognitive science will someday understand how the mind and nervous system manage to bring together all of what we are thinking, sensing, and feeling into one event. This "bringing together" is presumably a function, a psychological property, of consciousness. But it's difficult to imagine how one could explain the phenomenal event that occurs when these functional events cohere into a single unified experience. What is it about the function of bringing these sensations together that gives rise to a unified conscious *experience*? How and why do the lights go on? We might speculate that experiential unity adds significantly to the coherence of the functions from which it arises, and that this would in turn strengthen the phenomenal experience creating a kind amplifying feedback leading to a stable structure in consciousness. But this is an open question in the science of mind. It's not clear what work the inner experience actually does, indeed if it does any work at all. Most of the heavy lifting seems to be done by the functional properties of consciousness.

Some contemporary philosophers think that the idea that there *is* any unity in our internal experience is actually a kind of delusion.[23] If we look at the structure of the brain and its processes, they say, it doesn't seem to be organized around one central processing function where everything could be brought together. There's clearly many parallel processes happening at once, distributed across many interwoven neural networks. Moreover, when we look at our experience, in fact very little of it needs to be conscious for us to function in the world. Most of what we are experiencing is semi-conscious at best. There's an illusion of continuity created specifically by our *idea* of consciousness. According to this view, sporadic reflexive moments in our experience create this illusion of a false sense of a continuous self through time and a "stream of consciousness" playing out before our mind's eye. In actual fact this continuity in our experience probably doesn't exist. We just fill in the gaps. What we need to understand, according to this view, is not the *actual* unity in our experience but why we have this deluded idea that there *is* any such unity.[24] What function does this delusion serve? This critique attempts to address the hard problem of consciousness by rejecting it as a problem at all.[25]

Theories of system dynamics question the notion of an internal unified experience by challenging our presumption of its internality. If we look at emergent properties in complex systems, we don't need an answer to the question of how a system manages to respond to its environment as a unified whole. Spontaneous unity happens all the time in complex systems. As a system begins to function more cohesively, as its feedback mechanisms come on-line and it spontaneously organizes itself in relationship to the various inputs it

---

[23] Dan Dennett and Patricia Churchland are often cited as proponents of this view.

[24] For a nice overview of this objection, see Blackmore, Sue (2005) *Consciousness; a Very Short Introduction*, Oxford University Press.

[25] Chalmers, p. 188: "There is a certain intellectual appeal to the position that explaining phenomenal judgments [for example the 'judgement' that our consciousness is continuous] is enough. It has the feel of a bold stroke that cleanly dissolves all the problems, leaving our confusion lying on the ground in front of us exposed for all to see. Yet it is the kind of 'solution' that is satisfying only for about half a minute. When we stop to reflect, we realize that all we have done is to explain certain aspects of our behaviour. We have explained why we talk in certain ways, and why we are disposed to do so, but we have not remotely come to grips with the central problem, namely conscious experience itself."

receives from its environment, out of relative chaos a unified response spontaneously emerges. [26]   The structures that emerge through this process of self-organisation can seem miraculous[27], but generally, from the perspective of strict system dynamics, the external unity in a system's response to a change in its environment *is* what makes it a whole. Nothing internal is needed to make it so. In other words, whatever seems internal is just another layer of complexity within the system.

These critiques share the materialist assumption that we live in a dead universe made of dead stuff, that the only forces acting on this stuff are the fundamental forces of physics. According to this view, complexity doesn't need form or structure imposed on it to come together into self-organized complex systems which have some degree of unity in their response to their environment. Whatever we think our internal experience is, it must be merely the result of this complexity, because let's face it, proponents of this view would say, there's nothing else out there.

The Platonist would insist that there must be more to the picture than physical forces acting on complexity to make it into giraffes, rose

---

[26] Meadows (2008) p. 89. "The structure of a system is its interlocking stocks, flows, and feed-back loops. The diagrams with boxes and arrows (my students call them 'spaghetti-and-meatball diagrams' are pictures of system structure. Structure determines what behaviours are latent in the system. A goal-seeking balancing feedback loop approaches or holds a dynamic equilibrium. A reinforcing feedback loop generates exponential growth. The two of them linked together are capable of growth, decay, or equilibrium. If they also contain delays, they may produce oscillations. If they work in periodic, rapid bursts, they may produce even more surprising behaviours." This is an excellent overview of system theory. Meadows is happy to admit the limitations of systems theory especially when applied in a superficial way or in an effort to control complex systems like human society.

[27] Prigogine, Ilya and Stengers, Isabelle (1984) *Order out of Chaos: Man's new Dialogue with Nature*, Bantam Books. Nobel Prize winner, Ilya Prigogine, calls the unity that emerges spontaneously in this way a "dissipative structure". Such structures occur naturally in systems that are far from equilibrium. Prigogine explores the notion of an "active matter" and is open to the idea that matter carries with it more information about its organisation than we normally ascribe to it. "At all levels, be it the level of macroscopic physics, the level of fluctuations, or the microscopic level, nonequilibrium is the source of order. Nonequilibrium brings 'order out of chaos'". pp. 286-87.

bushes and human beings.[28] Emergence is not a satisfying answer to how things achieve their remarkable degree of unity. Just as Newton's idea of gravity was not really an answer to *why* two bodies are attracted to each other at a distance, emergence is not really an answer to why a system unifies a response to its environment out of chaos. Emergence is a description of what happens, not a reason, a description looking at the outside, not the inside of things.

Of course, evolutionary theory confirms that there *is* something acting on complexity to turn it into the panorama of form we see in the world, namely the constraints of the environment, but there is significant evidence in evolutionary science to question whether environmental constraints are really enough to explain the kinds of creative selection we see in evolutionary development.[29] Something else seems to be informing the process. Novelty itself may, as Darwin suggested, be spontaneous, but something *affirms* those spontaneous changes in a way that makes them stick. Something more than just the environment is saying "yes" to nature's experiments with form.

I think the Platonic notion of the internal unity of a thing, its participation in the Bound, presents us with a good reason *why* certain forms stick in evolutionary development and others don't. Yes, form and structure emerge naturally in complex systems through generative change and development, but the point is, those forms that achieve a level of internal unity persist in this process and those that don't, simply do not survive. The key word here is "internal". That crucial unity has to be some kind of "experience".

---

[28] This phrase is borrowed from evolutionary cosmologist, Brian Swimme. A dedicated student of cosmologist and "ecotheologian" Thomas Barry, Swimme is known for his compelling depiction of the "universe story".

[29] Evolutionary cosmologist, Brian Swimme, is fond of pointing out that life on earth developed the eye many different times and sometimes simultaneously in different environments with different mechanics. In a short overview called the 'Journey of the Universe', co-written with Mary Evelyn Tucker for a survey course by the same name offered through Yale University, he quotes evolutionary biologist, Ernst Mayr's estimate that the complex eye was constructed independently at least forty times. What is it about the sensing of light that was so critical to the development of life at a specific time in the development of the biosphere? Can we explain this without assuming that some degree of unity in experience had already been achieved? It is as if life itself demanded that this unity be illuminated. "Nothing will stop life's quest to absorb ever more of the universe's infinite depth." Swimme, Brian and Tucker, Mary Evelyn (2011) *Journey of the Universe*, Yale University Press, p. 62.

Chalmers argues that one way to explain the phenomenal nature of consciousness is to understand it as fundamental to the nature of reality. This means that regardless of how things are organized, some form of consciousness always comes with the package. As a fundamental feature of the universe, alongside space-time, mass-energy, charge, spin, etc. it's always there; it just manifests differently through different physical structures.[30]

This notion of consciousness as fundamental supports Plato's view that all things participate in the Bound internally. I would stress, however, that this is a consciousness that does real work in the world. Its primary effect is to create wholes out of disparate parts by generating a unified internal experience, which transcends and includes the parts. *Consciousness is that which unifies disparate experiences into one unified experience.* It does important work in the world by creating relationships between parts and wholes out of relationships. As such it acts as the ground from which all unity, i.e. being, emerges.

To embrace this conception of consciousness we have to look at things differently. We're thrown back on Plato's notion of Soul, pervasive in the universe, active in all things. If all things have some degree of internal experience, then some form of "life" may be in *absolutely everything around us.* A mountain, a river, a forest, a particular countryside, unlike the artefacts we surround ourselves with, these things have a kind of natural integrity, a certain unity generated out of their participation in larger ecosystems. If consciousness is fundamental, their unity, like ours, manifests internally as well as externally. A rain forest, an ocean, a continent, a planet, the solar system, the galaxy, these things are complex systems in their own right; if consciousness is fundamental, why could they not manifest the internal properties we recognise in other complex systems? Again, is a nervous system required for those internal properties to

---

[30] Chalmers, p. 128. "To capture the spirit of the view I advocate, I call it naturalistic dualism. It is naturalistic because it posits that everything is a consequence of a network of basic properties and laws, and because it is compatible with all the results of contemporary science. And as with naturalistic theories in other domains, this view allows that we can explain consciousness in terms of basic natural laws. There need be nothing especially transcendental about consciousness; it is just another natural phenomenon. All that has happened is that our picture of nature has expanded. Sometimes 'naturalism' is taken to be synonymous with 'materialism', but it seems to me that a commitment to a naturalistic understanding of the world can survive the failure of materialism."

manifest or does our nervous system just allow it to happen in a particular way?

This is wild stuff. It's way too radical for most of us to take seriously. But you have to go this far out there to challenge the materialist paradigm that is making human culture a cancer on this planet. You cannot go part way and expect it to make any real difference. We're so used to looking at the things around us as external events, it's just inconceivable to us that there could be a whole other dimension to them. But unless we recognise and honour some kind of "life" in the things around us, that they are in some sense participating in the same universal life that we are, we will continue to treat animals, plants, oceans, mountains, rivers, and countryside as dead for all practical purposes relative to our own needs and desires.

Where is the evidence for a conception of consciousness that is pervasive, manifests in all things, and is fundamental to the nature of reality? All around us, of course. A few examples: we feel certain that animals recognise us and know us in some way, not because we feed them, but because we have a relationship with them. A good gardener tunes into the likes and dislikes of individual plants, not just the properties of certain species. A good artist listens to the material he or she is working with to discover the particular form that "wants" to manifest through it. We feel the presence of an old oak tree in the forest more acutely than other plants. We choose to live near a specific mountain, a river, a forest, a seashore, because something about it resonates with us. Something about our dwelling place in the city makes it a home and not just a roof over our heads. Natural materials feel better in our environment than artificial ones. Even human artefacts take on qualities of presence if they are made or used with care. The 200-year-old violin, played by a lineage of masters, has a presence of its own. The old pair of blue jeans we have trouble throwing away. I could go on and on. We're "talking" to the world in this way all the time. The theme in these examples is a simple one: the universe values relationship. Even two subatomic particles maintain their relationship at a distance.

We don't normally think of Plato as being a proponent of panpsychism, but I think he clearly was. The belief that "all things are full of the gods" was the backdrop to Plato's whole philosophy. In a way, he makes the case for this in the *Symposium* where Diotima describes how even the basest expressions of love are at their core a desire for the Beautiful itself.[31]   If we allow Proclus' interpretation that matter is in essence a kind of insatiable desire for form, the picture is clearer. Diotima's ladder of love, by this measure, goes all the way up and all the way down the hierarchy of being.

Of course, Plato is not the only one who has been willing to commit to this idea that everything is conscious in some way. Contemporary academics are careful to avoid these deep waters. Chalmers was an important exception 20 years ago. He has more support now. Chalmers does not identify his philosophy with panpsychism, but because this is where his theory of consciousness naturally leads, he is willing to entertain it. The conclusion is natural: if consciousness is fundamental, then it must be active in all things.

> One might be attracted to the view of the world as pure causal flux, with no further properties for the causation to relate, but this would lead to a strangely insubstantial view of the physical world. It would contain only causal and nomic relations between empty placeholders with no properties of their own. Intuitively, it is more reasonable to suppose that the basic entities that all this causation relates have some internal nature of their own, some intrinsic properties, so that the world has some substance to it. . . There is only one class of intrinsic, nonrelational property with which we have any direct familiarity, and that is the class of phenomenal properties. It is natural to speculate that there may be some relation or even overlap between the uncharacterized intrinsic properties of physical entities, and the familiar intrinsic properties of experience.   Perhaps, as Russell suggested, at least some of the intrinsic properties of the physical are themselves a variety of phenomenal property? The idea sounds wild at first, but on reflection it becomes

---

[31] Plato (1997) *Symposium 208b*, Alexander Nehamas and Paul Woodruff (trans.) in *Plato: Complete Works*, John M. Cooper (ed.) Hackett Publishing Company, p. 491 ". . . everything mortal is preserved, not like the divine, by always being the same in every way, but because what is departing and aging leaves behind something new, something such as it had been. By this device, Socrates, what is mortal shares in immortality, *whether it is a body or anything else*, while the immortal has another way. So don't be surprised if everything naturally values its own offspring, because it is for the sake of immortality that everything shows this zeal, which is Love." (italics mine).

less so. After all, we really have no idea about the intrinsic properties of the physical. Their nature is up for grabs, and phenomenal properties seem as likely a candidate as any other.[32]

Environmental philosopher, Freya Mathews, is more explicit about it. In her book, *For Love of Matter*, she makes a case for panpsychism, arguing from a position of realism. This is not unlike Chalmers's position, but she is more forthright about it. Without some sort of inner subjective dimension to the world we have no way of distinguishing a thing's presence from its mere appearances and therefore no way to ground our belief that it's really there. She makes a distinction between two forms of panpsychism, 1) where the larger whole in which we play a part is conscious and 2) where all the parts of this conscious whole are conscious themselves, right down to the building blocks of reality. Mathews herself is prepared to defend the weaker version but not the stronger.[33]

Alfred North Whitehead's process philosophy is an example of the stronger version. It rests on a foundation of panpsychism committed to the idea that some kind of elemental pre-conscious "experience" must be present in inter-connected, relational entities all the way down to the subatomic level. For Whitehead, there are no "entities" in the materialist sense. There are "actual entities", but these are more like moments or "drops" of experience. What we perceive as material entities are in fact bundles of inter-connected elemental experiences in relational process. "[T]he actual world is a process, and the process is the becoming of actual entities."[34]

> "Actual entities" - also termed "actual occasions" - are the final real things of which the world is made up. There is no going behind actual entities to find anything more real. They differ among themselves: God is an actual entity, and so is the most trivial puff of existence in far-off empty space. But, though there are gradations of importance, and diversities of function, yet in the principles which actuality exemplifies all

---

[32] Chalmers, pp 153-154.

[33] Mathews, Freya (2003) *For Love of Matter: A Contemporary Panpsychism*, SUNY Press, Albany

[34] Whitehead, Alfred North (1978) *Process and Reality*, New York: Free Press, p. 22 as quoted in Mesle, C. Robert (2008) *Process-Relational Philosophy: An Introduction to Alfred North Whitehead*, Templeton Press, p. 95.

are on the same level. The final facts are, all alike, actual entities; and these actual entities are drops of experience, complex and interdependent.[35]

Whitehead's philosophy is perhaps the most comprehensive challenge to Cartesian dualism in the modern west. It is typically viewed as a radical Heraclitan challenge to Platonism, but ironically roots of it can be traced back to Plato's own notion of matter, intimate with the One, eternally desirous of form.

The popular philosophy of Ken Wilber is based, like Chalmers' position, on a theory of "property dualism" and as such would be supportive of Mathew's stronger version of panpsychism. Expanding on Alfred North Whitehead's conclusions, Wilber asserts that even the smallest physical systems, protons, electrons, atoms, and molecules, must exhibit properties of some kind of proto-consciousness.[36] Wilber's "Integral Philosophy" is founded on the observation that different knowledge disciplines have different ways of describing the same event, and if you line these descriptions up, they correspond nicely to each other. The various models of psychology, for example, describe individuals (Freud, Jung, Piaget, Plotinus) and collective groups (Kuhn, Gebser, Weber, Gadamer) with internal descriptions, whereas the social sciences and the hard sciences attempt to describe the same things with external descriptions (biology, behaviourism, empiricism, systems theory, Marxist theory, social theory). The argument for an internal dimension to all things, i.e. panpsychism, comes from the symmetry of this four-quadrant model (internal-individual, internal-collective, external-individual, external-collective), because the interior and exterior descriptions of things, individual and collective, line up nicely.[37] This doesn't prove anything, but it implies that there's

---

[35] Ibid, p. 95.

[36] Zimmerman, Michael E. (2012) 'Yes Virginia, Consciousness Goes All the Way Down. But Does It Go All the Way Up?' *Integral Life* website, 6 Aug 2012. <https://integrallife.com/yes-virginia-consciousness-does-go-all-way-down/

[37] Wilber, Ken (2001) *A Theory of Everything: An Integral Vision for Business, Politics, Science and Spirituality*, Shambhala, p. 49. "There is now occurring an extraordinary amount of research into organic brain states and their relation to consciousness – so much so that most orthodox researchers tend to simply *reduce* consciousness to brain mechanisms. But this reductionism devastates the contours of consciousness itself, reduces 'I' experiences to 'it' systems, and denies the phenomenal realities of the interior domains altogether. The insidiousness of this reduction of Upper Left

something fundamental about the internal dimension of reality. It's interesting to note that Wilber's argument is founded on the beauty of this symmetry and is not unlike Plato's own argument that a living, intelligent universe is the best universe and the most beautiful.

I think some version of panpsychism makes better sense of our experience of the world than a strictly materialist position. But if making sense of the world is all that matters here, then we haven't understood the point of this investigation. We're really talking about a fundamental change in our relationship to the world. We're talking about healing a sickness that is at the foundation of modernity, one that has caused enormous suffering in the world. When we treat the world around us as if it were dead it becomes something we can exploit. Tragically, this kind of ignorance ignites an obsessive cycle of desire and greed. The more of this dead stuff we possess and manipulate for our purposes, the more of it we want. There's nothing stopping our desire for more.

As Wordsworth demonstrates in the simple lines of his beautiful poem, when we treat the world as a whole, and the parts of it around us as participating in some kind of conscious experience, if we respect the life and integrity of that shared experience, we are more likely to be at ease with our part in it. Our desire to own and manipulate things is now checked by the recognition that we have a relationship with things that is important. That relationship, like all relationships, calls for our respect and gratitude. From this perspective, our life is lived in relationship with a panorama of other conscious events, and the more we're in touch with it, the more we participate in the beauty of this co-creation.

> For oft, when on my couch I lie
> In vacant or in pensive mood,
> They flash upon that inward eye
> Which is the bliss of solitude;
> And then my heart with pleasure fills,
> And dances with the daffodils[38]

[the internal-individual of the four-quadrant model] to Upper Right [exterior-individual] is avoided when we take instead an all-quadrant, all-level approach, which refuses unwarrantedly to reduce any level, line, or quadrant to any other."

[38] Wordsworth, William (1807) 'I Wandered Lonely as a Cloud'. Wordsworth's poem, forced on school children at an early age, is nevertheless still loved, and one

The recognition that everything has some degree of internal experience and participates in some larger form of conscious experience, has the potential to wake us up from the narcissistic dream of modernism and tune us into a deeper care for the whole. From this perspective, our life is not about us anymore it's about caring for the unfolding of this living universe, this happy God. What a stunningly beautiful idea this is. A powerful idea. Indeed, it might just have its own life in us.

Bibliography

Aristotle in 23 Volumes, Vol VIII, On the Soul, *Parva Naturalia*, On Breath, translated by W.S Hett, Harvard University Press, 1986.

Berryman, Sylvia (2016) 'Ancient Atomism' in *The Stanford Encyclopedia of Philosophy* (Winter 2016 Edition), Edward N. Zalta (ed.), URL = <https://plato.stanford.edu/archives/win2016/entries/atomism-ancient/>

Blackmore, Sue (2005) *Consciousness; a Very Short Introduction*, Oxford University Press.

Chalmers, David (1996) *The Conscious Mind: In Search of a Fundamental Theory*, Oxford University Press.

Descartes, Rene (1993) *Meditations on First Philosophy*, Donald A. Cress (trans.), Hackett Publishing.

Hannegan, Brother Justin (2015) 'How Augustine Made Us More than Matter – and Immortal' in <u>Homelitic and Pastoral Review</u>, 9th Aug 2015, URL = <http://www.hprweb.com/2015/08/how-augustine-made-us-more-than-matter-and-immortal/>

Iamblichus (2003) *On the Mysteries*, E.C. Clarke, J.M. Dillon and J.P. Hershbell (trans.) Atlanta: Society of Biblical Literature

Mathews, Freya (2003) *For Love of Matter: A Contemporary Panpsychism*, Albany NY: SUNY Press

of the most popular in the UK. A spark of life that does not die despite of our best efforts to trivialise it.

Meadows, Donella H. (2008) *Thinking in Systems: A Primer,* White River Junction, VT: Chelsea Green Publishing

Mesle, C. Robert (2008) *Process-Relational Philosophy: An Introduction to Alfred North Whitehead,* Templeton Press

Nagel, T. (1974) 'What's it Like to Be a Bat?' in *The Philosophical Review* 83 (4) pp 435-450

Plato (1997) *Philebus 16c,* Frede, D. (trans.), in *Plato: Complete Works,* Cooper, J.M. (ed.), Hackett Publishing Company

— (1997) *Symposium 208b,* Nehamas, A. and Woodruff, P. (trans.), in *Plato: Complete Works,* Cooper, J. M. (ed.), Hackett Publishing Company

— (2007) *Timeous, in The Works of Plato, Vol II,* Taylor T. and Sydenham F. (trans.), The Prometheus Trust

— (2001) *Timeous,* Peter Kalkavage (trans.), Hackett Publishing

Plotinus (2017) *Collected Writings of Plotinus,* Taylor T (trans.), Prometheus Trust

Prigogine, I. and Stengers, I. (1984) *Order out of Chaos: Man's new Dialogue with Nature,* Bantam Books

Proclus (1987) *Proclus' Commentary on Plato's Timeous,* translated by Morrow, G. R. and Dillon, J.M. (trans.) Princeton University Press

Swimme, B. and Tucker, M. E. (2011) *Journey of the Universe,* Yale University Press

Tze, Yuan (2015) *Wellbeing begins with You: Use Your Inner Resources to Heal Your Body and Your Life,* Yuan Tze Centre

Wilber, K (2001) *A Theory of Everything: An Integral Vision for Business, Politics, Science and Spirituality,* Shambhala

Wordsworth, W (1807) 'I Wandered Lonely as a Cloud'

Zimmerman, M. E. (2012) 'Yes Virginia, Consciousness Goes All the Way Down. But Does It Go All the Way Up?' in *Integral Life website,* 6 Aug 2012. <https://integrallife.com/yes-virginia-consciousness-does-go-all-way-down/>.

The Intelligible Intricacy of the Natural World

Ann van Ryn

> *... all things in it [the perceptible universe] are perfect,*
> *that it may altogether be perfect,*
> *having nothing which is not so,*
> *having nothing in itself which does not think;*
> *but it thinks not by seeking but by having.*

Plotinus.[1]

Introduction

At the Prometheus Trust Conference in 2017 the role of modern Western philosophy came into question with regards to the urgent nature of the current environmental issues. What impact if any, has philosophy had on the environment *and* humanity? Has it been relatively harmless or effectively toxic? Either way, the critical or objective nature of philosophical thought would have been lost sight of or even worse, strayed from the Truth of things. These and related questions were further explored by drawing upon ancient natural philosophy as a viable resource for better insight into the natural world.

Philosophy was once the thinking behind the doing. It informed mankind, and provided the fundamental, eternal principles to live by in the light of that knowledge. In the contemporary world however, it seems to be the other way around. More often, ever-changing ideologies determined within economic cultures are geared to feed the insatiable and greatly impact upon the way we think. "Is big, is good! Is more, is better!" *Not so*! Evidence is to the contrary and moreover, our so-called corrective measures have been predominantly short term and superficial, while the problems escalate. There must be more to it. Deep ecologists think so. They call for a radical revision of the

---

[1] Plotinus (2001) *Ennead V*, A. H. Armstrong (trans.), Cambridge, MA: Harvard University Press, *Enn* 5.1.4.13-14.

modern world-view, a call that echoes serious concerns expressed by scholars from many different disciplines.

At the 2010 Prometheus Trust Conference, the importance of being able to distinguish and then to judge effectively was discussed as critical to the far-reaching consequences of our decision-making. I presented a paper at that conference proposing 'A New View through an Ancient Lens' explored through certain themes in the Plotinian natural philosophy. These themes link Intellect which emanates from the One, as the causal power or Principle which gives rise to and permeates the sensible realm on a unifying, self-sustaining mode of consciousness, *synaisthēsis*. Since then, I have expanded upon those themes. The main focus has been on the Plotinian natural philosophy as universally representative of the ancient world-view. I have also turned to traditional symbolism in some instances, to elucidate features of the metaphysical structure of Reality. I draw on my recent thesis on the *noëtic* Unity of Nature focussing on the relationships underlying *synaisthēsis*. As a state in the natural world, *synaisthēsis* explains the integral role of the true Nature of each individual thing in the self-substantive life of the collective.

The aim remained in this paper, to strive towards the reconciliation between the ancient and the contemporary worldviews, by examining the natural unity of *homeostasis* as James Lovelock has identified, as *two* orders as David Bohm proposed, the Intelligible in the sensible realm, within the ancient metaphysical framework.

Step Outside

Clearly, to be able to entertain concepts and ideas beyond our current empirical paradigm would mean stepping outside our generally accepted framework. Similarly, as a writer and poet, Kathleen Raine initially warned against the limitations of the materialist hypothesis, which attributes to matter the great regions of consciousness. Furthermore, Raine noted that sadly and sometimes inadvertently, even the human being is increasingly treated as a mechanism while there is an absurd tendency to attribute human qualities to machines.[2] As an alternative to this, Raine pointed to

---

[2] Raine, Kathleen (2003) 'The Underlying Order: Nature and the Imagination' in *Seeing God Everywhere, Essays on Nature and the Sacred*, Barry McDonald (ed.), Bloomington: World Wisdom, pp 172-3.

many ancient traditions in the Eastern world where the whole of Nature is understood as "a system of appearances whose ground is consciousness itself"[3]. Indeed, as Raine explained, the meaning and values inherent in those traditions see life as Being and consciousness made expressible through the arts as Knowledge of the highest order.[4]

From a completely different discipline, scientist James Lovelock also expressed the urgent need for a reassessment of the modern world-view. Initially, Lovelock demonstrated through the *Gaia* Theory, a natural life supporting system in the physiology of the earth and in its biosphere. The theory included *all* life forms as integral to the life of the whole. It is a feature known as *homeostasis*, a type of wisdom found in living bodies which displays underlying governing faculties or powers. On that basis, Lovelock called for a combined approach by the separate sciences urging especially, a reassessment of the linear mode of thought that restricts our ability to accommodate concepts outside historicism and empiricism.[5]

Physicist David Bohm also saw the limited scope of the contemporary world-view. As early as 1978, he questioned the general approach to quantum physics, which, as a *calculus*, is drawn upon to predict a wide range of experimental results. Although Bohm acknowledged at the time that quantum theory was "the most revolutionary development in modern physics", he did recognize that a large part of its "potential impact on our world-view" had been lost owing to "its inability to accommodate any imaginative conception"[6]. Moreover, Bohm noted that there are essentially stable concepts that have been redefined over time in terms of new orders.[7] He drew upon Descartes who introduced a "precise mathematical form" to determine *two* coordinate orders.[8] On that basis, Bohm proposed an implicate order as First and causal, to an explicate order manifested in the sensible realm. To explain the relationship between the two orders, Bohm compared it to the projection of an image through a

[3] Ibid, p. 173.

[4] Ibid, p. 173.

[5] Lovelock, James (1995) *Gaia: A New Look at Life on Earth*, Oxford: Oxford University Press, p. 116.

[6] Bohm, David (1978) The implicate or enfolded order: a new order for physics in *Mind in Nature*, Washington, DC: University Press of America, p. 37.

[7] Ibid, p. 37.

[8] Ibid, p. 37.

hologram. The unique idea in a hologram is that the image remains complete if interrupted at any given point throughout the entire projection.[9] Bohm's theory is significant for two reasons. Firstly, it corresponds to the ancient idea of Intellect as the Principle of the reality of Being as it permeates the whole of Existence. Secondly, and notably, the hologram demonstrates how the image remains undiminished even at the end of its projection. This is a pivotal point to be taken up later in this paper in relation to the *noêtic* Unity of Nature.

While quantum physics is a subject outside the scope of this paper, Bohm's hypothesis is indicative of the continuing search by many scholars for answers to questions regarding the natural world. Philosophically speaking, I see that both accounts, Bohm and Lovelock, are practicable in the light of ancient epistemology, albeit on different levels of knowledge and both are potentially given life in the context of ancient cosmology. Such is the case for Bohm's *implicate order* that, he claimed, imaginatively captures the essence of a new situation in science, as Lovelock had encouraged. It is from that perspective that ancient natural philosophy offers the intellectual scope for both, and thus the potential to reveal what we desperately need to recover.

The Metaphysical Context

James Lovelock had a holistic view of life on Earth, and significantly his top down approach corresponds on the physical level to the Plotinian model. Lovelock maintained his position even under the constraints of the modern empirical sciences. Similarly, Plotinus' distinctive top down view of Reality set him apart from many of his contemporaries and the Stoics who maintained a material account from the bottom upward. And notably, both Plotinus and Lovelock maintained an all-inclusive approach towards the unity evident in the natural world.

In Lovelock's *Gaia* Theory, the role of all physiological life forms on Earth and in its bio-sphere were examined in order to explain the self-substantive unity, *homeostasis*, underlying the life of the collective. While Lovelock recognised the limitations of his theory, he acknowledged that it ultimately led to important questions on subjects

---

[9] Lovelock, James (2006) *The Revenge of Gaia*, New York: Basic Books, p. 138.

such as "consciousness, life, the emergence of self-regulation and a growing list of happenings in the world of quantum physics".[10] He stressed also, that "important concepts like God or *Gaia* are not comprehensible in the limited space of our conscious minds"; so that they are not rationally constructed, but emerge fully formed from "the seat of intuition".[11]

In a sense consciousness represents the common ground between the Plotinian natural philosophy and the *Gaia* Theory. The essential feature of *homeostasis* is the overall unity of the collective, which in the Neoplatonic account involves the relationships between parts to whole. Plotinus used the term *synaisthēsis* to denote those relationships as a mode of Being in all things, on all levels of Existence. It is the term *synaisthēsis*, understood as a mode of consciousness that provides us with considerable information about the *homeostatic* state of the natural world.

Very early in the Greek tradition, in Plato's *Timaeus*, the cosmos appears as a living creature featuring the First Principles of creation as "intelligence in soul and soul in body".[12] *To an extent*, the *Gaia* Theory corresponds to Plato's account by demonstrating the overall, physiological unity in the sensible realm and possibly, evidence of the Intelligible Unity in a living system. Five hundred years after Plato, Plotinus unpacked those First Principles in terms of an Intelligible hierarchy forming the Unity of Existence.

It was John Dillon who noted that the metaphysical system is implicit in the *Enneads*.[13] The eternal nature of the cosmos is based upon the First Principles in metaphysics. Furthermore, it is within the metaphysical context that the life of the sensible world can be understood as the emanation of its underlying Intelligible Principles. From the Absolute One, Pure Unity, to the Unity of Being in Intellect, then through Soul, to the living Cosmos, the Unity of Being permeates throughout. The system forms a chain of dependency, as each individual thing takes its Being from its prior and therefore has Being and naturally exists in accordance with Being. To reiterate, as

---

[10] Ibid, p. 138.

[11] Ibid, p. 138.

[12] Plato, *Timaeus 30B5* in *The Collected Dialogues of Plato (1964)* Edith Hamilton and Huntington Cairns (eds.), New York: Bollingen Foundation, pp 1162-3.

[13] Dillon, John (ed.) (1991) *Plotinus*, London: Penguin Books, p. xIviii.

each thing is a derivative of its prior, the Unity of Being in Intellect, is passed down. The system is all-inclusive. Plotinus elaborated on the unity of the All by specifically including the stone. As he explained, this is because, "existing for the stone is not [just] being but being a stone". [14] To return to an earlier point illustrated through the hologram, the image or, in this case Intellect, remains entire at any point including in the sensible realm and thus emanates as *noêtic* Unity through Nature. This is why Plotinus maintained that the cosmos "must be an intelligible [sic] universe". [15] At the beginning of *Ennead* 3.viii, *On Nature, Contemplation and the One*, he proposed a difficult and challenging concept. As an Intelligible Principle operating in two orders, Nature conveys Intellect to the sensible realm and on that basis, through its very Being, acts as agent and agenda to the natural world. Therefore, Intellect reaches everywhere for as Plotinus affirmed, "there is no point where it fails". [16]

In the Plotinian system, all things are determined on particular levels within the metaphysical context. Even the separate sciences form a part or aspect of the greater body of Knowledge and represent Truth in that context. In turn, within each discipline, the truth of a proposition is an aspect of the truth of its field, made possible *within the context of the whole* discipline. Thus, the relation of parts to whole as understood in the Unity of Being also applies to epistemology or Knowledge. In *Ennead* 4.ix.5, when Plotinus explained the relationship between Knowledge in Intellect and knowledge in the sciences, he also illuminated the interrelationships throughout Existence. [17]

In Intellect however, Knowledge is complete. On that level, "all the parts are in a way actual at once" and so, each one that you bring forward is complete. [18] In Intellect, cognition and Being coincide,

---

[14] Plotinus (2006) *Ennead VI*, Arthur H. Armstrong (trans.) Harvard University Press, *Enn* 6.2.5. 20-22.

[15] Armstrong indicates that Plotinus is alluding to Plato *Timaeus* 39E8, an allusion above (line 4) to 33B2-3 in Plotinus (2001) *Ennead V*, Arthur H. Armstrong (trans.) Harvard University Press, pp 307-9.

[16] Plotinus (1999) *Ennead III*, Arthur H. Armstrong (trans.) Harvard University Press, *Enn* 3.8.5. 14-15.

[17] Plotinus (2004) *Ennead IV*, Arthur H. Armstrong (trans.) Harvard University Press, *Enn* 4.9.5.5-9.

[18] Plotinus (2004) *Ennead IV*, Arthur H. Armstrong (trans.) Harvard University Press, *Enn* 4.9.5.16-20.

which means that the whole of Knowledge and Existence is identified in terms of its integral parts and conversely, Unity between the parts is integral to the whole. These relationships that begin in Intellect map out a type of spherical climbing frame involving the interconnectedness of all things on and between every level in the Unity of Existence. *This* is the context for the Plotinian natural philosophy.

The Principle Follows Through

In his book *Plotinus on Intellect*, Eyjólfur Emilsson introduced the Double Act Doctrine as critical to the unfolding of Being. The doctrine features the properties and relationships involved in generation and emanation explained as actual and potential states or internal and external Acts on all levels of Existence. Moreover, Plotinus attributed the two Acts to all things including those in the sensible realm, and as previously noted, even the stone.[19] The Internal Act is a state of Being, again in the Unity of parts as one living body. In turn, the External Act is the emanation of Being as the potential state prior to its actualisation in an entity. Thus, the stone contributes to the life of the whole through its own Being. Thus, the Principle, the Unity of Being in Intellect, follows through. The continuity of Intelligible Unity, as a mode of consciousness, is the central theme of my thesis on the *noêtic* Unity of Nature. The aim is to show how all life Forms exist in terms of Being or their true Nature as an Intelligible Unity in their own right on a self-substantive level of consciousness, *synaisthēsis*. Even though in the sensible realm the external Act does not produce new *levels* of Being or hypostases, by ever-renewing their own type, the particular Forms underlying the Unity or *homeostatic* state of the collective, ensure continuity.

Metaphysician, Rene Guénon made two significant points relating to the continuity of Unity. Each category draws its Reality from the preceding one and in doing so, participates in the Reality of its prior. Furthermore, there is the "continuity in distinction" carried through in the relationships between all successive categories. Here too is the recognition of the system as all-inclusive. Each entity is integral to the overall Unity. Guénon stresses that the decisive corollary is that the

---

[19] Plotinus (2001) *Ennead V*, Arthur H. Armstrong (trans.) Harvard University Press, *Enn* 5.4.2.29-32.

metaphysical Infinite, while transcendent and unique, principally participates in and is present to the entirety of its subsequent metaphysical categories, down to and including the entirety of Existence. Ultimately, there is only a single Principle: the metaphysical Infinite itself.[20]

Looking back to *Ennead* 3.iii.1 Plotinus noted the Unity in the living creature, as all genera are brought together.[21] As all belong to Being, there is a single common order as explained earlier, "with distinct parts, and each of the things in it, acts *according to its own nature* while being the same in the whole".[22] What is clear is that there is no separation of mind, as a particular state of consciousness, from body, Intellect exists in the true Nature of all things throughout Existence.

The Missing Link

On recollection, Lovelock did observe the pattern of activity in the distinctly different natural processes, although he knew that there exists an inexplicable unification evident in natural phenomena. Underlying his theory was the missing Intelligible link as recognized in Neoplatonism, connecting the physical processes to the Unity of the whole, in terms of Being. It was Dirk Baltzly who observed in Proclus the eternal nature of the universe that encompasses *all* the species that it presently contains.[23] It ought to be noted then that *homeostasis* as demonstrated through the *Gaia* Theory, is argued on the same basis. As a life-sustaining system, it takes the complexity of the diverse activity of all life forms in *Gaia*, to sustain suitable conditions for life on earth and according to Lovelock, it has done so for eons.[24]

Much earlier in *Timaeus*, Plato told of the Demiurge who combined the same and the different with Being, before dividing that combination into a *"as many portions as was fitting, each portion being a*

---

[20] Samsel, P. (2006) 'The Logic of the Absolute, The Metaphysical Writings of René Guénon' in *Parabola* Vol. 31, No. 3, p. 4.

[21] Plotinus (1999) *Ennead III,* Arthur H. Armstrong (trans.) Harvard University Press, *Enn* 3.3.1.8-28.

[22] Ibid, p. 115. (my italics)

[23] Baltzly, Dirk (2009) refers to Proclus In *Tim. II* 83.20; 84.29; 84.13. Ibid in 'Gaia Gets to Know Herself: Proclus on the World's Self–Perception' in *Phronesis*, Vol. 54, p. 271.

[24] Lovelock, James (1995) *Gaia: A New Look at Life on Earth,* Oxford: Oxford University Press, p. 117.

combination of the same, the different, and being".[25] Emphasizing the diversity of the things in the cosmos, mixed with Being, the mix is then divided proportionately in order to maintain the life of the whole body. It is perfectly designed. Here are three accounts, Proclus, Plotinus and Lovelock, who not only differ from their contemporaries, but also maintain that the dynamic nature of the collective is integral to the life of the whole as defined by the term *synaisthēsis* and therefore, as a *homeostatic* state.

Baltzly explored the idea of intelligence or *Nous*/Intellect in the World Soul in relation to perception in the sensible realm. He identified in Proclus, a vital link between the two. Proclus recognized in Plato's *Timaeus*, the difficult issue of perception in the cosmos where Truth is found within "different gradations of perception"[26]. The key point is in the attribution of Truth to *four* levels of perception, as John Dillon had observed.[27] It is important to note that in Neoplatonic terms, Unity in Intellect equals Truth. Dillon emphasized how Plotinus defended "Unity as the basic reality in the universe" by subjecting particular problems to "rigorous analysis". He noted that Plotinus attributed mind and intelligence to all levels of Existence and in the universe, recognizable on four levels: [1] superficially, as a congeries of physical objects, or [2] we can see in it the workings of Soul, or [3] we can penetrate to its Being, as a system of Forms, or ultimately we can apprehend it, mystically and ecstatically, as Absolute Unity.[28]

Baltzly found that within the range of perception, the cosmos perceives at the highest level. In turn, within the cosmos perception in things is in the form of *aisthēsis*, which as he noted, is "as close as possible in its structural features as cognition, to *noesis*".[29] This is thinking at its highest level. According to Baltzly, this is possible because the Neoplatonists admit Truth at the highest level of actuality in things *as well as their contents*. Moreover, the Neoplatonic

[25] Plato (1964) *Timaeus 35B3* in *The Collected Dialogues of Plato*, Edith Hamilton and Huntington Cairns (eds.) New York: Bollingen Foundation, pp 1164-5.

[26] Baltzly, Dirk (2009) refers to Proclus: *In Timaeus II* 83.16-84.5, in 'Gaia Gets to Know Herself: Proclus on the World's Self–Perception' in *Phronesis*, Vol. 54, p. 266.

[27] Dillon, John (1992) 'Plotinus at Work on Platonism' in *Greece and Rome*, Vol. 39, No. 2, pp 189-204, Cambridge University Press, p. 261.

[28] Ibid, pp 193-4.

[29] Ibid, p. 262.

epistemology is an account of knowledge that "makes being known or being perceived a matter of being that very thing" and not a matter of action or response.[30] On that basis, the Truth in sensible things can be understood as Being and therefore, existence for each thing is according to Being or, its true Nature, just like the stone.

Realities and Truth, a Matter of Perception

For the Neoplatonist, Knowledge and perception are matters of Being. Plotinus had clearly rejected the word perception if it involved the separation of subject from object, which is a feature of sense perception. Indeed, he insisted that "there must be an activity prior to awareness if thinking and being are the same".[31] He saw no reason why Intellect and Soul should not be active without sense perception or any sort of awareness of self or other, where Knowledge exists in the coincidence of Intelligible entities. As Emilsson explained, this one of the key features which highlights the Unity of the Intelligible Principles. As the Principle of cognition and Being, Unity begins in Intellect at a level where Being and Knowledge or, ontology and epistemology are one and the same.[32]

The perception of Realities and Truth rely on the understanding of the relationships within the Intelligible Order as qualitative and moreover, not spatially related to the universe. [33] As Intellect permeates Existence, there is no actual *other* or *above* or *beyond*, but only in terms of distinction, a distinctive way of seeing, seeing the Intelligibles. Initially, Dirk Baltzly observed that the modern worldview appears to be the antithesis of the Neoplatonic account. Plotinus dealt with the issue of perception or the lack of it, long ago. In *Ennead* 5.v.7, he wrote that "actual seeing is double" and so, as we look at things in the sensible world, his instructions were to reverse your way of thinking, or you will be left deprived of God, like the people at festivals who by their gluttony stuff themselves with things

---

[30] Baltzly, Dirk (2009) 'Gaia Gets to Know Herself: Proclus on the World's Self-Perception' in *Phronesis*, Vol. 54, p. 279.

[31] Plotinus (1978) *Ennead I*, Arthur H. Armstrong (trans.) Harvard University Press, *Enn* 1.4.10.8-9.

[32] Emilsson, Eyjólfur, Kjalar (2007) *Plotinus on Intellect*, Oxford University Press, p. 2.

[33] Also see Wilberding, J. (2005) 'Creeping Spatiality' in *Phronesis*, Vol. 50, no. 4, pp 315-334.

... [seeing] "only with the flesh; as if people who slept through their life thought the things in their dreams were reliable and obvious".[34]

While the eyes see the light of an object, "Intellect sees pure light".[35] For Plotinus, the Truth in "seeing" was not a physical matter. Although, he did not deny sense perception *per se*, it is just that true Knowledge is a matter of the perception of the non-material. As Baltzly observed, the Truth of Intellect is present in things throughout the universe, in the most obscure way. [36]

Kevin Corrigan elaborated on the perception of the Intelligibles, as more like a spontaneous identity. He noted as an example, the distinction in "the intelligible [sic] form of loving the other", not in the abstract sense, but for the other's sake and not for anything else.[37] Corrigan also spoke of the Plotinian use of light to symbolize the permeation of the Beauty of Intellect throughout Existence. He understood that seeing Intelligible Beauty is the way that we glimpse Intellect in Soul, Nature and art. From an ordinary reflexive experience, it is as though "the physical divide of two selves see each other".[38] So to *see* as Intellect does, depends upon the possession of and identity with the Intelligible Realities underlying Existence. To recognize their relationships within the universe is to know the *noêtic* Unity of Nature as agent and agenda to the Unity of the natural world.

Think of a hierarchical order of qualities. As Absolute Unity, Intellect emanates through Soul. Soul conveys the individual Forms, bringing the Unity of Being, also known through its qualities as Truth, to the sensible realm. For Plotinus, what this must mean is that overall, there is one nature, Intellect, all realities, and truth [sic]: if so, it is a great god; or, better, not just a god, but it demands as of right that this which it is universal god.[39]

---

[34] Plotinus (2001) *Ennead V*, Arthur H. Armstrong (trans.) Harvard University Press, 5.5.11.19-23.

[35] Ibid, p. 175.

[36] Baltzly, Dirk (2009) refers to Proclus In *Timaeus II* 83.16-84.5 in 'Gaia Gets to Know Herself: Proclus on the World's Self-Perception' in *Phronesis*, Vol. 54, p. 266.

[37] Corrigan, Kevin (2005) *Reading Plotinus*, West Lafayette, IN: Purdue University Press, p. 213.

[38] Ibid, pp 212-213.

[39] Plotinus (2001) *Ennead V*, trans. A. H. Armstrong, Cambridge, MA: Harvard University Press, *Enn* 5.5.3.1-4.

ॐ

An Intricate Web

Ananda Coomaraswamy brings to us from the Vedic texts, the beautiful metaphoric language that conveys the continuity of the Great nature of Brahman, as a single thread weaving all beings together.

> *I know the extended thread (sutram) whereas these offspring are woven:*
> *the thread of the thread I know;*
> *what else but the 'Great' (mahat, the Sun),*
> *of the nature of Brahman"*
> BU iii.7.1-2.

ॐ

> *He who knows the thread and the 'Inward Ruler' (antaryāminam iti),*
> *knows the Brahman,*
> *knows the worlds,*
> *knows the Devas,*
> *knows the Vedas,*
> *knows himself,*
> *knows All…*
> *By the Gale, indeed oh Guatama,*
> *as by a thread, are this and yonder world and all beings strung together*
> JUB 111.4.13-111.5.5.

ॐ

> *Even as the thread of a gem (manisūtram) might be threaded through a gem,*
> *even so is all this strung thereupon [upon the Sun, Vāyu, Prāna, Brahman],*
> *to wit, Gandharvas, Apsarases, beasts, and men*
> *All this is strung on Me,*
> *like rows of gems upon a thread.* [40]
> BG vii.7.

ॐ

---

[40] Coomaraswamy (1986) *1: Selected Papers, Traditional Art and Symbolism*, Roger Lipsey (ed.), Princeton University Press, p. 467.

Bibliography

Baltzly, Dirk (2009) 'Gaia Gets to Know Herself: Proclus on the World's Self-Perception' in *Phronesis*, Vol. 54.

Bohm, David (1978) 'The implicate or enfolded order: a new order for physics' in *Mind in Nature*, Washington, DC: University Press of America.

Coomaraswamy (1986) *1: Selected Papers, Traditional Art and Symbolism*, Roger Lipsey (ed.), Princeton University Press

Corrigan, Kevin (2005) *Reading Plotinus*, West Lafayette, IN: Purdue University Press.

Dillon, John (ed.) (1991) *Plotinus*, London: Penguin Books.

— (1992) Plotinus at Work on Platonism, *Greece and* Rome, Vol. 39, No. 2, pp. 189-204, Cambridge: Cambridge University Press.

Emilsson, Eyjólfur Kjalar (2007) *Plotinus on Intellect*, Oxford: Oxford University Press.

Lipsey, R. (ed.) (1986) *Coomaraswamy 1: Selected Papers, Traditional Art and Symbolism*, Princeton, NJ: Princeton University Press.

Lovelock, James (1995) *Gaia: A New Look at Life on Earth*, Oxford: Oxford University Press.

Lovelock, James (2006) *The Revenge of Gaia*, New York: Basic Books.

Plato (1964) 'Timaeus' in *The Collected Dialogues of Plato*, Hamilton E. and Cairns H. (eds.) New York: Bollingen Foundation.

Plotinus (1978) *Ennead I*, A. H. Armstrong (trans.), Cambridge, MA: Harvard University Press.

— (1999) *Ennead III, A. H.* Armstrong (trans.), Cambridge, MA: Harvard University Press.

— (2001) *Ennead V,* A. H. Armstrong (trans.), Cambridge, MA: Harvard University Press.

— (2004) *Ennead IV,* A. H. Armstrong (trans.), Cambridge, MA: Harvard University Press.

— (2006) *Ennead VI,* A. H. Armstrong (trans.), Cambridge, MA: Harvard University Press.

Raine, Kathleen (2003) 'The Underlying Order: Nature and the Imagination' in *Seeing God Everywhere, Essays on Nature and the Sacred*, McDonald, B., (ed.) Bloomington: World Wisdom.

Samsel, P. (2006) 'The Logic of the Absolute, The Metaphysical Writings of René Guénon' in *Parabola* Vol. 31, No. 3.

Wilberding, J. (2005) 'Creeping Spatiality' in *Phronesis*, Vol. 50, No. 4.

Anthropocene

An Ecstatic Naturalist Approach to the Anthropocene

Marilynn Lawrence

The earth is in trouble. The diversity of life upon the earth is in trouble. Human existence is threatened. For a long time, we've known about the alarming effects of carbon emissions, deforestation, nuclear waste and meltdown accidents, oil spills, pesticides and other pollutants in the soil and waters, and in more recent years, fracking. Optimism that it can all be turned around if we pull together has become an increasingly fragile trajectory. Human consumption is the primary cause of this crisis where the damage, particularly as caused by global warming, is most likely irreversible and the continuity of life on this planet is threatened at every angle.

In terms of geological epochs, the human impact on the ecosystem is known as the "Anthropocene", which follows from the previous epoch, the holocene, that began at the end of the last Ice Age approximately 11,700 years ago. Geologists debate about when this epoch begins and whether it should be officially recorded as following the holocene, or, if it is an extension of the holocene.[1] Earth's warming since the Ice Age is responsible for the thriving of human beings and other organisms. The anthropocene marks the end of thriving and the beginning of climate and ecological patterns that threaten life on this planet and has already cause extinction of numerous species of plants and animals.[2]

The human talent for denying reality has never been more obvious given the current political environment that normalizes anti-scientific and anti-intellectual attitudes. Conscious concern for the environment, and for the devastating impact we have on it, is not as widespread as it ought to be in order for us to collectively take effective actions such as developing green energy sources and

---

[1] See, for instance, Clive Hamilton, Christophe Bonneuil, and François Gemenne (eds.) (2015) *The Anthropocene and the Global Environmental Crisis: Rethinking modernity in a new epoch,* Routledge, pp 1-5.

[2] Ibid., pp 3-4.

agricultural practices. We can identify a multitude of obstacles to positive change (cultural, economic, political, and psychological). Diagnosing this illness does not require deeply philosophical reasoning or any particular theories about nature and human nature. Yet, philosophical theories have played a role in how we reached this global crisis and can help us cultivate ways of thinking out of it (if pessimism is to not take hold completely). We can fight for ecologically sound policies and economies; however, without changing the deep structures of our approach to the world and ourselves, on the whole, our relationship to nature will remain distorted and the threats to life on our planet will continue to worsen.

The goal of this essay is to introduce one of many contemporary philosophies, called *ecstatic naturalism*, that can be integrated with better ways of thinking and living than those theories and beliefs that lead to ecological destruction. Introduced by contemporary American philosopher Robert S. Corrington, ecstatic naturalism developed in dialogue with other alternative forms of naturalism that are together called "religious naturalism".[3] Forms of religious naturalism borrow ideas and methods from wide variety of philosophical traditions including American pragmatism, Continental thought, and Eastern philosophies. They also have a wide variety of expressions and differences among them. What they share in common is the emphasis on the natural world as the primary locus of inquiry while maintaining room for the reality of the sacred, spirit, God, or divinities. Naturalism, in general, is the position that nature is all that there is, and there is no separate world beyond nature. In some definitions of naturalism, there is also no God that resembles the omnipotent, omniscience and eternal force or person of traditional monotheistic religions, nor a God that is separated from or independent of nature.

In contemporary philosophy, the word "naturalism" has been co-opted by the New Atheism movement spearheaded by Richard Dawkins, Daniel Dennett, Sam Harris, and Alex Rosenberg.

---

[3] Because Corrington developed the metaphysical and ethical positions of ecstatic naturalism in a series of works extending over 25 years, the current author finds it difficult to recommend a single work as an introduction to the basic ideas. His texts on ecstatic naturalism include *Nature and Spirit* (1992), *Ecstatic Naturalism* (1994), *Nature's Self* (1996), *Nature's Religion* (1997), *A Semiotic Theory of Theology and Philosophy* (2000), *Nature's Sublime* (2013), *Deep Pantheism* (2016), and *Nature and Nothingness* (2017).

Proponents of this form of naturalism also self-consciously embrace "scientism" as a positive term and believe that nothing which is commonly (and perhaps mistakenly) described as supernatural exists or should be believed to exist.[4] This especially applies to God, angels, ghosts, an afterlife, psychic phenomena, and most beliefs within any religious tradition. This type of naturalism is aligned with classical scepticism of the unseen. It holds the view that science is on track to successfully describe and generate knowledge of the whole of reality, and that scientific inquiry is the only means to generate this knowledge. Proponents of this naturalism generally hold good intentions, particularly the desire to free people from superstitious beliefs and delusion, some of which may be very harmful to humane goals of equality and social justice. The proposed remedy, however, is to treat all religions and spiritual beliefs as a cancer that must be wholly eradicated for a mentally healthy society. This approach is not only insensitive to the values engendered in religious and spiritual traditions, but also paints an inadequate picture of reality based only on observations of nature up to this point. A hard-line atheistic naturalism does not break with but is an extension of the western Enlightenment project that views nature as something to be mastered and subdued for the sake of anthropocentric goals. It also dismisses millennia-long traditions, eastern and western, that have produced valuable metaphysical speculation and experiential information. Specific lines of metaphysical inquiry may ultimately be incorrect or provide incomplete pictures of reality, but they are a part of rich histories of speculative reasoning and attempts to envision the sublime experiences of nature and the divine.

Religious, sacred, and ecstatic forms of naturalism, on the other hand, do not reduce nature to mechanistic causality (while recognizing physical causality and valuing scientific research), and do not shy away from other values that are central to human beings such as religious or transcendental experiences. Each variation of these alternative forms of naturalism runs on a spectrum. On one end is an emphasis on natural processes that we know from science. Ursula Goodenough, a biologist and author of *The Sacred Depths of Nature*, and Wesley Wildman, an anthropologist who integrates neuroscience

---

[4] Rosenberg discusses his positive use of the term "scientism" in his description of New Atheism's naturalism in *The Atheist's Guide to Reality: Enjoying Life Without Illusions* (2011) New York: W.W. Norton & Company, pp 6-8.

in the study of religious experience, represent this end of the spectrum. [5] On the other end is a naturalism that emphasizes metaphysics or speculative philosophy and theology. This is represented by American pragmatist Charles Sanders Peirce's more religious writings, as well as a naturalism that uses the process philosophy of Alfred North Whitehead and Charles Hartshorne. [6] This more metaphysical end of the spectrum may also include contemporary theologian Robert Neville who seeks in his philosophical theology to preserve a creator god, though remains influenced by religious naturalism through his long-standing dialogue with it. [7] Robert S. Corrington's ecstatic naturalism (and deep pantheism) fall somewhere in the middle of this spectrum, holding stakes in evolutionary theory and observable natural processes, as well as in metaphysics and psychoanalysis. Ecstatic naturalism is differentiated from other naturalisms by the following ideas or claims: nature is self-transcending (hence, ecstatic), there is a soul or psyche of nature (concentrated in human existence), phenomenological and psychoanalytic methods are used to access the relation of the self to nature, and there is an underconscious or unconscious of nature.

The various forms of religious naturalism mentioned above set the context for a discussion of ecstatic naturalism. However, each version of religious naturalism could also be explored to yield a better philosophical approach to ecology and the natural world. It's important to note that naturalism is not synonymous with atheistic scientism but is alive with a considerable range of concerns and debates over the integration of the divine or sacred with nature. Ecstatic naturalism is one of these approaches that understands nature in a different way than we usually find in Western

---

[5] Ursula Goodenough (1998) *The Sacred Depths of Nature*, New York: Oxford University Press. For Wesley J. Wildman's neuroscientific approach to religious naturalism, see his *Religious and Spiritual Experiences* (2014), New York: Cambridge University Press.

[6] For more on Peirce as a predecessor of ecstatic naturalism, see Robert S. Corrington (1993) *An Introduction to C.S. Peirce*. Forms of process naturalism, particularly that of Henry Nelson Weiman, are discussed by C. Robert Mesle in *Process Theology* (1993) St. Louis, MO: Chalice Press.

[7] Although Neville doesn't identify himself as a religious naturalist, David Rohr has made an excellent case for such an identification through his commitment to a naturalistic cosmology in 'Neville's Ontological Creative Act: Two Interpretations' in *American Journal of Theology & Philosophy*, vol. 36.2 (May 2015): pp 168-189.

philosophical discourse. It incorporates metaphysics, psychoanalysis, semiotics, ethics, aesthetics and religious thought, and draws from a wide range of thinkers for inspiration. Its theological offshoot, deep pantheism, uses the framework of ecstatic naturalism to dive further into the meaning of the divine within nature and the process of "god-ing."[8] The present effort will outline only a few key ideas from ecstatic naturalism in order to apply them to an approach to our ecological crisis.

Natura Naturans / Natura Naturata

At the core of ecstatic naturalism is the notion that Nature has two dimensions. Nature, as both "nature naturing" *(natura naturans)* and "nature natured" *(natura naturata)*, originated with Ninth Century philosopher John Scot Eriugena, was revived by Benedict Spinoza, treated again by early Nineteenth century German philosopher Arthur Schopenhauer, by American Transcendentalist Ralph Waldo Emerson, and again by mid-twentieth century naturalist Justus Buchler.[9] This view of nature has not been central in the history of philosophy, but it has continued to return as a viable metaphysical option. Nature naturing is an active, perennial, and unpredictable process. It is an organizing power that provides the potencies *(dunameis)* of all things. Nature natured is the multitudinous orders and complexes that result from the potencies of nature naturing. This includes all observable phenomena. What we typically call "nature", as, for instance, our green and blue planet, along with its sand, rocks, soil, microbes, animals, and human beings, is a part of nature *natured*.

The meaning of this twofold and encompassing nature can be further illuminated by unpacking two quotes from Corrington's work. The first one is about the replacement of Heidegger's ontological

---

[8] The concept god-ing won't be discussed here but it is tied to the selving process discussed below. In *Nature's Sublime*, Corrington introduces it as a process in which "extra-human, but not extra-natural, energies enter into the selving process at key junctures helping it to evolve in more decidedly creative ways. God-ing is not *a* god or *the* god in a theistic or even panentheistic sense but is the potency within nature that has a special relationship to the heart of human evolution." (p. 71)

[9] Corrington situates his own understanding of nature naturing/nature natured closer to that of Schopenhauer than of Spinoza (*Deep Pantheism*, 7-10), however, Emerson's appropriation of nature naturing is also a strong influence on ecstatic naturalism (*Nature's Sublime*, pp 123-125).

difference (the gulf between Being/*Sein* and beings/*Seindes*) with the "natural difference".[10] "From the standpoint of ecstatic naturalism, the ontological difference is that between nature naturing and nature natured. The former term refers to the presemiotic potencies of a self-transforming nature, while the latter refers to the innumerable orders of the world."[11] One might immediately notice in this formula that metaphysics (speculative theory about reality and the relations of its components at the most abstract level) and semiotics (the study of signs and meaning available for human beings and other life forms) are treated as compatible, integrated philosophical concerns. Metaphysics and semiotics are usually treated as separate topics, as the former asks about the nature of reality and the latter about the nature of meaning. Corrington notes three intentions for forming this juncture between metaphysics and semiotics. The first is a "revival of pragmatism" without either neo-pragmatic relativism or the divorce of signs from nature;[12] the second is "a transformation of naturalism" away from its materialism and emphasis on efficient causality; and the

---

[10] The 'ontological difference' is a central to Heidegger's project, described in *The Basic Problems of Phenomenology* (1982) as the purpose of philosophy: "Only by making this distinction—*krinein* in Greek—not between one being and another being but between being and beings do we first enter the field of philosophical research." (p. 17). The function of Heidegger's "Being" to dispensate Worldhood to individual beings is that of nature naturing in ecstatic naturalism. For Corrington, Being "continues to invoke static conceptions of space-time particulars and their traits" (*Nature and Spirit*, p. 126).

[11] Corrington, *Ecstatic Naturalism*, p. 3.

[12] Corrington expresses a worry that postmodernism, in the form of the neo-pragmatism of Richard Rorty or the truth-relativity of Foucault clashes with naturalism. For example: 'The contemporary obsession with conventional and arbitrary semiotic codes violates the spirit of naturalism and puts nature and its orders into eclipse. Ecstatic naturalism affirms the absolute supremacy of nature and its internal tensions as manifest in the fundamental divide between nature naturing and nature natured.' *Ecstatic Naturalism*, 60. Twenty years or so since this was written, the extremes of postmodernism are no longer central to academic discourse. However, postmodernism has been blamed for providing intellectual fuel to the alt-facts, fake news and public mistrust of experts (For instance, "Daniel Dennett: 'I begrudge every hour I have to spend worrying about politics'," *The Guardian*, 17 February, 2017. https://www.theguardian.com/science/2017/feb/12/daniel-dennett-politics-bacteria-bach-back-dawkins-trump-interview, retrieved October 29, 2017.) Have postmodern ideas become so pervasive in society that we now question all facts, or were postmodern authors prescient of cultural values that would eventually lead to the widespread destruction of education about critical scientific facts, particularly about the effects of human activity on the environment?

third is "an even more radical transformation of psychoanalysis".[13] As defined here, metaphysics can tell us about nature's scope and definition vis-à-vis the whole of reality, and about the structures and orders that make all beings and the significations among them possible. Pragmatism, especially that geared toward the semiotics of Peirce, keeps metaphysical speculation in check and aligned with human experience and community-based validation that is admittedly fallible.[14] Psychoanalysis, which uncovers emotional forces and drivers in the lives of human beings, reveals similar structures and moods for a world semiosis and, more extensively, for a semiotics of nature itself.[15] This combination of pragmatism, non-reductive naturalism, and psychoanalysis results in "psychosemiosis", a critical component to an ethics of individuals, communities, and the world, as I'll touch upon momentarily.

Nature naturing is described as presemiotic (prior to significations) and self-transforming, or "self-othering". This activity of nature should not be misunderstood as a demiurgic creator god or a producer, whereby nature natured is the product.[16] Nature is still a unified and encompassing whole, but one with a dialectic interaction between its two dimensions; this whole includes human processes, selves or psyches, within nature natured.

A second quote about the twofold or fissured nature touches upon the relation of nature to god or the divine: "One can understand nature naturing as the great unconscious of nature and, as such,

---

[13] For a more complete discussion of these three points, see Corrington, *Ecstatic Naturalism*, pp 4-12.

[14] Ibid. p. 4.

[15] Ibid. p. 10.

[16] Corrington argues that treating nature naturing as a creator god is the panentheistic position held by process theologians. He defends his turn to pantheism in 'My Passage from Panentheism to Pantheism', *American Journal of Theology & Philosophy*, v. 23, n. 2, May 2002: p. 129). I would add to his arguments that a panentheistic view of divinity does not necessarily 'move the dial' toward a philosophical position on nature that centralizes ecological ethics because a divine will or intelligence is still separate from the natural world and is ultimately in charge of the fate of the earth in a traditionally providential way. Nevertheless, it could also be argued that the panentheism of process theology still offers a better approach to nature than traditional monotheisms, because the divine is also immanent in nature and dependent upon it, or intelligent aspects of it. The quarrel between the schools over metaphysics may itself indicate movement in the right direction away from philosophies and theologies that have objectified the natural world.

[nature natured] to the innumerable orders of the world, including god in its many ordinal locations."[17] There's much to decode in this dense statement, including nature's unconscious, the meaning of god or gods within nature (as a feature of deep pantheism), and the meaning of ordinality in ecstatic naturalism. I'll start with the simplest of these, the ordinal metaphysics which can speak of "god in its many ordinal locations."

Ordinal Metaphysics and Ordinal Phenomenology

Ecstatic naturalism incorporates feature of the "ordinal metaphysics" of American naturalist philosopher Justus Buchler. This metaphysical system centres on the interrelated concepts of ordinality, ontological parity, and natural complexes. In Buchler's own words, "Nature as ordinality is *natura naturans*; it is the providing, the engendering condition. Nature as "orders" is *natura naturata*; it is the provided, the ordinal manifestation, the World's complexes."[18] Nature naturing itself is not an order but makes orders possible. Ontological parity, Corrington tells us, "insists that all orders are equally real. Differences between and among orders are not differences of reality but differences of location."[19] In this context, location does not mean a spatial place, but represents a relationship among "things" and traits (including nonmaterial concepts and all that can be conceived or imagined). Not all beings, concepts, or properties are related to all other ones, but they are relevant to or cluster around certain cases. For example, in describing a book on my shelf, the book participates in various orders such as publications by a university press, green objects, hard covered, about the topic of neoplatonism, books containing translations from another language, etc. The book is not related to other orders such as edible things and objects that don't burn easily. For Buchler and Corrington, traditional metaphysical terms such as being, entity, reality, and existence are replaced with "natural complexes", which include whatever is, in whatever way that it is. Complexes cannot be reduced to any essence, universal, or simple component. They are arrangements of relevance, patterns, and

---

[17] Robert S. Corrington (2015) 'Ecstatic Naturalism' in *A Philosophy of Sacred Nature* L. Niemoczynski and N. Nguyen (eds.), p. 14.

[18] Justus Buchler (1990) *Metaphysics of Natural Complexes,* p. 276.

[19] *Ecstatic Naturalism*, p. 13.

clustered traits within natured natured. In this regard, ordinal metaphysics moves away from foundationalism (such as the hierarchical metaphysics of Aristotle or the *cogito*-based foundation of Descartes) toward a pragmatic pluralism.

By linking high-level metaphysics with pragmatic first-person experience, Corrington extends the concept of ordinality to the methods of phenomenology and psychoanalysis. His ordinal phenomenology is influenced less by the methods of Husserl and more by those of William James and Charles Peirce.[20] This approach opens the way to a pluralism of religious experience, and even covers the complexes underlying what is traditionally designated as supernatural or beyond nature. Anyone who has practiced a form of divination, for instance, experiences the insight gained as *real* in a pragmatic sense; hence, the practice relates natural complexes in particular ways. In this sense, the ordinal phenomenology of ecstatic naturalism is a more generous approach to personal experiences which are not readily accessible to scientific scrutiny yet play a significant part in individual and shared reality. Such experiences do not point to something beyond nature but may reflect glimpses of the "engendering condition" of nature naturing.

To return to our second quotation on nature naturing, God (or gods or goddess), it would appear, is considered one natural complex among many. This consideration provides Corrington with a launching point from Buchler's descriptive naturalism into ecstatic naturalism and deep pantheism. Corrington maintains that aspects of the divine are on both sides of the natural difference. Within nature natured, divinity is emergent as a complex or complexes, and is limited or fragmented, as can be said when one experiences a glimpse of a god in a newborn baby or through the genius of a musical performance. On the side of nature naturing, the divine is the providing and sustaining function of the orders and complexes, and so is transcendent of those orders, but not outside of nature.

---

[20] In *Nature and Nothingness* (2017), Corrington describes James as a "master at doing ordinal phenomenology" through his "descriptions of consciousness and the stream of awareness that has 'flights' and 'perchings' throughout." Peirce, on the other hand, "developed his own rich form of phenomenology that he called 'phaneroscopy' . . . Both were ordinal phenomenologist insofar as they went beyond some kind of transcendental ego (pure self-constituting awareness) and rooted the phenomenological enterprise in the orders of nature. This is where pragmatism and naturalism join hands." (p. 110)

Nature's Unconscious

Divinity as emergent from the fissure between nature naturing and natured natured can be labelled as a type of pantheism, but not the Spinozistic monism in which nature and God are identified as the same substance. Corrington calls his version "deep pantheism" where, as he notes, "the term 'deep' signals that this kind of pantheism goes beyond many traditional forms by its strong stress on the unconscious of nature".[21] What does it mean for nature to have an unconscious, and how does it relate to the human unconscious and psychology in general? Corrington identifies nature's unconscious as an element of its "ecstatically self-transforming" character and as "the source for both the human and sentient collective unconscious and the human personal unconscious". [22] We may be in danger of anthropo-morphizing nature by attributing an unconscious to it. However, this attribution brings processes that aid in understanding the psyche, such as dream analysis and the interpretations of symbols, closer to a re-enchanted natural world. Psychoanalytic methods are often considered abstract, intellectual exercises that are geared toward an individual, and divorced from consideration of the whole that is beyond the self. However, *ordinal* psychoanalysis, while still concerned for the health and healing of the psyche, moves away from Freudian drive theory and object relations that focus exclusively on the early experience and symbolization of the parents.[23] It also recognizes that the self's unconscious is an integrated aspect of the unconscious of communities and nature.[24]

One thing to note about nature with an unconscious is that nature could not be equated with an all-wise and omniscience deity or force, and is not to be idealized or romanticized as having an intelligence that is ultimately working toward its Good in a teleological way, as

---

[21] *Deep Pantheism*, p. 95.

[22] *Deep Pantheism*, p. xxiii.

[23] Corrington discusses Heinz Kohut's self-object theory as it relates to one's parents in *Nature's Sublime*, pp 59-63. Ordinal psychoanalysis extends the self-object to "non-human realms of nature insofar as those realms become transparent to the primacy of the natural difference; namely, the perennial fissuring that is the *way* of nature". (p. 62)

[24] "Key to *ordinal* psychoanalysis is its insistence that all analytic work, on both theory and practice, begins and ends with the vast infinite unconscious of nature from out of which the differently infinite unconscious of the human self emerges." (*Nature's Sublime*, p. 29)

Aristotle's acorn is working toward becoming an oak tree. Nor is the providingness (a term coined by Justus Buchler) of nature naturing like the divine providence that has the welfare of human beings in its care. In ecstatic naturalism, nature remains indifferent to human ends, and its unconscious is an "unruly ground" (a concept from F.W.J. Schelling), an abyss lying between the interaction of nature naturing and nature natured.[25] Gustav Mahler, as a proto-ecstatic naturalist, describes his experience with such a nature in a letter where he discusses his monumental Third Symphony:

> That this nature hides within itself everything that is frightful, great and also lovely (which is exactly what I wanted to express in the entire work, in a sort of evolutionary development)—of course no one ever understands that. It always strikes me as odd that most people, when they speak of "nature", think of only flowers, little birds, and woodsy smells. No one knows the god Dionysus, the great Pan. There now! You have a sort of program—that is, a sample of how I make music. Everywhere and always, it is only the voice of Nature![26]

We can consider Pan and Dionysus to be symbols of the unconscious of an encompassing nature that is beyond good and evil. This unconscious is not to be thought of as purposive, but is the ground of purposes, intentions and significations that emerge from it, as from a *chora*, a place where significations are born in the world of nature natured. Corrington refers to *chora* as the "active dimension of the unconscious of nature because it is fundamentally ejective of its own

---

[25] While Schelling's idealism trumps his naturalistic tendencies, his concepts of unruly ground and will of the ground serve as predecessors of nature's unconscious: "[Will of the ground] is not a conscious will nor one connected with reflection, although it is also not a completely unconscious one that moves according to blind, mechanical necessity; but it is rather of intermediate nature, as desire or appetite, petite, and is most readily comparable to the beautiful urge of a nature in becoming that strives to unfold itself and whose inner movements are involuntary (cannot be omitted), without there being a feeling of compulsion in them." *Philosophical Investigations into the Essence of Human Freedom* (2006) Jeff Love and Johannes Schmidt (trans.) Albany, NY: State University of New York, p. 59.

[26] Letter from Gustav Mahler to Dr. Richard Batka, 18 November, 1896. In Donald Mitchell's *Gustav Mahler: The Early Years, Vol. 1*, Revised Edition, (2003), Boydell Press, pp. 99.

rhythms and powers. The unconscious "surrounds" the *chora*, providing it with an infinite reserve of energy and semiosis."[27]

Natural Anthropōs

If nature is self-transcending, and perennially ejecting from its unconscious the materials or signs that are of significance to *someone*, what is the role of the human being within nature? And how does nature's unconscious relate to the unconscious and consciousness of humans and other animals?

Philosophical positions on the relationship of human beings to nature can often go to the extremes. At one end, we are simply more advanced animals, enslaved by our biology, neurology, and a closed system of physical causes. In an attempt to decentralize and de-anthropomorphize nature, the human being has been successful at survival on the global scale, but becomes as insignificant as our earth becomes in the context of many earths that may sustain life across the universe. On the other end of the spectrum, the human being is a temporarily embodied intelligence that can hold dominion over nature and all life within it. Both of these perspectives, a thoroughly decentralized nature and an intellect/nature dualism, in one way or another, support the dream (or nightmare) of artificial intelligence and/or uploaded brains that surpass or replace the human being with an artificial, immortal body.

Ecstatic naturalism addresses the relation of the human being to nature in a different way. It considers the relation of the self to communities and to nature through semiotics that is especially influenced by Peirce, as well as by the psychoanalytic tradition, particularly Jung's theory of the collective unconscious.[28] Semiosis, the giving of and receiving of signs and significance, the basis of communication, is a process available to all organisms. Human semiosis is "but one realm within the larger order of zoösemiosis".[29] Yet, anthroposemiosis, or "psychosemiosis", has unique features not available in other realms of meaning within nature.

---

[27] *Ecstatic Naturalism*, 48. This understanding of *chora* is adapted from Julia Kristeva, but without being confined to a representation of the earliest stage of life or linked to drive theory.

[28] Corrington discusses Jungian archetypes and their importance for ordinal phenomenology in *Deep Pantheism*, pp 57-67.

[29] *Ecstatic Naturalism*, p.181.

Corrington has referred to certain human processes, including the psychological exploration of the formation of selves and communities, that which moves toward both self-actualization and self-transcending, as "nature's psyche". Developing consciousness, starting with exploration of meaning and values while integrating contents of the unconscious, is called the "selving" process. The selving of a human being works at the edge of, or between, the fissure between nature naturing and nature natured. Humans have a unique role (or opportunity) of being in touch with the pre-semiotic potency of nature naturing, while operating in the semiotic realm of nature natured. Ordinal psychoanalysis is a tool for making sense of, and for healing, the individual's connection to the twofold nature.[30] The selving process is a step beyond evolution but emergent from it, toward *involution*.[31]

Selving

The pinnacle goal for the application of ordinal psychoanalysis is the selving process, which is not simply about the individual, but establishes a fluid relationship of the human being to nature. As an ideal, selving appears to be rare, just as freedom of will is limited and difficult to actualize (e.g., on account of entrenched habits or difficult circumstances). One reason for this is that many defense mechanisms prevent an individual from opening up to the personal unconscious, collective unconscious, and nature's unconscious. Openness to the pulsations of nature, of the unruly ground of nature, is a personal risk. As Corrington writes, "radical openness to the unconscious of nature requires courage and the willingness to founder and suffer shipwreck

---

[30] "What we call 'psychosemiosis' seeks a unified theory of the basic structures and behaviours of those signs that are relevant, directly or indirectly, to the human process. Ordinal psychoanalysis is that branch of psychosemiosis that focuses most directly on the pathology and healthy aspects of selving per se.'" (*Nature's Sublime*, p. 35)

[31] The concept of involution is fleshed out in a chapter in *Nature's Sublime*, pp 113-146. Corrington describes it as experienced "as a kind of stretching of the boundaries of experience, a kind of opening and clearing around the edges of the regular/regulated forms of semiosis. The moment of involution is felt to be a potency of an opening that has its source in something larger than human, something divine or religious" (Ibid., p. 115). This rare and transforming phenomenon indicates a brief connection to and insight on nature naturing.

in the face of the uncanny depths of nature naturing".[32] However, to not take this risk is a bigger danger:

> To lose contact with the unconscious of nature is to enter into a power system that can be deeply destructive of semiotic and human prospects. Consciousness becomes persuaded that it has abjected chaos, while it has merely attempted to encircle it with feeble and permeable defensive structures.[33]

Again, the human being, the self-in-making, is neither an insignificant product of natural evolution, nor a disembodied mind that can have mastery over nature. It has, rather, a symbiotic relationship with its origins—its processes, including *techne* or artifice, are deeply embedded within nature. The anthropocene is an epoch where human activity shapes the physical outcome of nature natured, but the relationship between humans and nature is not one-directional at the level of consciousness. Our psychological processes are not separate from nature, but play out the moods and impulses of nature's unconscious.

The self is not an isolated, lone creature in the wilderness, but is born into and contributes to communities. Even Henry David Thoreau, a predecessor of religious naturalism known for advocating solitude, placed value on society, but with a stance toward reform and resistance of its dehumanizing and denaturing configurations. [34] Communities can be psychologically healthy or unhealthy, peaceful or violent. Ecstatic naturalism addresses this by working out the semiotics and psychoanalytics of communities. Corrington begins such work with a distinction between "natural communities" and "communities of interpreters".[35] An example of a natural community

---

[32] *Deep Pantheism*, p. 95.

[33] *Nature's Religion*, p. 130.

[34] This is best exemplified by Thoreau's chapter in *Walden* on visitors to his home in the woods that begins with the statement, "I think that I love society as much as most, and am ready enough to fasten myself like a bloodsucker for the time to any full-blooded man that comes my way." (p. 94) His famous essay, 'Resistance to Civil Government', is itself his contribution and relation to society through sharp criticism of the weaknesses of civil law.

[35] These types of communities and the relations to selving is discussed in several works, particularly *A Semiotic Theory of Theology and Philosophy* (2000) p. 127 ff., and in *Nature's Sublime*, pp 75-112.

is one we are born into, such as a family, a culture based on ethnicity or geographical location, or a religious community. These communities are typically less flexible in terms of novel interpretations and in their extreme form, incline toward tribalism and exclusion of the Other, and can be dominated by an in-group/out-group dichotomy. Communities of interpreters emerge out of natural communities and are more rare and fragile. They value pluralism, novel interpretations, democratic principles, self-reflection, and the welfare of the whole over personal gain. The selving process flourishes in such communities, while is hindered by natural communities on account of a repression of the personal and collective unconscious, and the primal narcissism inherent in them. The self that has not begun to relate to a community of interpreters

> has no sense that a genuine unconscious exists. Its life world (or what there is of it) is all there is, and it makes no sense to probe into anything pre- or posthuman if these orders resist the imperial needs of the self. The distinction between the self and its governing community is so muted that it is almost as if self-consciousness refuses to lift itself out of communal consciousness.[36]

An excellent illustration of the relation of the selving process to the collective unconscious and nature's unconscious is provided by Elaine Padilla in her essay 'Landscapes of the Unconscious and the Longings of Nature'. [37] Padilla relates concepts from ecstatic naturalism to the work of Caribbean philosophers Edouard Glissant and Francisco José Ramos in order to understand deep-seated roots within the collective unconscious and nature's unconscious that are a result of the violence from colonialism and racism. [38] Patterns of

---

[36] Corrington, *A Semiotic Theory of Theology and Philosophy*, p. 133.

[37] In *Nature's Transcendence and Immanence: A Comparative Interdisciplinary Ecstatic Naturalism*, (2017) M. Lawrence and J.S. Oh (eds.), pp 103-119.

[38] Padilla notes the how Corrington grounds and deepens Jung's collective unconscious within nature: "Corrington progresses several steps deeper into the collective unconscious than Jung when darkening the enlivening processes of creative activity of the unconscious as it pertains to the infinite inter-relationality of nature. What for Jung is 'suprapersonal', in the sense of an ancestral archaic stock, is progressed by Corrington into the deepening of the unconscious through the pathways of the dead as the seedbed of an infinite relational soil. As if buried in the depths of nature, by adopting a Hindu-like stance, selves are reborn through the unconscious." (Ibid., p. 106)

oppression do not simply heal and end when the external sources of violence are removed. They sit deep within the nature's unconscious; yet they can transmute into a source of healing through the creative energies that emanate from nature naturing. Violence on the human level is deeply connected to the whole of nature. For this reason, human selving moves beyond individual concerns and toward the ecological. On this matter, Padilla writes:

> With the deepening into the womb of nature that is useful in overcoming the human impulse toward employing dominant masks and exclusive personifications, can also come expressions of interconnectivity with which to counter the prevalent androcentrism. The human who becomes conscious of her widespread entanglement can be an active communal member who minimizes practices that deplete resources or desecrate the land.[39]

Artistic and symbolic expressions can also work toward bringing individuals and cultures in touch with nature's semiosis to enable regional and global change.

Approaching Ecology Through Ecstatic Naturalism

The network of ideas from ecstatic naturalism may provide a better outlook for approaching the environmental crisis than traditional naturalisms and other modern Western philosophies that separate the human mind from its body, surroundings, and natural world. The concepts introduced here include: the natural difference of nature naturing and nature natured; ordinal metaphysics and ordinal phenomenology that leverage "natural complexes" rather than essences and a hierarchy of being; nature's unconscious and unruly depths; nature's psyche as the relationship between the human being and nature as a whole; and the selving process aided by communities of interpreters. While providing a metaphysical and semiotic framework for understanding nature, ecstatic naturalism alone may not offer a complete picture for understanding and acting upon our ecological reality. It works best when connected to other philosophies, disciplines, and ways of living.

---

[39] Ibid, p. 108.

As Plotinus reminded us, "All things are full of signs, and the sage is one who learns one thing from the other."[40] Nature's signs are not exclusively divinatory but express the language of a dynamic and self-transcending nature. The importance of semiotic theory for a philosophy of ecology cannot be understated. For example, a connection between the semiotics that inspires ecstatic naturalism and ecology was explored by Leon Niemoczynski, primarily through the concept of the "midworld" by twentieth century philosopher John William Miller.[41] The midworld is the environment, not as a place or container for subjects and objects, but as a "cosmic locus" constituted by the multiple active expressions of organisms and natural phenomena.[42] It is not a world that fills itself with signs of its will, per se, but sign and symbol-rich environments *created* by interconnected non-human and human agents who affect and are affected by these environments. As Niemoczynski concludes:

> [W]e must see that relations on the level of the cat, the cow, or the rat, the plant, and the insect, and the environment, for example, are not only just as real as but are also just as important as any human being's relation to its world and environment, because there is a facticity held in common among them.[43]

Miller's "midworld" bares the hallmark of the ontological parity of Buchler and Corrington's naturalism, in the sense that it supports a pluralism of perspectives and values beyond a dominant monocultural human view of reality.

Ecstatic naturalism can further extend its scope in ecological theory through dialogue with deep ecologists such as David Abram. For instance, Abram's description of shamanic experience bears resemblance to the ecstatic naturalist position that the supernatural is actually natural:

> Yet we should not be so ready to interpret these dimensions as "supernatural," nor to view them as realms entirely

---

[40] *Ennead* II.3.7.12-14. Μεστὰ δὲ πάντα σημείων καὶ σοφός τις ὁ μαθὼν ἐξ ἄλλου ἄλλο.

[41] See L. Niemoczynski, 'The Meaning of Nature: Toward a Philosophical Ecology' in *Nature's Transcendence and Immanence*, pp 93-102.

[42] Ibid., p. 94.

[43] Ibid, p. 101.

"internal" to the personal psyche of the practitioner. For it is likely that the "inner world" of our Western psychological experience, like the supernatural heaven of Christian belief, originates in the loss of our ancestral reciprocity with the animate earth.[44]

Abram's naturalization and sensualisation of the collective unconscious points to nature's unconscious as well as the reciprocity and interconnectedness of beings within nature. Another point of connection is Abram's incorporation of research by linguists such as Benjamin Lee Whorf on how different conceptions of reality are tied to language. Abram holds to Whorf's observation that the Hopi people make a distinction between the "manifest" and the "manifesting". The manifest is all perceived by the senses, the present and past, while the manifesting is described as forms in the "heart of nature" and all that is "gathering itself toward manifestation within the depths of all sensible phenomena".[45] This distinction could readily describe the natural difference (nature natured/nature naturing) of ecstatic naturalism. The heart of nature is made of the thoughts, feelings, and intentions of all organisms. Deep ecology and the ecstatic naturalism of Robert Corrington may differ, however, on the philosophical details about nature's interconnectivity. For Corrington, the interconnectedness of natural beings is not in such a way that every order is relevant to every other order—nor is it a panpsychism, if what is meant by this term is the priority and ubiquity of mind as a uniform substance in things (such as in Leibniz' monadology).[46]

---

[44] D. Abrams (1996) *The Spell of the Sensuous: Perception and Language in a More-than-Human World*, New York: Vintage Books, p. 300.

[45] Ibid., p. 190.

[46] Corrington's criticisms of panpsychism are primarily targeted at the philosophy of Charles S. Peirce. On Peirce's panpsychism he writes, "To elevate the mind to a generic category is to violate the basic insight that nature has no whatness. Innumerable 'whats' emerge from nature . . . but there is no reason to assume that nature is a vast pool of mind that links every 'what' together into a network of internal relations." *An Introduction to C.S. Peirce: Philosopher, Semiotician, and Ecstatic Naturalist* (1993) Lanham. MD: Rowman & Littlefield Publishers, p. 213. Panpsychism fits uncomfortably with the general premise of naturalism - nature is all that there is. However, insofar as panpsychism is conceived of as a type of consciousness or sentience that extends beyond higher level organisms to any natural being that participates in semiosis, this form's compatibility with ecstatic naturalism may be worth further consideration. This is at least implied in the contention of Nicholas L. Guardiano, who sees Corrington's critique of Peirce's panpsychism as unnecessarily restrictive on semiosis of animals and natural

Panpsychism, while an attractive alternative to Cartesian mind/body dualism and to naïve materialism, is not endorsed in Corrington's system. Nevertheless, the mysteries of divinity in the indirect glimpses of nature naturing remain honored. Humans and other natural beings are connected in ways that even manifest as sacred, but this does not mean that every natural entity holds consciousness, awareness, or intentionality in the same or similar way as human beings do.

To return to our global ecological crisis, journalists recently reported that the more optimistic among climate experts have concluded that we have only three years to halt the climbing global temperature before the trend toward an uninhabitable planet for most humans and non-humans is irreversible. [47] On the surface, our environmental crisis is inextricably tied to political and economic systems. The poor and disadvantaged suffer altogether in impoverished countries located in the harshest drought-stricken environments (such as South Sudan, Ethiopia and Somalia).[48] And, in more wealthy countries, the poor and non-white suffer climate change of the anthropocene more acutely due to lack of insurance for disaster recovery and lack of systemic support—New Orleans and Puerto Rico. The obstacles to global cooperation are, at root, clashes of community norms and values. The power struggle over the fate of our earth can be framed as that between "natural communities" that lack personal and community growth through insular tribalism and ignorance of nature's unconscious, and "communities of interpreters", which acknowledge the ancestral pain rooted deep in the soil and seek creative solutions to heal communities and the earth. Yet, we have to be realistic and admit that changes in dominant philosophical outlooks are slow, long-term revolutions. We can seek better ways of thinking about nature, such as through ecstatic naturalism, and be personally transformed by them; however, the urgency for widespread action required on the part of governments

---

processes that are supported by science. (See Guardiano's 'Groundwork for a Transcendental Semeiotics of Nature' (2017) in *Nature's Transcendence and Immanence*, pp 77-92.)

[47] Chris Mooney, 'These experts say we have three years to make changes that would halt the climbing climate change under control. And they're the optimists', *The Washington Post*, retrieved July 2, 2018.

[48] Althor, G. *et al.* (2016) 'Global mismatch between greenhouse gas emissions and the burden of climate change' *Scientific Report*, 6, 20281. https://www.nature.com/articles/srep20281 (retrieved November 14, 2017).

and powerful organizations is immediate, and philosophy is too slow for the current need. But that is no reason for not continuing this work at the philosophical level. Regardless of the political decisions in the next few years that will determine the severity and speed of climate change, what we do collectively, and how we think and form more enlightened communities, will continue to impact the planet for generations. The price of *not* embracing better psychological and philosophical approaches to nature is just too high.

Bibliography

Abram, David (1997) *The Spell of the Sensuous: Perception and Language in a More-than-Human World*. New York: Vintage Books.

Buchler, Justus (1990) *Metaphysics of Natural Complexes*, Second Expanded Edition, eds. Kathleen Wallace, Armen Marsoobian, and Robert S. Corrington. Albany, NY: State University of New York Press.

Corrington, Robert S. (1992) *Nature and Spirit: An Essay in Ecstatic Naturalism*. New York: Fordham University Press.

—   (1993) *An Introduction to C.S. Peirce: Philosopher, Semiotician, and Ecstatic Naturalist*. Lanham, MD: Rowman & Littlefield Publishers.

—   (1994) *Ecstatic Naturalism: Signs of the World*. Bloomington and Indianapolis: Indiana University Press.

—   (1997) *Nature's Religion*. Lanham, MD: Rowman & Littlefield Publishers.

—   (2000) *A Semiotic Theory of Theology and Philosophy*. Cambridge: Cambridge University Press.

—   (2013) *Nature's Sublime: An Essay in Aesthetic Naturalism*. Landham, MD: Lexington Books.

—   (2016) *Deep Pantheism: Toward a New Transcendentalism*. Lanham, MD: Lexington Books.

—   (2017) *Nature and Nothingness: An Essay in Ordinal Phenomenology*. Landham, MD: Lexington Books.

Goodenough, Ursula (1998) *The Sacred Depths of Nature*. New York: Oxford University Press.

Guardiano, Nicholas L. (2017) "Groundwork for a Transcendental Semeiotics of Nature," in *Nature's Transcendence and Immanence*, eds. M. Lawrence and J.S. Oh, 77-92.

Hamilton, Clive, Bonneuil, Christophe, and Gemenne, François, (eds.) (2015) *The Anthropocene and the Global Environmental Crisis: Rethinking modernity in a new epoch*. London and New York: Routledge.

Heidegger, Martin (1982) *The Basic Problems of Phenomenology*, Albert Hofstader (trans.) Bloomington and Indianapolis: Indiana University Press.

Lawrence, Marilynn and Oh, Jea Sophia (eds.) (2017) *Nature's Transcendence and Immanence: A Comparative Interdisciplinary Ecstatic Naturalism*. Landham, MD: Lexington Books.

Mesle, C. Robert (1993) *Process Theology*. St. Louis, MO: Chalice Press.

Mitchell, Donald (2003) *Gustav Mahler: The Early Years, Vol. 1*, Revised Edition. Boydell Press.

Niemoczynski, Leon (2017) 'The Meaning of Nature: Toward a Philosophical Ecology' in *Nature's Transcendence and Immanence* M. Lawrence and J.S. Oh (eds.) pp 93-102.

Niemoczynski, Leon and Nguyen, Nam T. (eds.) (2015) *A Philosophy of Sacred Nature: Prospects for Ecstatic Naturalism*. Landham, MD: Lexington Books.

Padilla, Elaine (2017) 'Landscapes of the Unconscious and the Longings of Nature' in *Nature's Transcendence and Immanence*, eds. M. Lawrence and J. S. Oh (eds.) pp 101-118.

Rohr, David (2015)'Neville's Ontological Creative Act: Two Interpretations' in *American Journal of Theology & Philosophy*, vol. 36.2 (May 2015) pp 168-189.

Rosenberg, Alex (2011) *The Atheist's Guide to Reality: Enjoying Life Without Illusions*. New York: W.W. Norton & Company.

Schelling, F.W.J. (2006) *Philosophical Investigations into the Essence of Human Freedom* (2006), trans. Jeff Love and Johannes Schmidt, Albany, NY: State University of New York.

Thoreau, Henry D. (1992) *Walden and Resistance to Civil Government, Second Edition*, ed. William Rossi. New York and London: W.W. Norton & Company.

Wildman, Wesley J. (2014) *Religious and Spiritual Experiences*. New York: Cambridge University Press.

Navigating the Anthropocene: Insights from the Wisdom of the Corpus Hermeticum

Dr. Sally Jeanrenaud & Jean-Paul Jeanrenaud MSc (Oxon.)

Abstract

What is nature? And what is humanity's role in the world? Such questions have been asked for millennia and constitute major themes of philosophical enquiry. However, they take on a special urgency for leaders in the context of the Anthropocene, a new geological era in which "human activities have become so pervasive and profound that they rival the great forces of nature" and have potentially catastrophic consequences for all life on earth.[1]

In this paper we review the characteristics of three meta-narratives that address human-nature relationships: Anthropocentric, Cosmocentric, and Theocentric. [2] We appraise their contested ontologies and epistemologies, or different assumptions about "being" and "knowing", which are embedded in contrasting worldviews, and which profoundly shape how global sustainability problems and solutions are framed and legitimized today.

The paper goes on to explore insights from ancient wisdom, and in particular ideas from the Hermetic tradition. It outlines the Hermetic idea of "The Three Heads of Knowledge'": Atum (or God), Cosmos, and Humankind, and argues that such a framework can help establish a more integral worldview today. The Hermetic system presents a broader view of human nature, of Mind (Nous), Soul and Body, with a capacity to have relationships with many planes of being – both spiritual and material; and a higher human purpose, related to fulfilling our spiritual potential.

---

[1] Steffen, W., Crutzen, P.J. & McNeill, J.R., (2007), 'The Anthropocene: are humans now overwhelming the great forces of nature' in *AMBIO: A Journal of the Human Environment* 36 (8): 614-621

[2] In this chapter the words 'Cosmocentric' and 'Ecocentric' are used interchangeably.

Hermetic wisdom outlines a spiritual path of "regeneration", cultivated through quiet contemplative practices and a pious life. This interior journey involves transcending the limitations of time, space and generation, and expanding the consciousness to merge with *Nous* – or the Mind of God. Self-realization implies oneness with the truth of divine intelligible causes, principles and powers. This knowledge is beyond human opinion, and the knowledge of the laws of nature.

We propose that the ancient wisdom of Hermes has several implications for addressing contemporary challenges. Its integral worldview provides a key to reconciling apparently contradictory philosophies and enriches our understanding of the paradox of what it means to be human: "a part of", as well as "apart from" nature. It also suggests methods of social and ecological regeneration. Unlike most sustainability solutions today, these methods focus on realising humanity's inner spiritual potential and role. These include but go beyond both Anthropocentric and Cosmocentric worldviews.

1. The Challenges of the Anthropocene

Scientists claim we have entered a new geological era they have named the Anthropocene, in which "human activities have become so pervasive and profound that they rival the great forces of nature".[3] We are warned that we face a "perfect storm" of interconnected social, environmental, and economic challenges, which have potentially catastrophic consequences for all life on earth.[4] These challenges relate to:

Planet. We are currently using the equivalent of 1.5 planet's worth of resources to fuel our economic growth, and consumption, generating risks for business.[5] Our fossil fuel based, linear, take-make-waste economy creates climate disruption, biodiversity loss, water shortages, resource scarcity, violent conflicts, and mountains of

---

[3] Steffen et al. (2007) Crutzen, P.J. & Stoermer, E.F., (2000), 'The "Anthropocene"' in *Global Change Newsletter*, 41, 17

[4] Jeanrenaud, S., Jeanrenaud, J-P. & Gosling, J. (eds.) (2017), *Sustainable Business: a one planet approach*, Chichester, UK: Wiley

[5] WWF (2016), *Living Planet Report 2016: Risk and Resilience in a New Era*, Gland, Switzerland: WWF

toxic waste. The "ecological disconnect" between people and nature is undermining our life support systems.[6]

People. Wealth is not trickling down. Just eight men own the same wealth as the 3.6 billion people who make up the poorest half of humanity.[7] Power and privilege are skewing the economic system, increasing extreme inequalities, and creating a "social disconnect" between the rich and the rest. This is unethical, unjust, socially divisive, politically corrosive, and ecologically and economically damaging in the long term.[8]

Profit. The financial sector is unstable, favouring speculation and "phantom wealth" over investment in real wealth.[9] This "economic disconnect" is driving boom and bust cycles, creating debt, holding governments hostage to corporations and financiers, and undermining efforts to invest in a sustainable economy.

Power. Corporations spend billions of dollars a year on lobbying governments, international trade and financial institutions, and influencing decisions relating to taxes, subsidies, trade deals and legislation. These support private gain at the expense of people and planet and threaten democratic processes.[10]

Person. Rates of stress and depression are increasing worldwide. Some 1 million people die by suicide each year, and it is the leading cause of death among young people.[11] Materialistic values and consumerism generate chronic dissatisfaction, do not fulfil our human potential, and create an inner 'spiritual disconnect'.[12]

Countless analysts point to the failure of outdated paradigms and worldviews that shape our perceptions of nature, and our place in the

---

[6] Scharmer, O. & Kaufer, K. (2013), *Leading from the Emerging Future. From Ego-System to Eco-System Economics. Applying Theory U to Transforming Business, Society and the Self*, San Francisco: Berrett-Koehler Publishers

[7] Oxfam (2017), 'An economy for the 99%', Oxfam Briefing Paper, January 2017

[8] Scharmer & Kaufer (2013)

[9] Korten, D. (2010), *Agenda for a New Economy: From phantom wealth to real wealth*, San Francisco: Berrett-Koehler Publishers

[10] Jeanrenaud et al. (2017)

[11] WHO (2014), *Preventing Suicide: a global imperative* (Geneva: WHO)

[12] Scharmer & Kaufer (2013)

world. Many argue for the need to rethink our eco-philosophies and eco-psychologies if we are to survive the Anthropocene.[13]

An influential line of debate is that arrogant anthropocentric mindsets and values need to be replaced with ecocentric approaches – ones which recognize that all life is interconnected and interdependent, and that humans are "part of nature". Some argue that western religious thought (particularly Christianity) [14] and modernistic philosophies, which have privileged human reason, and justified human control of nature, are the cause of our current ecological predicament.

This chapter recognizes the validity of such perspectives and agrees that they make important contributions to expanded awareness. However, in this chapter we argue that such positions can be further enriched by the wisdom of the ancients, which goes beyond anthropocentric and ecocentric worldviews, to embrace spiritual dimensions. We explore insights from the *Corpus Hermeticum* which help "re-member" deeper ways of seeing and being,[15] which may provide new outlooks for navigating the Anthropocene.

2. People Nature Narratives

What is "nature"? What is humanity's role in the world? And why do these questions matter? Such questions have been asked for millennia and constitute major themes of philosophical enquiry. Today, there are many contrasting and contested schools of thought, which have become the rich subject matter of eco-philosophy. This field of scholarship draws from philosophy, anthropology, ecology, ethics, psychology, linguistics, arts and theology.

---

[13] Heikkurinen, P., Rinkinen, J., Jarvensivu, T., Wile, K., Ruuska (2016) 'Organising in the Anthropocene: an ontological outline for ecocentric theorizing' in *Journal of Cleaner Production*. Vol. 113: 705-714; Montuori, A., Purser, R., Park, C. (1995) 'Limits to Anthropocentrism: Towards an Ecocentric Organization Paradigm' in *The Academy of Management Review 20(4):1053-1089*

[14] White, L. (1967) 'The Historical Roots of Ecological Crisis' in *Science* Vol. 155:1203-1207

[15] We use the verb to 're-member' to mean to reintegrate separated parts, and to recall our essential nature.

It is not the intention of this paper to examine the roots and variety of eco-philosophies in detail, which are well reviewed elsewhere (for example see Pepper, 1989, 1996). Rather, this section will outline three broad meta-narratives, which lie beneath this diversity, namely: the Anthropocentric, Cosmocentric and Theocentric. See Table 1 for examples of diverse people-nature narratives.

Table 1. Examples of Contemporary People-Nature Narratives

Deep Ecology: nature has intrinsic value that transcends human values (Naess, 1973).
Animal Liberation: non-human beings are part of the moral community with rights (Singer, 1975).
Social Ecology: ecological and social problems are rooted in problems of social hierarchy (Bookchin, 1980).
Ecofeminism: the Scientific Revolution is involved in the ecological crisis and the devaluation of women (Merchant, 1980).
Political Ecology: ecology is shaped by politics, economy, and society (Blaikie, 1985).
Spiritual Ecology: The universe is a communion of subjects rather than a collection of objects (Berry, 1988).
Ecological Modernization: the economy will benefit if economy and ecology are combined (Hajer, 1995).
Eco-Paganism: religious rituals and practices based on reverence for nature (Taylor 1995).
Indigenous Wisdom: indigenous cultures and knowledge are critical to the protection of biodiversity (Posey, 1999).
Environmentalism of the Poor: protecting nature is involved in the liberation movements of the poor (Guha, 1999).
Bright Green: sustainability solutions can be found through eco-technological design & social innovation (Steffen, 2003).
Panpsychism: sees the world as a communicative presence in its own right, capable of a dialogical congress with us (Mathews, 2003).
Dark Ecology: humans are waking up to their enmeshment with other beings as a result of the Anthropocene. 'Nature', as an idea, is no longer relevant (Morton, 2009, 2016).

Three Meta-Narratives

Jeanrenaud (1998) outlined three meta-narratives, or contrasting eco-philosophies, to help interpret diverse perspectives influencing international conservation policies and practices.[16] These help to expose different ontologies and epistemologies shaping ideas about what we think nature "is", and how we "know" it. They also help explain why sustainability problems and solutions are framed and legitimized in such diverse ways today. These are:

i.   Anthropocentric: the view that nature and god are contained in humans.

ii. Cosmocentric: the view that humans and god are contained in nature.

iii. Theocentric: the view that humans and nature are contained in god or father-mother mind.

i.   Anthropocentric

"Humans know nature through socially-constructed science. Nature per se does not exist. Nature is only the name given to a certain contemporary state of science."[17]

The Anthropocentric narrative puts "humans" centre stage. Humans are usually seen as apart from nature, due to human attributes of self-consciousness and reason. Some of its more technological roots can be traced back to the scientific revolution and the image of "nature as a machine", and Baconian scientific rationalism.[18]

More recently, constructivist philosophers have argued that what we consider to be "nature" and "natural" varies across cultures, and that we cannot know nature or god independently of a cultural lens. Rather, we make them in our image. We ascribe meanings to nature

---

[16] Jeanrenaud, S. (1998) *'Can the Leopard Change its Spots? Exploring People-Oriented Conservation in WWF'*, PhD Monograph, School of International Development, University of East Anglia; Jeanrenaud, S. (2002) *People-Oriented Conservation in Global Conservation. Is the Leopard Changing its Spots?* London: IIED & Brighton: IISD

[17] Larrère, C. (1996) 'Ethics, politics, science, and the environment concerning the natural contract', in J. Baird Callicott and Fernando J. R. da Rocha (eds.) 1996 *Earth Summit Ethics Toward a Reconstructive Postmodern Philosophy of Environmental Education.* Albany, NY: SUNY Press, p. 22.

[18] Pepper, D. (1989) *The Roots of Modern Environmentalism*, London: Routledge

and interact with it on the basis of those meanings.[19]   Such perspectives do not necessarily appeal to objective science for the facts in defining sustainability problems. Rather they are inclined to ask, "what *counts* as a problem, and to whom?".

The root causes of sustainability problems are framed in social, political or economic terms. For example, they highlight how social inequalities and injustices are driving some forms of environmental degradation. Sustainability solutions are likewise framed in these sociological terms, and emphasise cultural, economic and political answers.[20] From this perspective it can be argued that *nature and god are contained in people, and it is culture that mediates nature and god.*

On the positive side, Anthropocentrics are receptive to plural knowledge systems; analyze the inter-connections between social and ecological issues, and importantly, expose the link between knowledge and power. However, from an extreme post-modern epistemological position, nature appears to have no value or significance beyond our perception of it, and all knowledge systems become equal. Critics have pointed out that this over-socialized view of nature can be used to justify a hubristic pursuit of human interests at the expense of all other life forms, a trend which some claim is undermining planetary life support systems.[21]

ii.   Cosmocentric

" . . . *the truth is we ARE nature. In fact, biomimicry works precisely because there is no difference between what we do and what other organisms do — the boundary between us and the rest of the natural world is a false one and dissolves when you consider what's really important, what makes life worth living.*"[22]

The Cosmocentric narrative puts "nature" centre stage. Pepper outlines how some early cosmocentric streams of thought shaped

---

[19] Evernden, N. (1992) *The Social Creation of Nature*, London: John Hopkins University Press; Seeland, K. (ed.) (1997) *Nature is Culture: Indigenous Knowledge and Socio-cultural Aspect of Trees and Forests in Non-European Cultures*, London: Intermediate Technology Publication

[20] Bookchin, M. (1980) *Toward an Ecological Society*, Montreal: Black Rose Books; Merchant (1980); Blaikie, P. (1985) *The Political Ecology of Soil Erosion in Developing Countries*, New York: Longman

[21] Benton, T. (1994) 'Biology and Social Theory in the Environmental Debate' in *Social Theory and the Global Environment*, Redclift, M. & Benton, T. (eds.)

[22] Benyus, J. (2012) p. 10

nineteenth century romanticism, and poetic conceptions of nature.[23] The influential philosophy of "deep ecology"[24] claims that nature has intrinsic value that transcends human values, and that our estrangement from nature is a root cause of environmental problems. More recently, and influenced by the evolution of systems thinking, Cosmocentric philosophers claim that humans are part of nature, the product of evolution and subject to the same laws as the rest of nature, and that there is no dividing line between humans and non-humans.[25] Indeed, our self-realization is dependent on recognizing our interdependence and oneness with nature.   More recently, anthropocentric categories of thought have been critiqued for separating humans from nature, suggesting that even the concept of "nature" is redundant.[26]

Cosmocentric solutions to global sustainability problems focus on the need for humans to live in ways that do not to exceed the earth's carrying capacity or transgress planetary boundaries. It is argued that we need to reclaim our connection with non-human nature and develop ecocentric ontologies[27]. From a Cosmocentric standpoint, it can be argued that *god and people are contained in nature*, and that it is *nature that mediates humanity and god.*

On the positive side Cosmocentrics challenge the arrogance of the Anthropocentric position, and our separation from nature. They promote an understanding of the interdependent character of natural systems, and foster respect for other life forms. However, where Cosmocentrics stick narrowly to the science of the material realms, they tend to overlook the socially constructed nature of knowledge, and the knowledge of transcendent or spiritual planes. Taken to an extreme, such views can support biological determinism (we are simply products of nature or our genes), which has been used to justify and excuse any human behaviour, including violence and

---

[23] Pepper (1996)

[24] Naess, A. (1973) 'The shallow and the deep long range ecology movement, a summary' in *Inquiry* 16: 1-4

[25] e.g. Benyus (2012)

[26] Mathews, F. (2003) *For Love of Matter, a Contemporary Panpsychism*, Albany NY: SUNY Press; Morton, T. (2009) *Ecology without Nature, Rethinking Environmental Aesthetics*, Cambridge MA: Harvard University Press; Morton, T. (2016) *Dark Ecology: for a Logic of Future Co-existence*, New York: Columbia University Press

[27] Heikkurinen et al. (2016)

euthanasia. It is also critiqued for its undertones of paganism, and association with quasi-fascist Aryan movements.[28].

iii.   Theocentric

"In our inner world there is something not bound by the laws of nature, by the laws of time and space. In the inmost of our soul there is the world of spirit, and the world of spirit is free."[29]

The Theocentric narrative puts God or Divinity centre stage. It assumes the subsistence of a spiritual source, preserver and goal of all life, which is a reality behind and beyond existence. This transcendent and immanent reality is beyond time, without boundaries, and non-material, but is the cause of all finite and corporeal beings. Nature is valued because it is an outward expression and symbol of God. Humanity has the capacity to know and relate to this realm through spiritual insight or noesis.[30] Sustainability problems are seen as the result of inner human perversions, such as greed, aversion or delusion.[31] Sustainability solutions are framed in terms of inner work, purification and transformation, and living in conformity with the Way, the Dhamma, or Divine Wisdom. From this perspective it can be argued that *people and nature are contained in God,* and that it is *God that mediates people and nature.*

On the positive side, Theocentrics challenge the scientific materialism of both Anthro- and Cosmo-centric positions, and have ideas, which resonate increasingly with post-material science.[32] Theocentric approaches foster a reverence for the sacredness and mystery of life and see the transcendent reflected in nature. However, when taken to an extreme, deferral to God, or an over-emphasis on the impermanence of existence, can undermine responsibility towards manifested nature, and produce limiting fatalistic attitudes with

---

[28] Schwartz, W. (2009) 'Obituary: Arne Naess' in *The Guardian* Thursday 15th January 2009 https://www.theguardian.com/environment/2009/jan/15/obituary-arne-naess (accessed 8/11/17)

[29] Mascaro, J. (1965) *The Upanishads*, London: Penguin, p. 20

[30] Mascaro, J. (1965)

[31] Batchelor, S. (1992) 'The Sands of the Ganges. Notes towards a Buddhist and Ecological Philosophy' in *Buddhism and Ecology*, Batchelor, M. & Brown, K. (eds.), London: Cassell

[32] Beauregard et al. (2014)

respect to environmental degradation. Emphasis on reforming "interior" nature can be used to excuse passivity in relation to "exterior" nature. Furthermore, a doctrinaire approach, at the expense of reason, can support unchallenged religious dogmas, which support repressive theocratic political regimes.

Table 2. People, Nature and God in Different Meta-Narratives

	Anthropocentric	Cosmocentric	Theocentric
Ontology	Subjective being	Objective being	Spiritual being
Epistemology	Socially constructed	Positivist science	Noesis
Human position	Apart *from* nature	A part *of* nature	Humans engage with spiritual and material realms
Value of nature	Use Values	Intrinsic value Scientific value	Sacred value
Sustainability Problems	Social-political-economic injustice	Transgressing planetary boundaries	Inner transgressions; greed, hate, delusion
Sustainability Solutions	Social-political-economic reform	Protection of nature; nature based solution	Spiritual / Inner transformations

While such eco-philosophies rarely constitute pressing everyday concerns for decision-makers, they are deeply embedded in the ways we see ourselves and the world, and shape leadership and management approaches. How we perceive nature is not ethically neutral. Philosophical subtexts contain moral and normative arguments with different political and economic agendas, which drive social movements, influence policy and funding decisions, and affect lives. They therefore need to be made visible and carefully examined.

For example, WWF's mission is to "achieve the conservation of nature" and "to build a future in which humans live in harmony with nature".[33] But conservation practitioners interpret the concepts of "nature", and how to "live in harmony with nature" in contrasting ways. Conservation history reveals that ideas about what constitutes a threat to nature, how to protect it, and how conservation is legitimized have evolved over time, privileging the interests of some groups over others.[34]

The three meta-narratives confront us with several versions of reality and ways of knowing. Each narrative appears true in certain senses. Our experiences may draw us to each worldview, yet the extremes of each seem repelling. To hold one perspective seems to deny the truth of the other. From the standpoint of contemporary science, and logical argumentation, they can't all be true. Can such views ever be reconciled? The next section explores insights from ancient wisdom, with a focus on the Hermetic tradition, a perennial philosophy, which helps establish a more integral model.

3. Insights from the Hermetic Teachings

3.1   Background to the Hermetic Tradition

This section outlines a theoretical framework inspired by the Hermetic Tradition, one of the world's oldest wisdom traditions, which may offer fresh perspectives on how to navigate the contemporary Anthropocene. The Hermetic texts were compiled in the early centuries CE but their origins are lost in antiquity. Scholarship believes the Hermetic writings to be based on oral wisdom teachings originally derived from ancient Egypt.[35]

These wisdom teachings are attributed to Hermes Trismegistus, also known as Thrice Greatest Thoth (the Ibis-headed Egyptian god). The Greeks of the classical and Hellenistic period considered Thoth and Hermes to be one and the same.[36]

---

[33] WWF (2016)

[34] Jeanrenaud (2002); Corry (2015)

[35] Salaman, C. van Oyen & Wharton, W.D. (1999) *The Way of Hermes. The Corpus Hermeticum*, London: Gerald Duckworth & Co.

[36] Hart, G. (2005) *The Routledge Dictionary of Egyptian Gods and Goddesses*, London: Routledge

The teachings were originally never written down, but the precepts and axioms were later collected together in narrative-style. The major philosophical or religious texts of the Hermetic doctrine include:

The *Corpus Hermeticum*, which consists of seventeen short texts composed in Greek, and which are presented in dialogue form between three generations of teachers and disciples.

The *Asclepius* (or The Perfect Sermon), composed in Latin.

The *Definitions of Hermes Trismegistus to Asclepius*, composed in Armenian.

The *Emerald Tablet*.

It is widely accepted that the *Corpus Hermeticum* was produced between the first and third centuries AD in Alexandria, a then cosmopolitan city including a mix of Greek, Egyptian, Jewish and other traditions. The origin and authenticity of the texts have been much debated, with some scholars rejecting the works as a miscellany of Hellenistic thought ascribed to an ancient Egyptian sage, but with little native Egyptian origin. More recent scholars have recognized the specific contributions of Egyptian thought to the texts.[37]

A Greek manuscript of the *Corpus* was translated into Latin by Ficino in 1471, where it subsequently had influence on Renaissance thinking. There have been several English translations including the first by Dr. John Everard in 1650; J.D. Chambers in 1882; W.W. Westcott in 1894; G.R.S. Mead in 1906; Nock and Festugière 1946; Copenhaver 1992; and Salaman, van Oyen & Wharton, 1999; Freke, T. & Gandy, P. 2008. There have also been various arrangements of the *Corpus*, including one by the Editors of *The Shrine of Wisdom*, First Edition 1923, based on several of the earlier translations. This arrangement has shaped the conceptual framework presented in this paper.

The Hermetic tradition greatly influenced early Christian and Renaissance thought and science, although its main principles can be found in all the world religions. The teachings are not associated with any particular religion or creed, but are considered a "Master Key", which opens the doors to the mysteries.[38] The Christian Church later

---

[37] Quispel, G. (1999) 'Preface' in Salaman, C. van Oyen & Wharton, W.D. (1999) *The Way of Hermes. The Corpus Hermeticum*, London: Gerald Duckworth & Co.

[38] Three Initiates (1940) *The Kybalion: Hermetic Philosophy,*. London: Yogi Publications Society.

distanced itself from Hermetic philosophy, and it subsequently went underground and became associated with esoteric and secret societies and teachings.

There are many good reasons for bringing this profound philosophy to light in the context of current global sustainability challenges. One powerful idea – that of an "integral world view" – is explored below. Section 3.2 outlines its major features; while section 3.3 considers some of its implications, and perhaps fresh perspectives for navigating the challenges of the Anthropocene.

3.2 An Integral Worldview

Hermetic wisdom provides a basis for developing an integral worldview based on its model of Three Heads of Knowledge, which provides a key to understanding, and perhaps even a reconciling of divergent eco-philosophies.

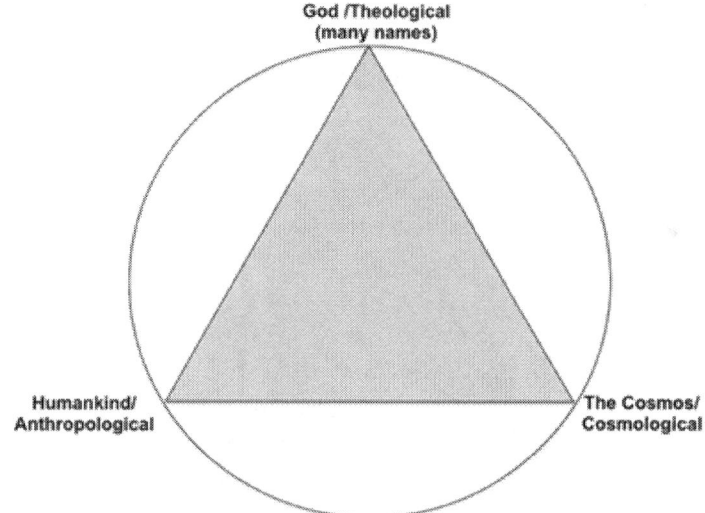

Fig 1. The Three Heads of Knowledge

The Hermetic wisdom presents three fundamental and interrelated philosophical principles of reality, within *one worldview* (rather than competing worldviews). These have been called the Three Heads of Knowledge; Three Worlds; or Spheres of Being; the Theological, Cosmological and Anthropological; or God, Cosmos, and Humankind. In fact, the Hermetic tradition is perhaps the earliest known doctrine to philosophically distinguish between these ideas. It includes the three ideas of God, the Cosmos and Humankind as one interconnected and interdependent whole. *God (many names)*. The Hermetic tradition recognizes a non-material reality that substands, and lies hidden behind, the manifested universe, but is also mirrored and manifested within it. Some writers describe it as an "Infinite Living Mind", which transcends our ordinary understanding of life and mind.[39] It is an ineffable but intelligible source, beyond names, although it has been called Atum; the One; the ALL; Light and Life; Father-Mother Mind; God (many different names). It is considered Eternal (outside time); Infinite (without boundaries); Immutable (not subject to change). It is prior to all things, but it is also immanent within the manifested, materialized Cosmos. While it is an undifferentiated unity, beyond categories and distinctions, it is within all particularized things. It is the creative source of being, the power of life, and the intelligible principle of all things, upon which all things depend and by which they are sustained. It interpenetrates all things, and yet retains an eternal, exempt transcendence. It moves all things, but is Itself neither moved nor subject to birth, decay, and death.

The Cosmos. In Greek, the idea of Cosmos literally denotes order and beauty (in contrast to Chaos meaning empty and void), but it is also often associated with the actual material world contacted by the senses. In the Hermetic tradition the Cosmos can be contemplated as an all-inclusive unific idea, as well as a multiplicity of diverse existences, lives, and intelligences. It *subsists* as a oneness, which some call the Cosmic Mind, or the image of God; and *exists* as the physical cosmos, which is a perfect reflection of this unity. The Cosmos is the principle by which all lives proceed and are manifested, held together and related to each other, and to their ends. It is the totality of all that is objective to God. It is filled with the energy of God, which it expresses and manifests in an infinite variety of existences. It gives rise to an outer world of change, time, space, generation and decay; but is distinct from the everlasting and creative source of all manifestation, which is beyond time, space and motion.

Humankind. In the Hermetic system, humankind is endowed with Mind (or Nous), Soul and Body. Humans are said to be microcosms of the macrocosm – a blend of both spiritual and corporeal principles.

---

[39] Three Initiates (1940), p. 65

As said in the *Corpus Hermeticum*: "From Life and Light, Man became Soul and Nous; from Life – Soul, and from Light – Nous."[40] The Soul is considered to be the non-material life-force of human beings. Nous is the power of Mind, the light of intellect, through which humans come to know the Cosmos and God. Both Nous and Soul are of the same immortal essence as God. Humankind also has Body, made of physical elements, which is mortal and subject to birth, growth, decay and death.

Humans have a unique blend of both matter and spirit, with both a mortal and immortal nature, which gives them a position as intermediary, a "blessed station in the midst"[41], and the capacity to participate in both the material and spiritual worlds. They are the only physical beings said to be able to bridge these dimensions, which gives humankind special roles and responsibilities.

Humans can be distinguished from other creatures because they possess the potential to participate in higher mind (Nous, or the Mind of God). The Hermetic spiritual journey focuses on participating in higher levels of mind and consciousness, and on understanding the mirrored relationships between the spiritual and the concrete phases of reality. This participation can only be achieved by purifying the mind and life, by living piously, through contemplative practices, and by developing right knowledge (*gnosis*), speech (*logos*) and mind (*nous*). Indeed, it is said that humankind can embrace the whole Cosmos through Nous, and was created to appreciate and wisely tend and embellish the beauty of creation.

It is important to emphasise that the Hermetic system presents three Heads of Knowledge as interdependent principles in one integral worldview, or plural-unity, rather than as contested or competing worldviews. This is why they are presented diagrammatically as three points within one circle in Figure 1, and in "*logoi*" terms, rather than in "*centric*" terms, which tend to prioritize one worldview over the others (i.e. Anthropo*logical*, rather than as Anthropo*centric*).

---

40 *Corpus Hermeticum*, Ch. I:17
41 The Shrine of Wisdom (eds.) ([1923] 2015) p.49

Extracts on the Three Heads of Knowledge from Hermetic Texts

Atum (God)

God as Unmanifest: "But the unmanifest for ever is. Because it has no need to manifest, being eternal, it is that which makes all other things manifest. It makes all things manifest, but is never itself manifest, and generates without itself being generated, and makes all things apparent but itself is unapparent. For appearance is only in things which are brought into being. For coming into being is nothing other than appearance." (*Corpus Hermeticm*, 5:1 Hermes to Tat)

God as Most Manifest: "God is always immanent in His work, being Himself that which He creates. For if they were separate from Him, all things would collapse, all would perish of necessity, since there would be no life. But if all things are living, and life is one, then God is one." (*Corpus Hermeticm*, 11:14 Nous to Hermes)

God as the Unmanifest-and-the-Most-Manifest: "This is God, greater than any name. This is the unmanifest, this the most manifest. He is that which is contemplated by Nous, yet which may be seen by the eyes. He is the incorporeal, the many-bodied, or rather the all-bodied. There is nothing, which He is not. For all that is, He also is. And for this reason He possesses all names as they are from one Father, and because of this He has no name, because He is the Father of all things." (*Corpus Hermeticm*, 5:10 Hermes to Tat)

Relationships between God, Cosmos and Man: "So there are these three: firstly, God, Father and the Supreme Good. Secondly the Cosmos. And thirdly, Man. God contains the Cosmos, and the cosmos man. The Cosmos is the son of God, and Man the son of the cosmos, and as it were the grandson of God." (*Corpus Hermeticm*, 10:14)

The Cosmos

"Therefore Eternity is in God; the Cosmos is in Eternity; Time is in the Cosmos; Generation is in time . . . Therefore the source of all things is God; Eternity is their essence; and the Cosmos is their matter. The power of God is Eternity; the work of Eternity is the Cosmos, which has never come into being, but is forever coming into being through Eternity. Therefore the Cosmos will never be destroyed (for Eternity is indestructible), nor will anything in it cease to be, for the Cosmos is encompassed by Eternity." (*Corpus Hermeticm*, 11: 5, 7-9)

"Everything must always be begotten at exactly the right place. The Creator is in everything. He does not dwell just in one thing, nor does He create in one. He begets them all. His power being active is not separate from what He has begotten, for all that is begotten exists by reason of Him. Through me (said the Pymander) behold the Cosmos open to your vision and contemplate deeply its beauty; its body without taint. Nothing is more ancient. It is ever new and ever in prime; indeed it exceeds its prime." Salaman, C. van Oyen & Wharton, W.D. (1999) (*Corpus Hermeticm*, 11:6).

Humankind

"Nous, the Father of all, who is life and light, brought forth Man, the same as himself, whom he loved as his own child, for Man was very beautiful, bearing an image of his Father. It was really his own form that God loved, and he handed him over to all his creatures." Salaman, C. van Oyen & Wharton, W.D. (1999) (*Corpus Hermeticm*, 1:12)

"Man beyond all living things on Earth, is twofold: mortal because of his body, but immortal through the Essential (i.e. Archetypal) Man. For though he is immortal and has authority over all things, yet he suffers the conditions of mortals, being subject to Fate." Salaman, C. van Oyen & Wharton, W.D. (1999) (*Corpus Hermeticm*, 1:15 Nous to Hermes)

"Man is a mighty wonder for he passes into God's Nature as though he were himself divine. How happy is the blend of human nature. Joined to God by his resemblance to Divinity, he looks down upon the part by which he is common with the earth. Man has his place in the blessed station of the midst; so that he loves those below himself, and, in turn, is loved by those above. Heaven seems not too high for him; for it is measured by the wisdom of his Mind (Nous) as though it were quite near." Salaman, C. van Oyen & Wharton, W.D. (1999) (The Perfect Sermon, *Corpus Hermeticm*, 5. 1-2)

The Pymander to Hermes: "Grow to immeasurable size. Be free from every body, transcend all time. Become eternity and thus you will understand God. Suppose nothing to be impossible for yourself. Consider yourself to be immortal and able to understand everything; all arts, sciences and the nature of every living creature. Become higher than all heights, lower than all depths. Sense as one within yourself the entire creation: fire, water, dry, moist. Conceive yourself to be in all places at the same time: in earth, in the sea, in heaven; that you are not yet born, that you are within the womb, that you are young, old, dead; that you are beyond death. Conceive all things at once: times, places, actions, qualities, quantities; then you can understand God." Salaman, C. van Oyen & Wharton, W.D. (1999) (*Corpus Hermeticm*, 11:20)

But why is it significant to differentiate Three Heads of Knowledge?

Firstly, teasing out three principles expands the field of science and ideas, to include: the spiritual and concrete worlds, the noumenal as well as the phenomenal, the incorporeal as well as the corporeal. It thus helps avoid the limitations of either predominantly spiritual or materialist worldviews. This approach resonates with the emerging field of post materialist science, in which "Mind represents an aspect of reality as primordial as the physical world. Mind is fundamental in the universe, i.e. it cannot be derived from matter and reduced to anything more basic."[42]

Secondly, it helps avoid confusion between principles. If these principles are conflated with each other, the field of thought, and science, narrows; and insights into important phases of being, and their relationships are overlooked. The very fact that we can distinguish between Humankind, the Cosmos, and God reveals these fundamental distinctions. Indeed, even the act of asserting that 'they are one', implies that they are intuitively perceived separately. But:

Humankind is not God, because otherwise humans would be omnipotent, omniscient and omnipresent, which they clearly are not.

Humankind is not the Cosmos, because humans are self-conscious and self-determining and can decide to consciously work with (or against) the laws of the Cosmos.

God is not the Cosmos, because this would make God the totality of finite, changeable and mortal existences, without infinite, immutable and immortal essence and attributes.

God is not the Soul or Life-Force of the Cosmos, because it would make God a huge animal, with the Cosmos as a body, subject to birth, decay and death.

The Cosmos is not God, because it is not the eternal source of Being, Life and Intellect, beyond time, space and motion.

The Cosmos in not the Soul, because the Cosmos contains matter, and the Soul is non-material and unitary.

---

[42] Beauregard, M., Schartz, G.E., Miller, M., Dossey, L., Moreira-Ameida, A., Schlitz, M., Sheldrake, R. & C. Tart (2014): 'Manifesto for a Post-Materialist Science' in *Explore: The Journal of Science and Healing*, 10 (5): 272–274

Thirdly, the Hermetic tradition also presents the correspondences and inter-relations between these principles. While they may be considered distinct ideas or heads of knowledge for the sake of analysis, in certain senses they can all be seen as part of each other. God contains the Cosmos, and the Cosmos contains Humankind (see Figure 2). However, in the Hermetic framework, while Humanity is within the Cosmos, it is distinct from it, just as God is within the Cosmos but distinct from it.

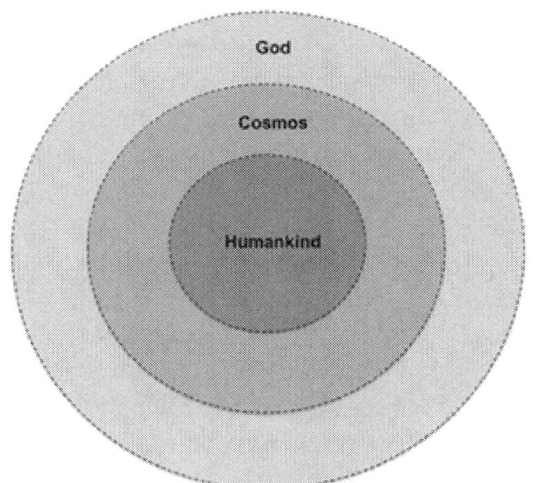

Fig. 2 Correspondences Between the Three Heads

The Hermetic framework presents manifested worlds as mirrors of an intelligible, eternal Divine reality, and presents inter-related planes of truth as subjective and objective to each other, in a cascading spectrum. The Hermetic axiom, "As Above, so Below; As Below, so Above", suggests one set of universal principles, but operative in different phases of manifestation. In the Hermetic system, it is humankind's prerogative to penetrate to worlds beyond the Cosmos, through participating in Mind or Nous (see Figure 3).

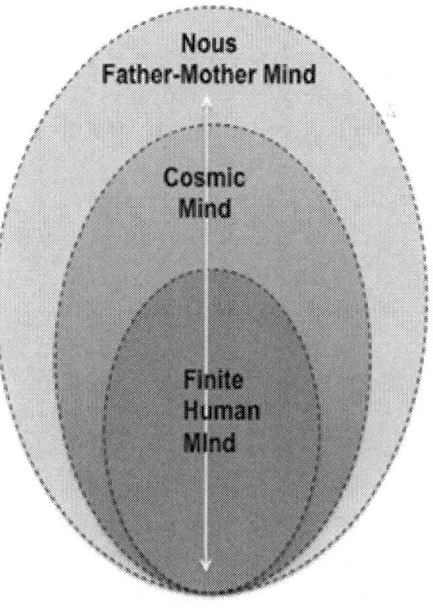

Fig. 3 Humankind's potential to expand consciousness

3.3   Some Implications of an Integral Worldview

3.3.1   Source of all Eco-Philosophies

One consequence of an integral worldview is that every particular eco-philosophy can rediscover its roots within it, and learn to appreciate the contribution of the others.

The Anthropocentric perspective, which focuses on Humanity, is one which recognizes the self-conscious, self-determined and creative power of humans, to imagine and construct their own worlds. But, without recognizing its interrelationships with theological and cosmological principles, humanity's infinite potential is limited, as is the harmony and prosperity that would result from living in accordance with cosmic laws.

The Cosmocentric perspective, which focuses on Nature, is one which recognizes the inter-relationships and inter-dependencies of life in all its diversity, and the wisdom of living according to life principles in solidarity with all other beings. But when it does not acknowledge its interrelationships with anthropological and theological principles, it reduces human beings to just another species among many, and fails to recognize humans' unique attributes and roles, which give humans the capacity to make ethical choices in the light of reason. It risks remaining limited to materialist approaches.

The Theocentric perspective, which focuses on God, is one which recognizes the eternal transcendent source of all being, life and intelligence, and which fosters reverence and a recognition of the sacredness of creation. But without recognizing its interrelationships with the anthropological and cosmological principles, it risks seeing humans as fallen and in need of salvation, and can result in transcendentalism, which fails to see God immanent *in* humans and *in* nature.

When each is considered in isolation it is difficult to reconcile these different ontologies and epistemologies scientifically. Science relies on rules of thought based on the "law of excluded middle term", which states that "a thing either is, or is not another thing". Those who see reality under only one aspect are inclined to disagree with those who see it under another, supposing their worldview to be contradictory, rather than complementary.

However, from an integral perspective, if any one Head of Knowledge is taken alone, the truth becomes one-sided.

Hermeticism suggests a way of reconciling these diverse ontologies and epistemologies because it recognizes different planes of being and ways of knowing them. From the perspective of Three Heads of Knowledge, it is not a matter of choosing "either/or", but rather of choosing "and/and", by applying the law of paradox, which states that "a thing is and at the same time is not, in different senses". For example, by integrating the three perspectives, we may understand that humanity is paradoxically both "part of nature", as well as "apart from" nature.

Cosmocentrics might claim that it is this latter way of thinking that has encouraged a sense of separation from nature, which is at the root of our current ecological crisis. The fact that we do not see ourselves as part of nature is the reason that nature has been abused and degraded. However, drawing distinctions between the principles of God, Cosmos and Humankind is *not* the real problem, rather it is how humanity is living in the absence of an integrating worldview, and is therefore not fulfilling its spiritual role.

3.3.2   The Spiritual Path to Enlightenment

Another consequence of integrating Three Heads of Knowledge, is that human enlightenment and final liberation is conceived of at the highest level: as oneness with Nous or Divine Mind.

The Hermetic concept of human "regeneration" or "rebirth" involves an expansion of consciousness above the realms of time and space, and the laws of nature. It includes, but goes beyond the Cosmos and self-realization "in nature".

The human mind can turn in two directions, towards matter and towards spirit. When turned outwards the consciousness can gather knowledge of the material and phenomenal realms through the senses. But by contemplating inwards and upwards, the human consciousness can transcend the material planes and come to understand more subtle intelligible layers of reality, including the primal nature of being, life and intelligence itself.

This expansion takes place in the silence of profound contemplative practice, in which the consciousness ultimately enters eternity and understands all things at once.

The key to the ascent to Nous is undertaking the deep work of inner purification, and overcoming all the hindrances, which keep humankind attached to the mundane worlds. In the *Corpus Hermeticum* these hindrances are known as the Twelve Tormentors, which cause humans to suffer and include: ignorance, grief, lack of self-control, desire, injustice, greed, deceit, envy, treachery, anger, rashness, and malice. But they can all be transmuted by becoming "God-like" through the contemplation of the beauty of Primal Goodness, "for like is intelligible only to like".[43] As it says in the *Corpus Hermeticum*, only pious souls enter Nous. Nous is set up as 'a prize before Souls'.[44]

The Alchemists always insisted that the art of transmutation depended upon the transforming influence of a superior principle. For example, hate can only be transmuted by love; divine knowledge casts out ignorance; joy replaces grief; intemperance is expelled by temperance; falsehood by truth, as so on. The Twelve Tormentors, are said to be driven out by the ten powers of the Decad (a Divine number containing the keys to all creation). The alchemical stories of 'turning base metal into gold' can be seen as allegories of the inner spiritual work that needs to be done for the Soul to know God. In relation to the self, the greatest obstacle was seen as covetousness, or put a different way, attachment to one's own limited ego in thrall to passion[45].

Finally, as Hermes declares: "Nous enters the pious Soul and leads it into the light of divine knowledge". Once regenerated in Nous, it is said that the Soul never tires of hymning praises and gratitude to God, "and pouring blessings upon humankind, both in words and deeds – in imitation of its own Divine Father-Mother".

Figure 3 (see above) indicates that in the ascent to Nous, the human mind can expand interiorly beyond the limitations of the finite mind and penetrate deeper and higher layers of consciousness into what is called Cosmic Mind, and then Father-Mother Mind, the root and eternal source of all perfections, principles and powers.

3.3.3   Ecological and Social Regeneration

Our final consideration is whether humankind can use Hermetic wisdom to serve and heal people and the planet, in the context of the Anthropocene. Can humankind borrow Hermetic principles to transform wider ecological and social sustainability challenges?

---

[43] *Corpus Hermeticum*, 11:20

[44] *Corpus Hermeticum*, 4:3

[45] Burckhardt, T. (1997) *Alchemy, Science of the Cosmos, Science of the Soul*, Kentucky: Fons Vitae

Hermetic wisdom suggests that hindrances can only be transmuted through the transforming influence of a superior principle. But if a cosmocentric worldview is adopted and humans are seen simply "as part of nature" (as many eco-philosophers suggest today); or if an anthropocentric worldview is maintained, and humans are viewed as the supreme intelligence, we will continue to be the victims of our partial views of reality. Rather, a Hermetic perspective suggests that social and ecological regeneration ultimately depends upon recognizing a principle superior to both humans and nature – the third Head of Knowledge – the Theological.

Hermetic wisdom also suggests that the path of regeneration and rebirth begins with a simple life coupled with inner contemplative practices on the nature of the Divine. This proposes a radically different approach to sustainability, which usually focuses on solving problems "out there". We would argue, however, that learning to cultivate the inner-place from which we operate, through such reflective practices, is key to achieving a deeper and lasting shift in mindsets and values. Put simply, we need to change from the 'inside-out' and restore the balance between being and doing.[46]

The inner journey and ascent to Nous brings wisdom, imbues life with higher purpose, and a conscious awareness of the non-material but intelligible, causes, archetypes, prototypes and paradigms informing nature. It may help develop humanity's potential for cooperation with these higher principles or cosmic intelligences. As a consequence, humans would become more effective healers of, and co-creators with, nature.

The Hermetic tradition teaches that humankind is meant to wisely tend the beauty of the Cosmos; and that nature is incomplete and waiting for humanity to play its part in its upliftment. If humanity works with higher purpose, purity of intention, and knowledge of a wider sphere of principles and intelligences, it could work to transform current challenges into opportunities, overcoming the cycles of poverty, and the degradation of the natural world, by mimicking the abundance and power of the divine (Theomimicry).

---

[46] Jeanrenaud, S. & Jeanrenaud, J-P. (2017) 'The Mindful Promise: Leading with Integrity for a Sustainable Future' in Mabey, C., & Knights, D., (eds.) (2018) *Leadership Matters: Finding Voice, Connection and Meaning in the 21st Century*, New York and London: Routledge

Burckhardt emphasizes that such alchemical work requires purity of intention, and the aspiration to benefit wider creation. As he puts it:

> ...the requirement that the pupil of Hermes must only seek to transmute elements in order to help the poor – or nature herself – in need, recalls the Buddhist vow to seek the highest enlightenment only with a view to the salvation of all creatures. Compassion alone delivers us from the artfulness of ego, which in its every action seeks only to mirror itself.[47]

4. Conclusion: "Re-Membering" the Way

Can Hermetic wisdom teach us anything today, to help us navigate the challenges of the Anthropocene? We draw the following conclusions:

1. Hermetic wisdom provides a key for establishing an Integral Worldview, rather than competing worldviews. The Three Heads of Knowledge: God, Cosmos and Humanity expand the field of science and ideas. It provides the basis for understanding relationships between different sets of principles, and for reconciling contested eco-philosophies, which tend to prioritize one principle only. From an integral worldview, each eco-philosophy contains an element of truth, but not the whole truth. Each errs when taken to an extreme, or when considered alone. The Three Heads of Knowledge need to be reintegrated or re-membered.

2. Hermetic wisdom presents a larger view of human nature as Mind, Soul and Body, and explains that humankind uniquely blends spirit and matter. This perspective helps reconcile a current contention about whether humans are 'part of nature' or 'apart from nature'. Each statement is true, but only a half-truth; we need to integrate these two dimensions of human nature. We cannot hold this point of view in either/or terms (law of excluded middle term); but it can be held in the mind through the law of paradox.

3. The Hermetic tradition emphasizes a spiritual path of personal regeneration, involving participation in Nous or the Mind of God. We all have the potential to access this higher knowledge, but the path requires right intention, inner purification and contemplative practices. The inner journey leads to liberation and bliss, as well as to

---

[47] Burckhardt (1997) p. 32

a knowledge of Divine Archetypes, Prototypes, and Paradigms, which underpin all life principles. Hermetic wisdom suggests that we need to 're-mind' ourselves of our potential, and of *who* we truly are.

4. We suggest that Hermetic wisdom also has relevance in the wider work of ecological and social regeneration in the context of the Anthropocene. Hermetic tradition teaches that the art of transmutation involves the transforming influence of superior spiritual principles. From this perspective, we need to reintegrate the Divine Head of Knowledge, and consciously cooperate with all levels of being, life and intellect for the regeneration of all. In other words, to successfully navigate the Anthropocene we need to ultimately go beyond the principles of the Anthropos and the Cosmos.

Finally, we agree with Lamborn *et al* who propose that we need a new sacred contract between God, Cosmos and Man, in their book *Green Hermeticism, Alchemy and Ecology*: they explore the idea that we need a new universal, ecological, ecumenical, holistic culture in which humanity, nature and the divine renew their collaboration in the sacred work of earth.[48]

Glossary

Anthropos   Human beings

Cosmos   The Universe considered as an ordered whole.

Nature   From the latin 'nasci' – that which 'is born', and is subject to generation and dissolution.

Nous   Usually associated higher or spiritual mind, that knows truth by being at one with it. (In the system of Plotinus it is presented as comprising of Being, Life and Intellect)

Noesis   Intuitive, direct cognition of truth, without the process of discursive reason.

Soul   The animating and formative principle of the Universe and of humanity, which is self-motive, self-vital, and self-subsistent.

God   The indefinable, infinite, immutable source of all being, life and intelligence.

---

[48] Wilson, P.L., Bamford, C. & Townley, K. (2007) *Green Hermeticism. Alchemy and Ecology*, Great Barrington, MA: Lindisfarne Books

Bibliography

Batchelor, S. (1992) 'The Sands of the Ganges. Notes towards a Buddhist and Ecological Philosophy' in Batchelor, M. & Brown, K. (eds.) (1992): *Buddhism and Ecology*, London: Cassell.

Beauregard, M., Schartz, G.E., Miller, M., Dossey, L., Moreira-Ameida, A., Schlitz, M., Sheldrake, R., & C. Tart (2014) 'Manifesto for a Post-Materialist Science' in *Explore: The Journal of Science and Healing*, 10 (5): 272–274.

Benton, T. (1994) 'Biology and Social Theory in the Environmental Debate' in Redclift, M. & Benton. T. (eds), *Social Theory and the Global Environment*, London: Routledge.

Benyus, J.M. (2012) 'A Biomimicry Primer' in Baumeister, D., *Biomimicry Resource Handbook. A Seedbank of Knowledge and Best Practices. Biomimicry 3.8*, Missoula MT, USA http://static.biomimicry.org/wp-content/uploads/2012/02/Biomimicry_Resource_Handbook_Excerpt.pdf

(accessed 7/11/ 2017).

Berry, T. (1988) *The Dream of the Earth*, San Francisco: Sierra Club Books.

Blaikie, P. (1985) *The Political Ecology of Soil Erosion in Developing Countries*, London: Longman.

Bookchin, M. (1980) *Toward an Ecological Society*, Montreal: Black Rose Books

Brown, K.W., Ryan, R.M. & J.D. Creswell (2007) 'Mindfulness: Theoretical foundations and evidence of its saluatary effects' in *Psychological Inquiry*, 18, 211-237.

Burckhardt, T. (1997) *Alchemy. Science of the Cosmos, Science of the Soul*, Kentucky: Fons Vitae.

Chambers, J. D. (1882) *Theological and Philosophical Works of H Trismegistus*, Edinburgh: T. & T. Clark

Copenhaver, B. (1992) *Hermetica: The Greek Corpus Hermeticum and Latin Asclepius in a New English Translation: With Notes and Introduction*, Cambridge: Cambridge University Press.

Corry, S. (2015) 'Wildlife Conservation Efforts Are Violating Tribal Peoples' Rights' in *Truthout News Analysis*. http://www.truth-out.org/news/item/28888-wildlife-conservation-efforts-are-violating-tribal-peoples-rights (accessed 6/11/17).

Crutzen, P.J. & Stoermer, E.F. (2000) 'The "Anthropocene"' in *Global Change Newsletter*, 41, 17.

Crutzen, P.J. & Steffen, W. (2003) 'How Long Have We Been in the Anthropocene Era?' in *Climate Change* 61(3): 251–257.

Davidson, R.D., Kabat-Zinn, J., Schumacher, J., Rosenkranz, M., Muller, D., Santorelli, S.F., Urbanowski, E., Harrington, A., Bonus, K., Sheridan, J.F. (2003) 'Alterations in Brain and Immune Function Produced by Mindfulness Meditation' in *Psychosomatic Medicine* 65.

Eisenstein, C. (2013) *The More Beautiful World Our Hearts Know is Possible*, Berkeley, CA: North Atlantic Books.

Everard, J. (1650) *The Divine Pymander of Hermes Trismegistus*, London: Bruster and Moule.

Evernden, N. (1992) *The Social Creation of Nature*, London: The John Hopkins University Press.

Freke, T. & Gandy, P. (2008) *The Hermetica. The Lost Wisdom of the Pharaohs*, London: Penguin.

Ficino. M. (1471) *Corpus Hermeticum* (First Latin Edition/14 Tracts), Amsterdam: Bibliotheca Philosophica Hermetica.

Govinda, L.A. (1960) *Foundations of Tibetan Mysticism*, London: Rider and Co.

Guha, R. & Martinez Alier, J. (1997) *Varieties of Environmentalism. Essays North and South*, London: Clarendon Press.

Hajer, M. (1995) *The Politics of Environmental Discourse: Ecological Modernization and the Policy Process*, Oxford: Oxford University Press.

Hart, G. (2005) *The Routledge Dictionary of Egyptian Gods and Goddesses*, London: Routledge.

Heikkurinen, P., Rinkinen, J., Jarvensivu, T., Wile; K., Ruuska, (2016) 'Organising in the Anthropocene: an ontological outline for ecocentric theorizing' in *Journal of Cleaner Production*, Vol. 113: 705-714.

Jeanrenaud, S. (1998) '*Can the Leopard Change its Spots? Exploring People-Oriented Conservation in WWF*' PhD Monograph, School of International Development, University of East Anglia.

—   (2002) *People-Oriented Conservation in Global Conservation. Is the Leopard Changing its Spots?* London: IIED & Brighton: IISD.

Jeanrenaud, S., Jeanrenaud, J.-P. & Gosling, J., (2017) *Sustainable Business : A One Planet Approach,* Chichester : Wiley.

Jeanrenaud, S. & Jeanrenaud, J.-P. (2017) 'The Mindful Promise: Leading with Integrity for a Sustainable Future' in Mabey, C. & Knights, D. (eds.) (2018), *Leadership Matters: Finding Voice, Connection and Meaning in the 21ˢᵗ Century,* London: Routledge.

Kabat-Zinn, J. (1991) *Full Catastrophe Living: Using the Wisdom of Your Body and Mind to Face Stress, Pain, and Illness,* New York: Bantam Books.

Korten, D. (2010) *Agenda for a New Economy: from phantom wealth to real wealth,* San Francisco : Berrett-Koehler.

Larrère, C. (1996) 'Ethics, politics, science, and the environment concerning the natural contract' in J. Baird Callicott and Fernando J. R. da Rocha (eds.) *Earth Summit Ethics Toward a Reconstructive Postmodern Philosophy of Environmental Education.* Albany, NY: SUNY Press, p. 122.

Macy, J. & Johnstone, C. (2012) *Active Hope. How to Face the Mess We're in Without Going Crazy,* Novato, CA: New World Library.

Mahé. J-P. (1999) *The Definitions of Hermes Trismegistus to Asclepius,* with Salaman, C. van Oyen & Wharton, W.D. (1999) *The Way of Hermes. The Corpus Hermeticum,* London: Gerald Duckworth.

Marturano, J. (2015) *Finding the Space to Lead. A Practical Guide to Mindful Leadership,* London: Bloomsbury Press.

Mascaro, J. (1965) *The Upanishads. Translations from the Sanskrit with an Introduction,* London: Penguin Classics.

Mathews, F. (2003) *For Love of Matter. A Contemporary Panpsychism,* Albany NY: SUNY Press.

Mead, G.R.S. (1906) *Thrice-Greatest Hermes. Studies in Hellenistic Theosophy and Gnosis. Being a Translation of the Extant Sermons and Fragments of the Trismegistus Literature, with Prolegomena Commentaries, and Notes,* London: Theosophical Publishing Society.

— (2016) *The Corpus Hermeticum: Initiation into Hermetics, The Hermetica of Hermes Trismegistus,* Create Space Independent Publishing Platform.

Meadows, D. (1999) *Leverage Points: Places to Intervene in a System,* Hartland, VT: The Sustainability Institute.

Merchant, C. (1980) *The Death of Nature. Women, Ecology and the Scientific Revolution*, San Francisco: Harper One.

Montuori, A., Purser, R., Park, C., (1995) 'Limits to Anthropocentricism: Towards an Ecocentric Organization Paradigm' in *The Academy of Management Review 20(4):1053-1089.*

Morton, T. (2009) *Ecology without Nature. Rethinking Environmental Aesthetics*, Cambridge, MA: Harvard University Press.

—   (2016) *Dark Ecology: For a Logic of Future Co-Existence*, New York: Colombia University Press.

Naess, A. (1973) 'The shallow and the deep long range ecology movement. A summary' in *Inquiry* 16 (1-4).

Nock, A. D. & Festugière, A.-J., (1946) *Corpus Hermeticum*, Tome 1, Poimandrès. Traités II-XII, Paris: les Belles Lettres, Collection des Universités de France.

Oxfam (2017) 'An Economy for the 99%' *Oxfam Briefing Paper*, January 2017.

Pepper, D. (1989) *The Roots of Modern Environmentalism*, London: Routledge.

—   (1996) *Modern Environmentalism. An Introduction*, London: Routledge.

Posey, D. A. (ed.) (1999) *Cultural and Spiritual Values of Biodiversity*, London: Intermediate Technology Publications.

Quispel, G. (1999) 'Preface' in Salaman, C. van Oyen & Wharton, W.D. (1999) *The Way of Hermes. The Corpus Hermeticum*, London: Gerald Duckworth & Co.

Rockström, J., Steffen, W., Noone, K., Persson, Å., Chapin, F. S. III, Lambin, E., Lenton, T. M., Scheffer, M., Folke, C., Schellnhuber, H., Nykvist, B., De Wit, C. A., Hughes, T., van der Leeuw, S., Rodhe, H., Sörlin, S., Snyder, P. K., Costanza, R., Svedin, U., Falkenmark, M., Karlberg, L., Corell, R. W., Fabry, V. J., Hansen, J., Walker, B., Liverman, D., Richardson, K., Crutzen, P. and Foley, J. (2009) 'Planetary boundaries: exploring the safe operating space for humanity' in *Ecology and Society* 14(2): 32.

Salaman, C. van Oyen & Wharton, W.D. (1999) *The Way of Hermes. The Corpus Hermeticum*, London: Gerald Duckworth & Co.

Scharmer, O. and Kaufer, K. (2013) *Leading from the Emerging Future. From Ego-System to Eco-System Economies. Applying Theory U to*

Transforming Business, Society and Self, San Francisco: Berrett-Koehler Publishers.

Seeland, K. (1997) *Nature is Culture: Indigenous Knowledge and Socio-cultural Aspects of Trees and Forests in Non-European Cultures,* Bradford, West Yorkshire: ITDG Publishing.

Segal, Z., Williams, J.M.G., & J. D. Teasdale (2013) *Mindfulness-Based Cognitive Therapy for Depression,* New York: The Guildford Press.

Schwartz, W. (2009) 'Obituary: Arne Naess' in *The Guardian,* Thursday 15th January 2009. https://www.theguardian.com/environment/2009/jan/15/obituary-arne-naess (accessed 8/11/17).

Singer, P. (1975) *Animal Liberation: A New Ethics for our Treatment of Animals,* London: Harper Collins.

Steffen, W.; Crutzen, P. J. & J. R. McNeill (2007) 'The Anthropocene: Are Humans Now Overwhelming the Great Forces of Nature' in *AMBIO: A Journal of the Human Environment* 36(8): 614-621.

The Mindfulness Initiative (2016) *Building the Case for Mindfulness in the Workplace,* The Mindfulness Initiative. Private Sector Working Group. www.themindfulnessinitiative.org.uk.

The Shrine of Wisdom (Eds) ([1923] 2015) *The Divine Pymander of Hermes Trismegistus. A Guide to the Hermetic Teachings.* Godalming: The Shrine of Wisdom.

Three Initiates (1940) *The Kybalion. Hermetic Philosophy,* London: Yogi Publications Society.

Westcott, W.W. (1894) *Collectanea Hermetica Vol. II - The Pymander of Hermes or The Divine Pymander,* London: Theosophical Publishing Society.

White, L. (1967) 'The Historical Roots of our Ecological Crisis' in *Science* Vol 155:1203-1207.

WHO (2014) *Preventing Suicide: a global imperative,* Geneva, World Health Organization.

Wilber, K. (1997) 'An Integral Theory of Consciousness' in *Journal of Consciousness Studies* 4 (1): 71-92.

Wilson, P.L., Bamford, C., & Townley, K., (2007) *Green Hermeticism. Alchemy and Ecology,* Great Barrington, MA: Lindisfarne Books.

WWF (2016) *Living Planet Report 2016: Risk and Resilience in a New Era,* Gland, Switzerland: WWF.

Thinking:

Western, Eastern, Ancient

How Lockean Influence May Contribute to an Ecological Ethos

Paul Fagan

1. Introduction

I was delighted to be invited to present a paper at the twelfth annual conference of The Prometheus Trust and at the time I was busy researching the possibility of defining an ecological ethos, based upon the work of the Enlightenment philosopher John Locke. I had recently completed a doctorate researching the way renewable energy may be owned; and to my own personal amazement, Locke's work satisfied the criteria for providing fair access to energy for all.

I had started my doctorate under the naïve impression that a socialist school of thought would be the best for the advancement of humanity and I was surprised, when at the end of my research, the very individualistic philosophy of Locke had effectively fended off libertarianism, liberalism, socialism, Marxism, egalitarianism and, last but not least, communitarianism.

Spurred on by the revelation, I set about my own research to see whether aspects of Locke's work could be furthered to provide a whole environmental *ethos*; and by ethos I hasten to add that I mean the characteristic habits accepted by a group of people; whether that group is a community, society or nation. Although it is accepted here that an ethos is not necessarily exclusive to one group of people and may be transportable to other groupings.

Unfortunately, due to the increasing environmental damage that this planet is sustaining and the extent of the damage, I came to the conclusion that an ethos based upon the work of Locke may have a limited suitability: if we consider this planet to be in a parlous state, a Lockean-influenced ethos, which requires individuals to voluntarily adhere to it, may only have a limited tenure before it becomes imperative to replace it. Hence, a different philosophy may need to be applied to solving this planet's problems; and as it stands, I feel that a consequentialist one, veering towards utilitarianism, is now a likely contender.

Within this work I have upheld the concept of sustainability described in 1987 by the United Nations' Brundtland Commission in its publication *Our Common Future*; where sustainability was defined as "development that meets the needs of the present without compromising the ability of future generations to meet their own needs". [1] The United Nations' guidance, with its emphasis on refraining from mitigating the needs of future generations, would indicate that humanity should adopt a path that preserves the goods that people enjoy today for the enjoyment of future humanity. In its widest sense, this may be practically interpreted as producing current goods that do not damage the environment, improving common goods such as the atmosphere that have already been damaged, and monitoring environments for potential damage. Here, my work concurs with these principles but particularly agrees that anticipating the needs of future generations is essential when constructing an ecological ethos. Furthermore, this chapter also upholds the spirit of the United Nations' work in that it is globally inclusive and assumes that all persons from all backgrounds should benefit from it.

An investigation of the relevant tracts of Locke's *Two Treatises of Government* is presented, followed by some criticisms that may be levelled at the approach taken, before concluding.

2. An investigation of a Lockean influenced ethos

Here, in the following subsections, a three-pronged exploration of how Locke's theorising may be incorporated into an ecological ethos in the modern world is provided. Firstly, the applied theory is noted; then the extent of its appeal is discussed; followed by a demonstration of its practical introduction.

2.1 Adapting Locke's provisos concerning property ownership

Locke's work, with its inherent individuality, is often taken on board by those who we may group as "libertarians" and who often highlight discrete aspects of his work to support their own cause. Certainly, his work is widely used to provide arguments as to how individuals may acquire physical goods in the world. I hereby follow in this tradition of isolating aspects of his work, but instead apply

---

[1] United Nations WCED (1987) *Our Common Future*, Oxford University Press, p. 43

them to using the Earth's resources with the end goal of providing an ecological ethos.

The background fuelling Locke's individualist stance may be taken by focussing on the chapter 'Of Property' in his *Two Treatises*. Locke considered the Earth to be a common asset to be shared by all persons:

> The earth and all that is therein, is given to men for the support and comfort of their being [...] all the fruits it naturally produces, and beasts it feeds, belong to mankind in common, as they are produced by the spontaneous hand of nature; and nobody has a private dominion, exclusive of the rest of mankind [...].[2]

Furthermore, individuals were free to use their own talent and benefit from the Earth:

> [...] everyman has a property in his own person. This nobody has any right to but himself. The labour of his body, and the work of his hands, we may say, are properly his. Whatsoever he removes out of the state that nature hath provided, and left it in, he hath mixed his labour with, and joined to it something that is his own, and thereby makes it his property.[3]

However, an oft-quoted expression that limits the acquisition of goods that one may take from the world is Locke's "enough, and as good" proviso: whereby one may take goods provided that one leaves enough for others to benefit themselves to the same extent as oneself. The operation of this proviso is described thus:

> Whatsoever, then, he removes out of the state that Nature hath provided [...] being the unquestionable property of the labourer [...] at least where there is enough, and as good left in common for others.[4]

With regards to ecological living and particularly sustainability, a proviso such as this may provide a device to prevent the excessive usage of the Earth's resources. This way of thinking may be made more acute by taking a societal view: for instance, if eating fish from

---

[2] Locke, J. (1993) *Two Treatises of Government*, London: Orion Publishing Group, p. 127

[3] Ibid. p. 128

[4] Ibid. p. 128

the North Sea has depleted fish stocks then perhaps we are not leaving "enough" fish in the Sea. And if we deplete those stocks so that they become extinct, then perhaps we have not left "as good" for future generations.

Moving to focus upon a second proviso in Locke's chapter 'Of Property', he was adamant that we should not waste resources:

> [one may acquire as] much as anyone may make use of to any advantage of life before it spoils; so much he may by his labour fix a property in. Whatever is beyond this, is more than his share and belongs to others.[5]

This proviso is very stringent in that it explains that, if one has no intention of using an asset and an unspecified other does then one does not possess it in the first place. Returning to the North Sea, if you are not going to eat the fish you have caught then you do not own them; and it follows that you should be gifting those fish to others. This action would aid sustainability as the recipients of gifted fish would not now need to catch their own fish and more fish remain swimming in the sea.

Locke further provided what may be considered to be a third proviso concerning charitableness. Earlier in his *First Treatise* he laid the foundations of what may be considered to be a proviso when he noted that:

> [God has given] his needy brother a right to the surplusage of his goods [...and it is a] sin in any man of estate, to let his brother perish for want of affording him relief out of his plenty.[6]

Placing emphasis upon the word "estate", this may be interpreted as a duty to allow one's property to service the needs of others when one's compatriots find themselves in a dire position. Hence, Locke's commitment to charity may be interpreted as stronger than merely giving away one's goods that would go to waste: we should go the extra mile and positively act to prevent the suffering of the needy. And once again returning to the example of fishing, the boat owner should lend her boat to the needy in order for them to reap the rewards of the high seas.

---

[5] Ibid. p. 130

[6] Ibid. p. 31

Hence, a triumvirate of provisos could provide the basis for an ethos, which may be summarised as the adoption of a culture of reducing consumption accompanied by sharing both goods and equipment.

2.2 Who would support a Lockean-influenced, ecological ethos?

But after the establishment of an applicable theory, the question remains, who would find a type of Lockean-influenced, ecological, thinking favourable? At first glance, it would seemingly appeal to those who have a conscience and wish to directly and positively take part in environmental action at a grass-roots level. In addition, this cohort may be joined by those who are attracted to the anthropocentric nature of the philosophising: those who would consider the needs of persons before fauna, flora, ecosystems and the environment. Further attraction may be found for those who appreciate the voluntary nature of the ethos: those who wish to minimise governmental intrusion into one's life and recoil from "big government".

But with more thought it should really have a greater appeal than these rough categories. I would expect that the Lockean-influenced ethos would err towards a "strong" type of sustainability in theory.[7] To elucidate: the "enough, and as good" proviso would limit the amount of goods acquired; the "waste" proviso would encourage the donation of goods to the needy; whilst the "charitableness" proviso would encourage the sharing of equipment. The combination would be expected to act as a limitation upon exploiting the Earth's resources and thereby leave much of this planet intact for future generations.

And overall, the bequeathing of a healthy planet to future generations should have great appeal. To explain, most people would want a state of affairs where we should be providing a healthy environment for those alive today; in order for them to flourish and lead decent lives. In addition to this, most people wish to have

---

[7] Connelly *et al* discuss the differences between 'strong' and 'weak' sustainability in greater detail (Connelly *et al* 2012, 238-241). Quite simply, 'weak' sustainability may be defined as theory that allows natural resources to be converted into human-made assets; such as roads and schools etc.: 'strong' sustainability may be characterised by denying that the conversion of natural goods is always to humanity's advantage; and certain goods that benefit all, such as climate-regulating oceans and rainforests, may never be subject to bargaining as they are crucial to this planet's survival.

children and grandchildren, and wish for them to live in decent conditions. Therefore, on balance, the concern for future generations should include both our own descendants and the descendants of others. Looking into the near future, as immediate offspring would wish to procreate and leave decent conditions to their descendants it may be concluded that considering future generations should be an essential and ongoing part of being human. And if this is the case, then a Lockean-influenced ethos that assures future persons their needs, albeit inadvertently, should have a very wide appeal.

However, for any philosophically based project, the prospect of considering future generations is fraught with difficulties. Bearing this in mind, one commentator, namely Ernest Partridge, in his essay 'Future Generations' has summarised how various moral philosophies would deal with the concept of our responsibility to future persons. One point he makes, that would be applicable to all philosophies, is that we cannot know where future people will place value,[8] and therefore cannot plan for this: future persons may prefer desert to rainforest and would therefore implore us to act to bequeath this situation. Hence, some may conclude that it is an impossibility to cater for future generations and therefore we should not attempt to do so.

However, if we accept that we should consider future persons' needs but we cannot know what future persons will need, then we should err on the side of caution and preserve all goods for them. Hence, if a natural asset is to be used it should only be used to the extent that it will replenish itself; and if it cannot replenish itself an attempt should be made to leave enough of the resource for future generations' usage but ensure that all products derived from its current usage are recyclable and reusable. But to augment this, if we accept that human beings can gain more comfort, entertainment and health benefits when a greater quantity of goods is provided, or there is a greater chance of this occurring when a greater quantity of goods is provided, then we should leave the maximum amount of resources to increase the possibility of future generations attaining their *desiderata*. Hence, put simply, if we accept that it is a natural human duty to care for future generations, then I feel it is a safe bet to bequeath the same planet in which persons evolved and leave the

---

[8] Partridge, E. (2001) 'Future Generations,' in *A Companion to Environmental Philosophy*, Dale Jamieson (ed.), Oxford: Blackwell, p. 380

variety of goods that this planet offers. Therefore, we should attempt to leave this planet as we first found it and the Lockean-influenced ethos would contribute to this.

Moving from future generations to concentrate upon the present, we may consider whether the ethos would be globally beneficial. It has already been noted that an ecological ethos should benefit all of this planet's inhabitants and it is expected that the combination of the three provisos would act to uphold this assertion and this will now be explained.

Certainly, if we are to consider this ethos to be internationalist in outlook, then goods should be donated to developing nations; and the proviso concerning "charitableness" should assist here. An example is provided by solar power, where, if a culture of assisting developing nations were to be introduced, then it is possible that moves such as gifting solar panels would pay dividends. Even equipment, considered "obsolete" in the developed world, may work far more efficiently when donated to sunny, tropical latitudes where most developing nations lie. However, such regions could already have benefitted from merely the *good of knowledge*: for instance, by now, everyone in tropical areas could have a solar powered cooker as the most basic are made from cardboard and tin foil.[9] Such devices are easily constructed and could have provided energy to the world's poor for at least the past sixty years. Imagine the amount of time saved searching for firewood that could have been used more constructively; let alone the amount of forest saved from felling. Hence, the Lockean-influenced ethos could be attractive for those who demand more equality in the world.

Overall, if the Lockean inspired ethos is packaged and presented alluringly, then it should provide another tool by which environmentalists can enlist supporters to their cause. As demonstrated above, it may contain an appeal for a wide assortment of persons ranging from libertarians to egalitarians.

2.3 The practical introduction of a Lockean-influenced ethos

Although, the ethos may potentially have a very wide appeal, we may ask, how could this thinking practically manifest itself in societies? But possibly more importantly, when embarking upon

---

[9] Black, R. accessed April 8, 2017, http://news.bbc.co.uk/1/hi/sci/tech/7991654.stm

introducing a new ethos in the first instance, how would this basis for ecological living be introduced? Certainly, a solution based around the work of Locke, with its emphasis upon the individual, would require that persons choose this path of their own volition. To assist this, first may come education, where persons are informed of the damage that this planet has sustained; and that the amount of pollution is now perilous. Moreover, frank discussion concerning ways of solving the problems would need to be aired. From this, one may hope that a resultant desire would emerge where the vast majority of persons would wish to live in an environmentally-friendly manner.

How this state of affairs may be achieved sociologically is now demonstrated by borrowing from the work of the late Gerald Cohen. Cohen described how individuals have the freedom of choice to change social practices within liberal societies.[10] These choices may cause incremental changes in social *ethi* as follows: pioneers change their behaviour; laying down a pathway for others to follow; until the vast majority holds the new attitude.[11] From this, it may be concluded that an ethos should allow persons an enormous amount of individuality in how they relate to it; and it is expected that *any society* which allows individuals to change the way they behave, or change their opinions concerning varying goods or situations, would be considered to allow a change in ethos. Cohen further and helpfully gave the example of how persons of yesteryear were considered "freaky" by recycling their waste materials but noted that at the time of writing, it was acceptable behaviour.[12] Since then such recycling has become even more commonplace; and overall this provides an example of how one strand of an ecological ethos is arising in our midst.

Turning to focus upon the practicalities of introducing an ethos in more detail, it may be achieved by making slight adjustments to our lives on the one hand, and then by paying for the changes on the other: however, neither change should be considered to be a Herculean task. Firstly, looking at the adjustments to our lives, these may be accomplished by a whole slew of actions and a few are now noted: reducing consumption; supporting environmentally-friendly,

---

[10] Cohen, G. (1997) 'Where the Action is: On the site of Distributive Justice' in *Philosophy and Public Affairs*, 26:1, pp 3-30

[11] Ibid. p. 26

[12] Ibid. p. 26

political parties; avoiding purchasing environmentally-damaging goods; and signing petitions to voice concern over environmental damage. All of these are easily attainable and would not cause too much discomfort to people's lives.

However, some discomfort may be caused by the changes to our ways of life that cost more. For instance, with regard to wastage, moving from the West's throwaway lifestyles and embracing full recycling would be expected to be more costly; possibly researching recyclable alternatives for plastics, metals and porcelains would incur more cost and the process of recycling itself may incur cost. Added to this, supporting developing societies is almost certainly likely to accrue costs: for instance, donating goods to the developing world would incur expenses associated with transporting goods due to the distances involved. Furthermore, preserving goods for future generations may cause extra expense by limiting the usage of finite goods and using more expensive alternatives.

Now some may initially be intransigent due to either the sacrifices or costs that may be involved, but where education and discussion have been permitted, people should understand that their actions are very necessary in the modern world. The narratives must emphasise that the developed world has caused most of the pollution and is therefore arguably obliged to rectify this. Furthermore, future generations are an inevitability, and in the same way we would exercise due consideration for persons who are geographically distanced, we must bear some costs today on their behalf. But eventually and hopefully, persons would become accustomed to this new way of life and accept such costs.

And this begs the question, how would these costs be funded? Well the answer may be provided in the form of taxation, to which, Locke agreed in principle, provided the populace agreed:

> [Governments] must not raise taxes on the property of the people, without the consent of the people.[13]

The notion of agreeable taxation is a beautiful concept in that it can be used, if arranged progressively, to alleviate changes to Western ways of life so that discomfort is minimised. But in addition, could it not be used to negate the environmental problems that this planet is

---

[13] Locke, J. (1993) *Two Treatises of Government*, London: Orion Publishing Group, p. 188

suffering? For instance, could it not be used to construct a device to remove greenhouse gases from the atmosphere? Moreover, could it not levy the funds required to monitor environments and ensure that any future progress made in humanity's endeavours remain environmentally-friendly? And the answer to these questions is, that if a consensus of persons wished to fund such actions, then the Lockean-influenced ethos could accommodate them.

The problem that some may foresee, is that extra taxation is not necessarily an "agreeable" concept. However, where taxation is needed, the environmentalist ethos should possibly concentrate upon solving problems close to home so taxpayers can see how their taxation is actively solving environmental problems; and also advertising that potential future problems are being addressed. After this, it is possible that only modest amounts of taxation may be used to solve inherited problems such as restoring the atmosphere; and transporting goods abroad. Hence, solving these latter two examples may be considered to be long-term projects.

In summarising this section, it may be observed that we have the basis for an ecological ethos that society could introduce, based upon introducing the spirit of Locke's work. Its establishment in society would be underwritten by modifying behaviour in one's everyday life so that one acts to support environmentalism. The initial basic ethos, based upon a triumvirate of provisos, could be supported and augmented via consensually agreed taxation to forge a more practical ethos.

3. Some potential weaknesses of Locke's work

The casual reader of this work may feel that Locke is not a suitable choice upon which to base an environmental ethos. He has provided the individualism upon which liberalism is based and this characteristic was incorporated by the economic creed of capitalism. And in turn, capitalism begot extremely wealthy individuals exploiting others; not to mention its "dark, satanic mills" and pollution. Additionally, some may ponder whether a person from the past has anything to offer the modern world with more complex societies and an inherent anticipation that we are now capable of interfering with the lives of future persons. Over the next two subsections I will attempt to assuage such critics.

3.1 Isn't Locke an unusual choice?

Certainly Locke does not enjoy an esteemed reputation amongst those with left-leaning politics. We have already seen that Locke's political philosophy was based upon freedoms the individual should enjoy. Furthermore, he may be held accountable by some, for encouraging capitalism: Locke's pamphlet of 1691, designed to petition Parliament and entitled "Some Considerations of the Consequences of the Lowering of Interest and the Raising the Value of Money" contained early capitalist theorising opposing price controls. However, there may be those who would exclaim that Locke was also a promoter of slavery, imperialism and colonialism: a brief review of *The Fundamental Constitutions of Carolina* of 1669, to which Locke was a major contributor, seemingly contains an endorsement of all three.

In defence of my usage of Locke's work, I would like readers to note that I have appropriated only what I need to forge an ecological ethos: any contradictory writings, that Locke may have penned, I feel to be irrelevant to this main purpose.

Additionally, I feel that Locke's work concerning persons acting with a benevolent individualism, represents the true spirit of his political philosophising and it is from this essence that we should build an ecological ethos that is associated with Locke.

Furthermore, writings concerning Carolina's early constitutions were written at the behest of Locke's employers; Locke was what may be now termed a "civil servant", working as the 'Secretary to the Lords Proprietors of Carolina'.[14] And when Locke wrote his tract concerning embryonic capitalism, it may be interpreted as his cries to establish sensible governance in the society in which he found himself. As such, these writings may be contrasted with the way he would really have liked society to be constructed and recounted in his *Two Treatises*.

3.2 Isn't Locke's work too archaic?

Some may say that Locke's work cannot possibly be relevant to the modern age. Locke lived in a sparsely populated world where resources were seemingly unlimited and could not be foreseeably

---

[14] Goldie, M. (1993) 'A Chronology of Locke's Life and Times' in *Two Treatises of Government*, London: Orion Publishing Group, pp. viii-xiii

denuded by humanity's actions. It would be an impossibility to anticipate greenhouse gases warming the atmosphere, mass extinctions or deforestation. In fact, in Locke's time, the wilderness was considered to be a dangerous place inhabited by wild animals and cutthroats; and for Locke himself, land left in a state of nature represented an under used asset that should be put to good use by humanity to "increase the common stock of mankind".[15] Certainly, it will be volunteered here that an ecological ethos based upon the work of Locke cannot be truly labelled Lockean; but may *claim influence* from Locke. This will be explained over the next few paragraphs.

For example, ardent Lockeans may stipulate that Locke's work featured here, was meant to guide our actions in the *present*; they may ask, is it not unfair on the memory of Locke to extend his remit into the future and consider such concepts as *future generations*? The answer to this is that firstly, all of Locke's provisos when combined within an ethos are enacted in the present; and secondly, it *is possible* that his remit is being extended and therefore the resulting ethos only *claims influence* from Locke.

Secondly, with regard to being charitable to geographically distant persons, it may also be claimed that the provisos were only measures devised to ensure the continued operation of a *discrete society*, and once more Locke's remit is being unfairly extended. To which the reply would be that if Locke were alive today, being a benevolent person, he would almost certainly wish to alleviate suffering, even where it occurs at a distance. That said the parochial nature of Locke's work is *undeniable* and therefore it is acknowledged that only the *spirit* of his work is being extended.

However, there remains one aspect of Locke's thinking that is arguably more relevant today when most of the world's property, including land, is now owned: as opposed to Locke's day and age when there were seemingly large tracts of wilderness that went unowned. Hence, his thoughts concerning taxation may be considered to be a far more important factor today, where taxes govern many of life's transactions; such as sales taxes, property taxes and income taxes. Overall, there now exists more opportunity to fund goods for the global needy and finance the instituting of sustainable lifestyles, which may all be funded by moderate and progressive

---

[15] Locke, J. (1993) *Two Treatises of Government*, London: Orion Publishing Group, p. 133

methods of taxation to make the process as fair and painless as possible.

Overall, as the ecological ethos portrayed here extends what are traditionally understood to be Locke's provisos it would not be wise to label it "Lockean". However, the ethos retains Locke's influence and the characteristic importance he placed upon individuals actioning decisions.

4. The continuing denudation of the environment

The state of the environment continues to worsen and as I prepared a presentation another major piece of environmental devastation was brought to my attention; and it is seemingly as atrocious as the travesty of global climate change. Recent news reports recounted at least four million metric tonnes of plastic entering the oceans every year, with each piece of plastic needing 450 years to degrade and resulting in at least six floating "garbage patches" in the oceans.[16] Abrasion wears the plastic down into smaller pieces, often to a microscopic size, and plays havoc with wildlife by entering the food chain. Of course, this will also enter humanity's food chain.

This brought forth the question; have we enough time to introduce a Lockean-influenced ethos? Returning to Cohen's example of recycling, it took years for persons engaging in recycling to be considered normal and not deviant; and still, not everybody recycles. It may yet take many years to instil the habit of recycling in the vast majority and according to the example of the Lockean-inspired, voluntary ethos provided above; there could remain persons who *never* recycle.

According to the old adage, *desperate times call for desperate measures*; and if we consider ourselves to be living in desperate times, without the window of opportunity to introduce a voluntary, ecological ethos, then possibly we must seek a more authoritarian method of solving the problem. From a philosopher's standpoint, this may indicate moving to a consequentialist or utilitarian solution where, relatively speaking, the *end justifies the means*.

And although such bold statements may initially seem shocking, it should be noted that governments have both strategies and

---

[16] Evans, A. accessed 6 October 2017, http://news.bbc.co.uk/1/hi/sci/tech/7991654.stm

underlying policies at their disposal to bring about change quite rapidly. I would think that introducing this within the aforementioned example of recycling, would simply and quickly give a reasonable strategic outline of how to progress. The first step along this path would require governments deciding to rid their respective territories of the wasteful concept of *disposability*. Then, four main component policies may be implemented, and they are hereby categorised as: regulations; economic measures; permits; and social pressures. The policies will be explained in the following paragraphs.

With regards to regulations, society may enact legislation to outlaw behaviour. [17] For example, during the production of goods, manufacturers may be charged with ensuring that all parts are recyclable.

Looking at economic measures, society may use taxation to control environmental damage.[18] Manufacturers who insist on using non-recyclable materials may be taxed for this action: whilst "tax-breaks" may be given to manufacturers using recyclable materials. Overall, this would provide an incentive to use recyclable materials by making it more economically viable for business.

Within industry, companies may be allowed to pay for permits; which they may trade between themselves;[19] such permits may allow the usage of a limited amount of non-recyclable production. However, this has the effect of managing and delimiting the element of disposability. Furthermore, it acts to prevent economic growth via polluting methods: for industry to expand it would need to move to renewable means.

Less coercive measures would include a society endorsing social pressures to facilitate the emergence of a new environmentally-friendly ethos: consumers and communities alike may be provided with the information to make such benign life-choices.[20] Furthermore, businesses may be encouraged to engage in a culture of voluntarily moving to environmental-friendly behaviour.[21]

---

[17] Connelly, J. et al (2012) *Politics and the Environment: From Theory to Practice*, London: Routledge, p. 178

[18] Ibid. pp. 181-2

[19] Ibid. p. 188

[20] Ibid. p. 196

[21] Ibid. pp. 197-8

The reader may note that the above policies guiding recycling are aimed primarily at big business. And I feel that this is a natural consequence of taking a consequentialist-cum-utilitarian approach: the problem is most rapidly solved by tackling the production process, which here may be considered to be the *heart of the matter*. That said, local governments and agencies will have their roles to play in ensuring adequate recycling facilities are situated in the areas under their sovereignty; this may include instituting whole recycling plants, executing the process of recycling and also ensuring that adequate opportunities exist for individuals to recycle. Of course, individuals should play their part at the lowest level and be expected to conform, although local authorities may also be expected to "police" matters and assert more coercive measures to ensure conformity. Casting the scope further, at an international level, all countries should be encouraged to follow the same environmental path. I would hope that the United Nations could exert pressure upon those lagging behind: whilst those who need the financial assistance are given aid.

However, the example of recycling sketched here, hopefully displays an attitude that may be extended to other areas of human endeavour such as transport, building or energy production, as three examples. Overall, I feel that when all is said and done, adhering to an environmentally-friendly lifestyle will consist of incentives being offered on one hand: and on the other, enforcement by coercion.

5. Conclusion

An interpretation and application of Locke's work has provided a potential ecological ethos which would be underwritten by an individual's action. It should have wide appeal and be practicable to introduce; and when the majority of people have accepted it, and acted upon it, it could provide quite a strong variant of sustainability. It should be considerate to persons in the developing world and allow them to enjoin in an environmentally-friendly lifestyle. In turn, future generations should inherit a planet in which they may flourish. The ethos should be supported by consensually agreed taxation: but this should not be problematic where consensus dictates that this is necessary to live ecologically.

However, recent events have occurred that have necessitated drawing a veil over the original research into Locke. It is possible that the environment has now been damaged to the extent that an environmental ethos based initially upon the individual's own choice is quickly becoming irrelevant as it may be too slow to respond to pressing problems.

Taking into account the continual damage that the Earth has suffered, an investigation into Locke's work has paradoxically provided, what may be termed, *a self-negating negative element of a negative syllogism:* an ecological ethos influenced by Locke will not be rigorous enough to tackle ongoing problems and therefore discounts itself. Possibly, it could have been successfully introduced twenty or thirty years ago when environmental problems were not as severe as they are today. But the ethos as defined, threatens to be too lethargic when more dynamism is needed.

However, on a more positive note, this investigation has shown that another way of constructing an ecological ethos must be sought. With time of the essence, it is possible that a consequentialist philosophical theory may be favoured; although this may manifest itself as political practise, which some members of today's liberal societies will feel to be authoritarian. More research would prove beneficial to define this new approach.

Bibliography

Black, R. (2009) 'Prize for "Sun in a box" cooker' in *Science and Environment*,
http://news.bbc.co.uk/1/hi/sci/tech/7991654.stm (accessed 8 April 2017).

Cohen, G. A. (1997) 'Where the Action is: On the site of Distributive Justice', *Philosophy and Public Affairs*. 26: pp 3-30.

Connelly, J., G. Smith, D. Benson and C. Saunders (2012) *Politics and the Environment: From Theory to Practice*. London: Routledge.

Evans, A. (2017) 'If you drop plastic in the ocean, where does it end up?' in *The Guardian*,
https://www.theguardian.com/environment/2017/jun/29/if-you-drop-plastic-in-the-ocean-where-does-it-end-up (accessed 6 October 2017).

Goldie, M. (1993) 'A Chronology of Locke's Life and Times' in Locke, J. (1993) *Two Treatises of Government,* pp viii-xiii. London: Orion Publishing Group.

Locke, J. (1669) *The Fundamental Constitutions of Carolina,* https://quod.lib.umich.edu/e/eebo/A48880.0001.001/1:2?rgn =div1;view=fulltext (accessed 30 September 2017).

— (1691) 'Some Considerations of the Consequences of the Lowering of Interest and the Raising the Value of Money', http://la.utexas.edu/users/hcleaver/368/368LockeSomeConsi derationsAlltable.pdf (accessed 30 September 2017).

— (1993) *Two Treatises of Government.* London: Orion Publishing Group. (first published in 1698).

Partridge, E. (2001) 'Future Generations', in Dale Jamieson (ed.), *A Companion to Environmental Philosophy*, pp. 377-389. Oxford: Blackwell.

United Nations WCED (1987) *Our Common Future.* Oxford: Oxford University Press.

Thinking Ecologically: a post-Enlightenment perspective

Eccy de Jonge

We suffer from the delusion that the entire universe is held in order by the categories of human thought, fearing that if we do not hold to them with the utmost tenacity, everything will vanish into chaos.

Alan Watts, *The Wisdom of Insecurity*

The western Enlightenment of the 17th and 18th centuries is regarded as having changed the worldview of European thinking, by replacing superstitious belief with scientific rationalism. Whilst it is undoubtedly true that the Enlightenment led to a new intellectual openness and radical transformations in science, it held onto two fundamental aspects of the religious worldview which still permeate our value system today: a belief in the anthropocentric attitude, which places humans as separate and superior to nature (with some humans superior to others); and a belief in the strict dichotomy between mind and body or mind, body and soul, with the body regarded as inferior.[1]

This paper will show that in order to think ecologically we must examine and dispense with both the anthropocentric worldview and the denigration of the body. To achieve this aim requires a metaphysical solution that recognises the body as the essential being that connects us to others, including non-human nature, without placing humans at the centre of the world.

The criticism that focusing on the body contradicts the idea that human beings are interconnected with others is only the case, if we

---

[1] Steiner, Gary (2011) 'Toward a Non-Anthropocentric Cosmopolitanism' in Rob Boddice (ed). *Anthropocentism: Humans, Animals, Environments*, Leiden and Boston: Brill, pp 81-114

regard *mind* as distinct from body and feeling as distinct from thought. When feeling is recognised as corresponding to thinking and not inferior to it, the individual can recognise mind as dependent upon a body that exists in the world alongside others who are no longer seen apart from it. In order to realise a thinking that is non-separate (from body, feeling or others), it is only necessary to accept that we are *essentially* physical beings that depend for our existence on the world around us, without the necessity of inventing a moral theory or code. This then forms the basis of an ecological thinking that has the focus of a *deep* ecology as its base.

Deep Ecology's Non-Anthropocentric Stance

The term "deep ecology" was coined by the Norwegian philosopher, Arne Naess, in a lecture given in Bucharest in 1972. Rather than define the *deepness* of "deep ecology," Naess sought to distinguish deep from shallow ecology.[2] Though the term "shallow" suggests a trivial school of thought, Naess used the term to denote a distinct way of dealing with the environmental crisis. While shallow ecology focuses on establishing a philosophy of moral oughts – of what human beings should or should not do to resolve ecological catastrophe, Naess saw such a project as dealing only with the "symptoms" of environmental harm (e.g. pollution, urban expansion and global warming) whilst failing to establish its underlying cause. It was this failure which defined the "shallowness" of shallow ecology since Naess believed that unless people were prepared to recognise the underlying attitude that creates ecological catastrophe in the first place, the process of exploitation and repair would be non-ending. It was only a deep ecology, Naess argued, that could stop the revolving door of environmental harm by asking deeper questions about our relationships to both the human and the non-human world. Thus, what Naess advocated by initially using the phrase *"deep ecology"* was the need for human beings to examine the fundamental ways we see ourselves, others and the non-human environment.

Deep ecology took off in two distinct ways in the United States in the 1980s. Following the works of Bill Devall and George Sessions, it became both a political and an eco-activist movement with advocates

---

[2] Naess, Arne (1973) 'The Shallow and the Deep Long Range Ecology Movement' in *Inquiry* Vol.16 (1): 95-100

calling themselves "deep ecologists". Though the term "deep ecology" had only recently been coined, the ideas behind it had a long history in the United States, in the writings of, among others, Walt Whitman, Henry David Thoreau, John Muir and in the non-anthropocentric ethics of Alan Watts and Rachel Carson, the latter who wrote, "In the artificial world of his cities and towns [modern man] often forgets the true nature of his planet and the long vistas of its history, in which the existence of the race of men has occupied a mere moment of time."[3]

When Devall and Sessions introduced the term "deep ecology" across the Atlantic it was as if they had found a phrase to describe a particular description or critique of anthropocentrism that had been in existence for centuries but without clear definition. Though they took Naess' work in ways beyond the epistemological framework he proposed, it was the non-anthropocentric element of Naess' deep ecology that they utilised as setting it apart from other environmental philosophies.[4] They argued that it is precisely this view of seeing ourselves *as* separate and *as* superior to the non-human world that led to our divorce from nature.[5]

Anthropocentrism - the view that human beings are separate and superior to the non-human world - is thus regarded by deep ecologists as "the dominant worldview" which sees human centeredness as the underlying cause of the ecological crisis.[6] As not all humans play an equal role in the domination of the natural environment, nor can be said to maintain an anthropocentric stance, anthropocentrism represents the human will to dominate *in general* and thus threatens the human as much as the non-human world.[7]

This raises a number of questions: from how anthropocentrism originated, to why it became the dominant worldview and how a change in attitude, from one of domination to one of deep concern can be achieved. One of the major reasons given, elucidated in the

---

[3] Carson, Rachel (1961) *The Sea Around Us* New York: Signet, pp.29-30

[4] Devall, Bill and George Sessions (1985), *Deep Ecology: Living as if Nature Mattered* Salt Lake City: Peregrine Smith Books, p. 70

[5] *Ibid.,* p. 66.

[6] de Jonge, Eccy (2003) *Reinstating the Infinite: Arne Naess and the Misappropriation of Spinoza's God*, Delft: Eburon, p.4

[7] de Jonge, Eccy (2004) *Spinoza and Deep Ecology: Challenging Traditional Interpretations of Environmentalism* London: Routledge, p. 10

works of the philosopher, Alan Watts, is the disparaging of the body for a so called higher state of human identity. As Watts said:

> Deeply involved with our whole estrangement from nature is the embarrassment of "having a body." It is perhaps an egg-and-hen question as to whether we resent the body because we think we are spirits, or *vice versa* . . . Is it little wonder, then, that we seek detachment from the body, wanting to convince ourselves that the real "I" is not this quaking mass of tissue with all its repulsive possibilities for pain and corruption. It is little wonder that, we expect religions, philosophies, and other forms of wisdom to show us above all else a way of deliverance from suffering, from the plight of being a soft body in a world of hard reality.[8]

A focus on the body might seem to contradict the idea that human beings are interconnected with others including the non-human world. Yet we exist as bodies and become isolated egos only on the level of thought.[9] When feeling (sensation) is recognised as corresponding to thinking and not separate or inferior to it, the individual can begin to recognise thought as dependent upon the body that exists in the world alongside others who are no longer seen apart from it. It is not, after all, the body that has the problem. The body is always *here,* always a constant, located in the present. It neither imagines itself elsewhere nor reasons itself out-of-itself.

> The root of the difficulty is that we have developed the power of thinking so rapidly and one-sidedly that we have forgotten the proper relation between thoughts and events, words and things. Conscious thinking has gone ahead and created its own world, and, when this is found to conflict with the real world, we have the sense of a profound discord between "I," the conscious thinker, and nature ... What we have forgotten is that thoughts and words are *conventions.*[10]

---

[8] Watts, Alan W. (1991) *Nature, Man and Woman* New York: Vintage Books, p. 97 and p. 99

[9] Fox, Warwick (1990) *Toward a Transpersonal Ecology: Developing New Foundations for Environmentalism,* London: Shambala, p. 197

[10] Watts, Alan (2011) *The Wisdom of Insecurity: A Message for an Age of Anxiety,* New York: Random House, p. 44

The separation of our selves from our nature (that is, our bodies) has been addressed in much of the literature on deep ecology, in the works of Fox, Naess, Devall, Sessions, de Jonge, to name a few. To understand why the body remains denigrated in the 21st century requires an understanding of the roots of disparity. The European Enlightenment of the eighteenth century, can be seen to have most emphatically endorsed anthropocentric values, through its use of language and its prevalence of human rationality over feeling and nature, which still pervades modern thinking today, as we shall see.

The European Enlightenment

The historian Lynn White Jr. was one of the first environmentalists to link the root cause of the environmental crisis to the doctrine of anthropocentrism, which he saw as deeply rooted in the Judaeo-Christian tradition.[11] In his view this tradition positioned humans as guardians of the Earth, superior to non-human beings that exist not for their own sake but for the sake of humanity. In this sense, "anthropocentrism" denotes humanity's superiority over the nonhuman world, on the basis that humans occupy a higher position on the Great Chain of Being.

With the beginnings of enlightenment philosophy, the theistic/religious worldview was seemingly overthrown, supplanted by a dominant worldview of reason over nature; scientific rationalism over superstition. It failed however to change the basic premise that human beings are separate and superior to the non-human world. As Devall and Sessions argued, the Enlightenment simply reiterated the paradigm of domination that came to include *all* aspects of domination, e.g., masculine over feminine, the powerful over the poor, Western cultures over non-Western cultures, and so on. That this was nothing new – the Church had dominated the peasantry for centuries with its installing programme of guilt and original sin - the power-relations that existed between certain humans to each other shifted from priest to philosopher and from philosopher to scientist against the believer, the opinionator and the layman. It was no longer our souls that were superior to the physical world but our minds; animals, it was now argued, *may* have souls but it was human reason

---

[11] White Jr, Lynn R (1967) 'The Historical Roots of Our Ecological Crisis' in *Science*, 155: 3767, pp 1203–7

that separated us from non-human beings. Since animals *feel* it became the duty of human beings to extend moral concern from the human to the non-human world, with Jeremy Bentham famously declaring, *"the question is not, Can they reason? nor, Can they talk? but, Can they suffer?"* Adding, *"The time will come when humanity will extend its mantle over everything which breathes".*[12]

The superiority of human beings, even with consideration towards *sentient* animals thus remained clear. As primarily *moral*, it was our duty – our *humanity* to care and protect those who suffered and to show moral concerns for those unable to do so. Our reasoning faculty however was still seen as distinct from the emotions, creating the dichotomy that denigrated the "other" as body, woman, nature or non-Western.[13]

Spinoza, a pre-Enlightenment thinker, had held that the mind *is* the idea of the body; a view which was almost universally dismissed by most Enlightenment thinkers who preferred to follow Descartes' distinction between body and mind with the need for God to put the "thinker back into the being that thought."[14] This created the bizarre idea that the body was an "external world" outside the world of ideas which was said to constitute consciousness – philosophers' stating arrogantly that consciousness is a peculiar human element and not (as it is in most Eastern thought) that aspect of Being which connects us to the wider universe. There remained little else to say about the "body" and even less on the relation between emotions and reason - even David Hume, that exemplar of the Scottish Enlightenment, who critiqued Spinoza's mind/body parallelism insisting instead that reason is subject to the passions, could not bring himself to regard the human *being* - it's Self as the *body*; declaring instead that the "self" is simply a bundle of perceptions.[15] The recognition of ourselves as individuals – not as *embodied* creatures but actually *as* bodies – where "the mind is the idea of the body" – as Spinoza had declared, remained removed from the Cartesian perspective and thus from

---

[12] Bentham, Jeremy (1970) *An Introduction to the Principles of Morals and Legislation*, JM Burns and HLA Hart (eds.), Oxford: Clarendon Press, p. 283

[13] Jung, Hwa Jol (2002) 'Enlightenment and the Question of the Other: A Postmodern Audition in *Human Studies*, Vol. 25, pp 297- 306; p. 298

[14] *Ibid.* p. 299

[15] Hume, David (1946) *Treatise of Human Nature*, Oxford: Oxford University Press, p. 252

most Enlightenment thinkers. From Rousseau's notion of a general will to Kant's noumenal realm which we can think but not know – the basic feeling relation we have with ourselves - as subjective bodies - became lost. [16] Instead philosophers became entrenched with competing arguments on our knowledge or scepticism of, an external world – maintaining with some absurdity (as the existentialists would later point out) that our real identity – found in the realm of ideas – was non-dependent on the earth we inhabit.

For Immanuel Kant, whose paper 'What is Enlightenment' set out to show the fundamental flaw in blindly believing in church and state it was necessary for each person to think for themselves, to use their own reasoning faculty. As he argued:

> This enlightenment . . . nothing is required but freedom . . . freedom to make public use of one's reason at every point. But I hear on all sides, "Do not argue!" The officer says: "Do not argue but drill!" The tax collector: "Do not argue but pay!" The cleric: "Do not argue but believe!" Only one ruler in the world says: "Argue as much as you please, but obey!" . . . Everywhere there is restriction on freedom. Which restriction is harmful to enlightenment and which is not an obstacle . . .? I answer: the public use of one's reason must always be free, and it alone can bring about enlightenment among men. [17]

The problem that remained was that concerning the "external world" for the world we know, according to Kant, was only that of appearances and not "things-in-themselves". Let down by our sensory data, for which we remained ignorant of its cause, Kant rejected the idea that it might stem from the body. Simply put:

> A man may not presume to know even himself as he really is by knowing himself through inner sensation. For since he does not, as it were, produce himself or derive his concept of himself a priori but only empirically, it is natural that he gets his knowledge of himself through inner sense and

---

[16] DeLapp, Kevin (2011) 'The View from Somewhere: Anthropocentrism in Metaethics' in Boddice, Rob (ed.) *Anthropocentrism* (op. cit), pp 37-57; 45

[17] Kant, Immanuel (1950) 'What is Enlightenment' in *Foundations of the Metaphysics of Morals* and *What is Enlightenment* translated by Lewis White Beck, Chicago: University of Chicago Press, p. 287

consequently only through the appearance of his nature the way in which his consciousness is affected. But beyond the characteristic of his own subject, which is compounded of these mere appearances, he necessarily assumes something else as its basis, namely his ego as it is in itself.[18]

The position of many of today's shallow environmentalists however can be traced back to similar thinking echoed in the French Enlightenment particularly in the works of Jean-Jacques Rousseau. Rousseau held that in the state of nature, human beings are basically decent and good, live in harmony with the natural world but remain irrational and amoral. In a reversal of the position of Thomas Hobbes who had written a hundred years earlier that "natural man" was in a constant state of war, Rousseau argued that conflict had occurred with the rise of civilisation. Rousseau's solution was to demand that each individual pool that aspect of themselves which identified with the collective to form the general will that each could agree upon. This would be supreme and form the Legislature. The only sacrifice for the individual was the abandonment of her private will to that which transcended her selfish interests.[19] On this basis, laws and morality would benefit the individual as each person recognised that the sacrifice of their private (selfish) will was in their best interests, rewarded with the security of the state that would guarantee freedom from violence and other harms.

Whilst Rousseau's perspective seemed to provide a general consensus of ideal democracy, based on each persons' recognition of the collective good, at the same time, Rousseau argued, paradoxically, that those who refused to comply would be "forced to be free" that is, to accept the freedom of the general consensus that had been previously subscribed.[20] Furthermore, his notion of the general will depended on "heroic figures whose presence is required to rescue ordinary people incapable of taking care of themselves".[21] To this end Rousseau's discourse on 'The Virtue Most Necessary for a Hero'

[18] *Ibid.*, Kant, Immanuel (1950) 'Foundation of the Metaphysics of Morals' Part 3, p.106

[19] Rousseau, J-J (2008) *The Social Contract* translated by Christopher Betts, Clarendon: Oxford University Press, pp.54-56

[20] *Ibid.* p. 58

[21] Kelly, Christopher (1997) 'Rousseau's Case for and against Heroes' in *Polity* Vol. 30 (2) Winter: pp 347-366; 348

spoke of ordinary "people who make supreme sacrifices for their community", as "the sole virtue for heroes is 'strength of soul'."[22] Thus Rousseau's overall message was how "the autonomy of reason portends to rescue and emancipate humanity".[23]

Since the Enlightenment, many philosophers have focused, quite expressively on the body but without quite managing to speak of its *physicality*. Nietzsche, for instance criticised former philosophers and priests for dictating to the masses but only to redeem the role of particular will towards a will to power. Heidegger positioned *dasein* (human beings) most definitely in the world alongside-others, but could not quite find his way to thinking of "the body" except as a being moving towards death, whilst Sartre warned against treating the human body – particularly others, as mere "things". In one illustration, Sartre refers to a woman who, having agreed to go on a date with a man and knowing full well his intentions, refuses to recognise the man's flirtations because "she does not quite know what she wants". Thus, embarrassed by the man's sexual advances she pretends, when he takes her hand, that her body – her hand in his – is merely an object that she chooses to ignore thus disowning her own freedom of responsibility in order to divorce "the body from the soul".[24]

The feminist philosopher Luce Irigaray took aim with Sartre for thinking that the woman regarded her hand as an objective reality, arguing instead that she saw it as "a consciousness that is transcendent from the body." As she states, "Given that consciousness is transcendent with respect to the body – as Sartre and the majority of Western philosophers think – the other exists beyond what is perceived as a fact".[25] Irigaray thus drew a distinction between the so-called "transcendence of fact" and the Buddha's contemplation of a flower, remarking how the Buddha illustrates how "we can learn to perceive the world around us, that we can learn to perceive each other between us: as life, as freedom, as difference".[26] The irony of

---

[22] *Ibid.* p. 349 and p. 351

[23] Jung, Hwa Jol (2002) 'Enlightenment and the Question of the Other, p. 297

[24] Sartre, Jean-Paul (1950) *Being and Nothingness* translated by Hazel Barnes, London: Methuen, pp. 55-56.

[25] Irigaray, Luce (2004) 'The Wedding Between the Body and Language' in Luce Irigaray, *Key Writings*, London & New York: Continuum. p. 13

[26] *Ibid.* p. 17

Irigaray's remark (which does not in effect require eastern thought) is that far from escaping the rational prevalence of the Enlightenment and the bad-faith of Sartre's female protagonist (who Sartre makes clear knows all too well what she is doing) is that, in our everyday, ordinary lives we already *have* a perception of the world and a relationship with each other and the non-human world – not because it is around us but quite the opposite, it is because we are situated in it. The idea that we have to *learn to perceive the world* because (in Sartre's illustration) we are unsure *how* to react (because we are conditioned to accept a passive role for instance) is as negative a view towards the ever feeling body as the Enlightenment notion that human beings are by *nature*, flawed.

Dispensing with anthropocentrism

Our first relationship with the world is of our body and the bodies of others closest to us (primarily, but not always, the mother). Yet philosophers have gone to great lengths to ignore the basic feature of our humanity. It is as if we had to grow up, go to University and read philosophy only to discover that who we thought we were *in essence* was all wrong. And yet the anthropocentric viewpoint, which, in the West, most of us have been conditioned to accept, did not arise out of nowhere. Regarding any aspect of ourselves as superior to any other – e.g. reason over emotion – may not have been the starting point for anthropocentrism but it certainly reinforced human privilege over certain other humans heralding the birth of the prison and the insane asylum at almost the same moment in history. Once the body was dismissed as being inferior, insignificant, unreal or simply a matter of mechanics – this extended, *eo ipso* to other bodies as also inferior. This wasn't a consequence of the Enlightenment worldview (which led to industrialisation) – it happened simultaneously. Even Bentham's concern for sentient beings simply heralded the extension of a morality which posited human beings as special. As Alan Watt wrote in *The Wisdom of Insecurity*,

> Nothing is really more inhuman than human relations based on morals. When a man gives bread in order to be charitable, lives with a woman in order to be faithful, eats with a Negro in order to be unprejudiced, and refuses to kill in order to be peaceful, he is as cold as a clam. He does not actually see the other person. Only a little less chilly is the benevolence

springing from pity, which acts to remove suffering because it finds the sight of it disgusting.[27]

The assumption that every person pursues only her own interests and abandons any concern for others unless they are of benefit to oneself, is not only a false idea but cynical and self-righteous, a belief put forward by an insecure society that fears the general populace unless it can be controlled. Such a view conveniently forgets that what gives each of us individual pleasure are "relations with other human beings – conversation, eating together, singing, dancing, having children, and co-operation . . ." none of which require a moral theory to understand.[28] That imposing moral restrictions on human beings fails to work is an irony not ignored by Watts who wrote:

> This is where moralists make their mistake. If they want man to change his way of life, they must assume that he is free, for if he is not, all the raging and protesting in the world will make no difference. On the other hand, a man who is acting from the fear of the moralist's threats or from the lure of his promises is not making a free act! If man is not free, threats and promises may modify his conduct, but they will not change it in any essential respect. If he is free, threats and promises will not make him use his freedom.[29]

Morality then requires that human beings pay a heavy price one in which we no longer make our choices according to our usual motivations of pleasure or pain but accept that consciousness resides only in some mental state as if the stomach or head ache are not "really" pains but *ideas* of pain related to the stomach or head that we have somehow managed to construct. Why the mind should be any more conscious to us than the body, when the latter relates to us so directly, must therefore remain one of the more puzzling features of enlightenment philosophy since it would be just as easy to agree that there simply "is no 'unconscious' mind distinct from the conscious" except we have been led to believe otherwise.[30] The matter is one of content – of not accepting ourselves for who we are.

---

[27] Watts, Alan (2011) *The Wisdom of Insecurity*, p. 132

[28] *Ibid.* p. 121

[29] *Ibid.* p.122

[30] *Ibid.* p. 125

The urge is ever to make "I" amount to something. I must be right, good, a real person, heroic, loving, self-effacing. I efface myself in order to assert myself, and give myself away in order to keep myself. The whole thing is a contradiction. As long as there is the motive to become something, so long as the mind believes in the possibility of escape from what it is at this moment, there can be no freedom.[31]

To be seen as one among many is of course a terrifying thought for an individual who has been conditioned by the idea that she must *become someone* – to be seen as "special" either in relation to specific people (her parents, friends, children or spouse) or to a wider anonymous public, as holding a profession. To dispense with "specialness" breaks down one of the fundamental rules in any type of power relation that seeks to uphold that some beings (especially some humans) are of a higher order than others. Recognising there is no higher or lower order is problematic for those who seek to elevate themselves above others, whether it be to secure a place in heaven, or have one's hand printed on the Hollywood Walk of Fame. Less trivially, it is also problematic for those conditioned to believe that "being special" is required for human satisfaction, without considering the alternative. For brought into the desire *to be* special (a phrase which necessarily projects itself into a future) is the fear of being inadequate, of being *less than*, for it is not possible to be special unless there are others who fail.

Once we start asking what makes human beings superior to others, the response depends on what each of us regards as the defining feature of humanity. If we are part of the non-human world, as deep ecologists maintain, then "superiority" makes little sense since anything that sets us apart sees us as epistemologically and metaphysically separate from any other—not merely non-human beings but whites from blacks, west from east, men from women in ever increasing dichotomies that only go so far to being resolved until they fall back on the same old critiques. If each of us is merely an isolated individual with no relation to the other, at either a narrow level (the level of consumption say), or a deeper level (the level of intrinsic value or essence), then it will (again) be difficult to maintain a non-anthropocentric view of human nature, for moral egoism will be

---

[31] *Ibid.* pp 129-30

paramount. And yet, there is no reason to regard a peculiarly *moral* being as desirable.

The question is not whether we can ever entirely escape from some form of anthropocentric attitude for anthropocentrism is not a moral position. Nor does placing inter-human concerns at the forefront of ecology necessarily uphold an attitude of superiority over the non-human world for it simply requires a rejection of a certain type of thinking.[32] Whatever class of social actors one identifies as being most responsible for social domination and ecological destruction (e.g., men, capitalists, whites, Westerners), one tends at the most fundamental level to find a common kind of legitimisation for the alleged superiority of these classes over others and hence, for the assumed rightfulness of their domination of these others. Specifically, social agents have not sought to legitimate their position on the grounds that they are, for example, men, capitalists, white, or Western per se, but rather on the grounds that they have most exemplified whatever it is that has been taken to constitute the essence of humanness (e.g., being favoured by God or possessing rationality). This idea of favouritism can be seen to have extended to certain humans, not only the world of "priests" or "philosophers" or "scientists", but more generally, to those who "have faith", "believe", "cultivate themselves", "recognise that humans are born in original sin" are "good" or will "gain a place in heaven" as opposed to those heathens who "sin" are "deficient" or "inadequate" and /or fail to follow the prescribed path. Ironically, any supposition or claim of superiority depends on the idea of deficiency, lack or inferiority. And as such the idea of being *deficient* must also be seen as part of the anthropocentric view.

> There is and can be no "disembodied reason" insofar as perception is a nascent concept or logos . . . Thus it is wrong-headed to say that what is rational is real and what is real is rational. An event such as the Holocaust, according to Jean-François Lyotard, may not be rational, but it is real.[33]

---

[32] de Jonge, Eccy (2011) 'An Alternative to Anthropocentrism: Deep Ecology and the Metaphysical Turn' in Boddice, Rob (ed.) *Anthropocentrism* op.cit., pp. 308-339; p.310

[33] Jung, C. J. (2002) 'Enlightenment and the Question of the Other' p. 299

Dispensing with this "fact" means we might as well dispense with the view that any of us suffer or that the Holocaust (however defined) even occurred. Separating body from mind has just this affect; where the body is unreal, secondary or just a thing, it is open for exploitation. It also has the effect of creating the body-politic as hero where giving up one's body for the greater good is heralded as the highest sacrifice one can make. Paradoxically this cannot succeed without the belief in a transcendental human nature, hence the institutions of the collective ego e.g. the army and the police, rely on the belief in an afterlife and in salvation in order to be able to sacrifice themselves to the so called general good; the body being seen as having no intrinsic value as this is the essence of a higher self.[34]

The Body as a Feeling Consciousness

In order to develop a thinking that is non-separate from the body it is necessary to distinguish emotions (feelings) that depend on egoistical ideas (enforced by mental constructs, which are always general) from those that are in harmony with nature and that can be felt subjectively only in our own bodies. To do so does not require the adoption of any particular mental stance or spiritual belief but primarily an understanding of what has separated us from our bodies in the first place. In a study on the Eastern Taoist text the *I-Ching*, Carol Anthony and Hanna Moog suggest that understanding the distinction between the terms "unique" and "special" is a first step. As they state, "the difference between 'special' and 'unique' is one we can feel: while special creates a feeling of superiority, privilege, and 'being better than', the word unique gives dignity to all things, and makes it clear that no thing is to be compared to another".[35] That human beings are not particularly special except in our ability to use complex language does not however take much reflection if we think of the eagle, whose uniqueness allows it to spot its prey over two miles away or the cheetah that can reach speeds of up to 70mph. Confusing what is unique to one's species with being-special removes humans from any form of identification with the non-human world and even from its own kind in cases of muteness or severe disability,

---

[34] Chapman, Brian (1971) *Police State* London: Macmillan, p. 95

[35] Anthony, Carol K. and Hanna Moog (2009) *The Psyche Revealed Through the IChing*, Stow: IChing Books, p. 28

because either our commonality is regarded as "base"– the level of non-thought (corporeal bodies) – with feeling also derided as secondary, or we are nothing but rational beings, where thinking separates us from the rest of Nature, certain humans, and from any cosmic reality. Paradoxically "being special" also restricts any real or mystical relationship with the unknown and with a consciousness that is free flowing (e.g., "Cosmic", "Brahman" "the Tao" or even "eternal love") for what comes to us through bodily sensations transmuted into thought, is, without the body, merely some mental construct that is at base non-*sense* (without mood or empathy).

The self that regards its species as superior, special or powerful (which it can only do if some humans are *better than* others) and the self which recognises its physical nature as part of the natural world, as a being among many, is not a difference in *reality* then, nor in our perception, but in our actual experiential expressions of living.

> Most of the wisdom which we employ in everyday life never came to us as verbal information. It was not through statements that we learned how to breathe, swallow, see, circulate the blood, digest food, or resist diseases. Yet these things are performed by the most complex and marvellous processes which no amount of book-learning and technical skill can reproduce.[36]

Since words such as "special" automatically create their opposite – not special – "the idea of being not special introduced the original doubt in the wholeness and goodness of our true nature,"[37] being replaced by the seemingly intrinsic notion that we are not good enough, that we lack something which others have, that we are not clever or sufficiently attractive or a good enough parent or employee, or have enough wealth or belong to the right class and so on leading to the present day obsession with fitting in or "belonging" to the cultural paradigm and its obsession with celebrity - the empty idea that the more people who recognise one as distinct from others the more "special" one becomes for "underneath is the constant anxiety that we may be a 'nobody' after all".[38]

---

[36] Watts, Alan (2011) *The Wisdom of Insecurity* p. 56

[37] Anthony, Carol K. and Hanna Moog (2009) *The Psyche Revealed Through the IChing*, p. 32

[38] *Ibid.*

Such striving requires that we constantly measure our position in relation to others which "creates a mindset based on conflict and competition"[39]—a mindset, moreover, that requires a constant repeat of those myths concerning human nature – from those provided by the Enlightenment's focus on reason to the myth of the hero who is on the side of the good and will lay down his life if necessary. Since,

> people who seek glorification as a hero need to have something to fight ... they are constantly engaged in conflict with a perceived enemy and need to reinforce their beliefs, whether cultural, economic or political onto others. We can see this mind set prevalent even in today's society with the highest honours for heroism . . . given to those who give their lives to free the social structure from the perceived enemy.[40]

Not only is this mind set paranoid, it engages in what Orwell called in *1984* the need for perpetual war where there exists no particular enemy just the enemy out there, somewhere.

The egoistical self who holds anthropocentric concerns fails to recognise its relationship with others and with the whole of nature due to a social conditioning stemming back to the Enlightenment which chose to disregard the body and nature as being "inferior" whilst prevailing elusive ideas with no basis in reality but in what humans could impose as categories upon the world believing that the mere naming of things made them real. "As a consequence, we are at war within ourselves- the brain desiring things which the body does not want, and the body desiring things which the brain does not allow; the brain giving directions which the body will not follow, and the body giving impulses which the brain cannot understand."[41] Thus, Alan Watts asserts in one illustration, we have become estranged from our own bodily (animal) nature since, "the animal tends to eat with his stomach, and the man with his brain. When the animal's stomach is full, he stops eating, but the man is never sure when to stop."[42] When we thus get a stomach ache, we blame it on the food or our

---

[39] *Ibid.* p. 34

[40] *Ibid.* p. 33

[41] Watts, Alan (2011) *The Wisdom of Insecurity* pp 58-59

[42] *Ibid.* p.59

appetites or on the body itself, as if we had bothered to listen to it when it told us it was becoming full.

Since the cause of our over consumption is our own thinking, it is clear that left to its own devices, without the body limiting its use, as in communicating to us that it is full, or in pain or in a state that requires we should flee, our mental constructs actually put us at risk and not just from illnesses created by obesity. After all, it is the body which revolts from harming others, unless it is conditioned to do so; "not for nothing are *soldiers* trained to kill".[43]

Having obscured our "nature" – no longer in touch with the feeling aspect of ourselves except for what we can rationalise by ideas, our lives become obsessed with the goal of desiring something that would make us special since we are constantly reminded that our inner guidance of the feeling body which would fulfil our individual uniqueness should we listen to it, is a fiction, where only recognition from others has value-in-itself. Ironically then the very thing that makes us unique - our ability to think – has, when misused, created the deepest feelings of insecurity and danger to ourselves. This occurred because we elevated mind over body creating both inner conflict, anger, arrogance and isolation from ourselves and *mutis mutandis* from the non-human world of which we are a part. As Watts concludes,

> I feel cut off only because I am split within myself, because I try to be divided from my own feelings and sensations. What I feel and sense therefore seems foreign to me. And on being aware of the unreality of this division, the universe does not seem foreign anymore.[44]

Conclusion

A post-Enlightenment ecological thinking lies not in *adding* anything to human nature or reconstructing our thinking to develop a higher moral purpose, nor in the need to cultivate a caring or awe inspiring attitude towards the non-human world but only in stripping away those elements that substantiate the claim that we are, or need to be regarded as, special. Though it is beyond the scope of this paper to present ideas on *how* this maybe achieved, such ideas are nothing

---

[43] de Jonge (2004) *Spinoza and Deep Ecology*, p. 120
[44] Watts, Alan (2011) *The Wisdom of Insecurity*, pp 107-8

new – pertaining to practices in Yoga and Martial Arts, the Eastern philosophies of Taoism and Vedanta and contemporary works such as the books of Eckhart Tolle where the end (*telos*) is simply to locate ourselves where we actually are, that is, in the present.

Recognising that physical presence locates us in a now that is devoid of the need to become anyone does not require the additions of any moral imposition but rather an internal subjugation of all our individual prejudices, and those that we, as humans, share. Thinking *through* our bodies does not dispense with reason or rationality or the objective to analyse our physical or mental states, it simply grounds us to the earth and to others through our primordial way of encountering others, as beings-in-the-world. A philosophy concerned with criticising anthropocentrism in general is not interested in any *particular* environmental issue but with offering an alternative to the prevalent view that regards humans as superior to nature.   An ecological thinking then, lies not in *adding* anything to human nature, as in the need to cultivate a caring or awe inspiring attitude towards the non-human world but in stripping away those elements that substantiate the claim that we are or need to be regarded, as special.

Bibliography

Anthony, Carol K. and Hanna Moog (2009) *The Psyche Revealed Through the IChing,* IChing Books

Bentham, Jeremy (2009) *An Introduction to the Principles of Morals and Legislation,* Burns, J.M., & Hart, H.L.A., (eds.) Clarendon Press

Boddice, Rob (ed.) (2011) *Anthropocentrism: Humans, Animals, Environments,* Leiden: Brill

Carson, Rachel (1961) *The Sea Around Us,* New York: Signet

Chapman, Brian (1971) *Police State,* London: Macmillan

de Jonge, Eccy (2003) *Reinstating the Infinite: Arne Naess and the Misappropriation of Spinoza's God,* Delft: Eburon

   — (2003) *Spinoza and Deep Ecology: Challenging Traditional Interpretations of Environmentalism,* London: Routledge

   — (2011) 'An Alternative to Anthropocentrism: Deep Ecology and the Metaphysical Turn' in Boddice, Rob (ed.) *Anthropocentrism* op. cit., pp 308-339

DeLapp, Kevin (2011) 'The View From Somewhere: Anthropocentrism in Metaethics' in Boddice, Rob (ed.) *Anthropocentrism* op.cit., pp 37-57

Devall, Bill and George Sessions (1985) *Deep Ecology: Living as if Nature Mattered*, Salt Lake City: Peregrine Smith Books

Fox, Warwick (1990) *Toward a Transpersonal Ecology: Developing New Foundations for Environmentalism*, London: Shambala

Hume, David (1946) *Treatise of Human Nature*, Oxford: Oxford University Press

Irigaray, Luce (2004) 'The Wedding Between the Body and Language' in Luce Irigaray, *Key Writings*, London: Continuum

Jung, Hwa Jol (2002) 'Englightenment and the Question of the Other: A Postmodern Audition *Human Studies*, Vol. 25. pp 297- 306

Kant, Immanuel (1950) *Foundations of the Metaphysics of Morals* and *What is Enlightenment*, Lewis White Beck, (trans.), Chicago: University of Chicago Press

Kelly, Christopher (1997) 'Rousseau's Case for and against Heroes' in *Polity* Vol. 30 (2) Winter pp 347-366

Naess, Arne (2002) 'The Shallow and the Deep Long Range Ecology Movement' in *Inquiry* Vol. 16 (1), pp 95-100

Rousseau, J.-J. (2008) *The Social Contract* Christopher Betts (trans.), Oxford: Oxford University Press

Sartre, Jean-Paul (1950) *Being and Nothingness*, Hazel Barnes (trans.) London: Methuen, pp 55-56

Steiner, Gary (2011) 'Toward a Non-Anthropocentric Cosmopolitanism' in Rob Boddice

(ed.) *Anthropocentism: Humans, Animals, Environments*, Leiden and Boston: Brill, pp 81-114

Watts, Alan W. (1991) *Nature, Man and Woman*, New York: Vintage Books

Watts, Alan (2011) *The Wisdom of Insecurity: A Message for an Age of Anxiety*, London: Random House

White Jr., Lynn, R. (1967) 'The Historical Roots of Our Ecological Crisis' in *Science* Vol. 155: 3767, pp 1203–7

Re-printed by kind permission of *The Heythrop Journal.*

Returning to Wonder

Mary-Ann Crumplin

It is important in the philosophy of environmentalism to move from ethics to ontology and back. Clarification of differences in ontology may contribute significantly to the clarification of different policies and their ethical basis.[1]

Arne Naess, *The World of Concrete Concepts*

Introduction

I am interested in the way in which our metaphysical outlook conditions our ability to think and our way of being. In the West, our basic ontology, our basic framework for understanding how things are, is scientific rationalism. The fact that this is the case has no normative value. But it does have ethical implications.

This chapter picks up the claim that Arne Naess, the father of the Deep Ecology movement, makes when he says that "clarification of differences in ontology may contribute significantly to the clarification of different policies and their ethical basis" and will discuss what philosophers in the so-called "continental" tradition recognise as a fundamental ontological problem at the heart of Western thinking, and look at how this plays out in our conventional approach to ethics.

Then, bearing in mind the ecological crisis facing us now and the fact that we struggle to think our relationship with the natural world constructively rather than destructively, it will point out two

---

[1] Naess, A. (2008) 'The World of Concrete Concepts' in *Ecology of Wisdom*, London: Penguin, p. 77. [This essay is adapted from *Inquiry*, 1985]

conceptual tools that we have within the tradition of Western philosophy that could be used to recalibrate our thinking. These tools are an alternative ethics, that of Emmanuel Levinas, and an alternative approach to law, namely common law principles rather than a Napoleonic, codified system. Together these offer a productive way to approach ecological ethics.

The problem of deep ecology as articulated by Arne Naess

Our way into the problem begins with the fundamental disconnection that Western political man experiences in relation to the natural world. Arne Naess describes this disconnect when he outlines the conflict between ecologists and industrialists in his essay, 'The World of Concrete Concepts'. He writes:

> Confrontations between developers and conservationists reveal differences in estimating what is *real*. What a conservationist *sees* and experiences as *reality* the developer does not see - and vice versa. A conservationist *sees* and experiences a forest as a unity, a gestalt, and when speaking of the heart of the forest, he or she is not referring to the geometrical centre. A developer sees square kilometres of trees and argues that a road through the forest covers very few square kilometres, and so why make so much fuss? And if the conservationist insists, the developer will assert that the road does not touch the *centre* of the forest. The *heart* is then saved, he or she thinks. *The difference between the antagonists is one of ontology rather than one of ethics* . . . There is no way of making the developer eager to save a forest as long as he or she retains the conception of it as a set of trees.[2]

What Naess pinpoints here is the fact that the scientific, rationalistic, calculative approach to ontology does not always feel authentic when faced with an ethical dilemma in the real world.

Our Western love of cataloguing, counting and evaluating became the all-encompassing, modern, and scientific way to be in the Enlightenment. The Enlightenment disenchanted the natural world, continuing and exacerbating the weaknesses of a tradition which has read Plato's Ideas as the inauguration of a split between real and ideal,

---

[2] Naess, *Ecology of Wisdom*, p. 77 (my emphasis)

between subject and object. The rational revolution broke the existential and ontological bond with our environment that we naturally feel, so that now scientific rationalism establishes the fundamental framework of our ontology. It is a system that we could call "instrumentalism", or "technological thinking". On this view nature is a resource. Nietzsche, incidentally, calls this approach to thinking "nihilism" and identifies it with a general loss of meaning or direction. And it is as nihilists that we have, Nietzsche famously tells us, killed the gods, eradicated wonder and left ourselves lost and adrift.

So, modern talk about subjectivity typically sees the human being as a separate entity, at odds with the world and at pains to determine his own, distinct identity. European philosophers, Martin Heidegger foremost amongst them, have dug deeper to uncover the underlying structural foundations of this thinking. And they articulate the fundamental problem such that in the Western tradition of philosophy since Plato, man has muddled *ontology*, that it is his way of being in the world, with *theology* and so created a false ethics and a false conception of ontology.

Modern people seem uncomfortable with the idea that things are not under control, that nature is complex and largely mysterious. In order to create certainly, our ontology creates a schema that we can apply to affect a pseudo order on the cosmos. It places humans at the centre of being, as the reasoning, knowing animal charged with making sense of the cosmos. Heidegger calls this pseudo ontology, "onto-theo-logy" because it works by dropping an absolute, a *theos*, into the centre of being so that there is something against which everything else can be measured or interpreted or comprehended[3]. The *theos* is an ideal. It can take the form of a religious God, and for centuries the god of monotheism did perform this function. After monotheism, mankind, understood as the rational, knowing centre of

---

[3] Heidegger, M. (2006) 'Der onto-theo-logische Verfassung der Metaphysik' in *Gesamtausgabe 11, Identität und Differenz*, Klostermann, pp 51-79; English translation 'The Onto-theo-logical Constitution of Metaphysics' in *Identity and Difference* (2002), Stambaugh, J., (trans.) University of Chicago Press, pp 42-74. See also Levinas, E., (1993) 'Dieu et l'onto-théo-logie' in *Dieu, la mort et le temps*, Grasset & Fasquelle, pp 137-259; English translation 'God and Ontotheology' in *God, Death and Time* (2000) Bergo, B., (trans.) Stanford University Press, pp 121-239

being became the *theos* of the ontotheological worldview. But nowadays, the *theos* is technology.

Technological thinking goes further than a misplaced belief in the all-pervasive certainly of so-called objective facts. In his later works, notably his essay 'The Question concerning Technology', Heidegger describes how mankind and nature have now **both** become instruments of technology itself[4]. Enthralled by science, we are increasingly dehumanised so that a fundamental change has occurred not only in the relationship between man and the natural world, but in the very essence of man himself. We can see this played out in the atrocities and inhumanity manifest in the history of the twentieth century, and also in more mundane ways - for example the way that we speak nowadays of "human resources"[5], "human shields", and of people as "collateral damage". Describing how the philosophy of rationality feeds into our contemporary situation, the American philosopher, Bert Dreyfus writes:

> The essence of modern technology . . . is to seek to order everything so as to achieve more and more flexibility and efficiency . . . our only goal is optimal ordering, for its own sake . . . *We become part of a system that no one directs* but that moves toward the total mobilisation and enhancement of all beings, even us.[6]

---

[4] "The threat to man does not come in the first instance from the potentially lethal machines and apparatus of technology. The actual threat has already affected man in his essence." Heidegger (2013) *The Question Concerning Technology*, Lovitt, W., (trans.) Harper Perennial Modern Thought, p. 28. Heidegger (1949) 'Die Frage nach der Technik' in *Gesamtausgabe 7: Vorträge und Aufsätze*, (2000), Klostermann, p. 29

[5] "Only to the extent that man for his part is already challenged to exploit the energies of nature can this ordering revealing happen. If man is challenged, ordered, to do this, then does not man himself belong even more originally than nature with the standing-reserve? The current talk about human resources, about the supply of patients for a clinic, gives evidence of this. The forester who, in the wood, measures the felled timber and to all appearances walks the same forest path in the same way as did his grandfather is today commanded by profit-making in the lumber industry, whether he knows it or not. He is made subordinate to the orderability of cellulose . . ." Heidegger, *The Question Concerning Technology*, p. 18; *Gesamtausgabe 7: Vorträge und Aufsätze*, pp 18-19

[6] Dreyfus, H. (2006) 'Heidegger on the connection between nihilism, art, technology and politics' in *Cambridge Companion to Heidegger*, Cambridge University Press, pp 361-2 (my italics)

This approach to ontology is not rich enough to capture reality

Clearly this is way out of sync with deep ecology. In fact, it is this kind of thinking that led to the ecological crisis in the first place. What is more, it also does not feel very ethical to speak of human beings as simply part of the system. The fact that instrumental thinking is ontologically dubious as well as ethically distasteful offers us a clue as to where to begin.

If we understand the problem to be, as Naess said, to find a way to get the two groups that he talked about in the quote at the beginning of this paper - that is to say, the ones who see the heart of the forest in quasi-spiritual terms and the ones who see it as a geometric centre - to speak the same language, then we need to recognise that there is a "diachronic rupture"[7] in logic at play here. The "ontotheological" approach will not work because the two groups have different *"theos"*. We need to articulate an alternative and yet equally compelling logic if we are to find a way to persuade consumers to care about the environment in its own terms, not merely as a commodity. Because as Naess says, "We need environmental ethics, but when people feel that they unselfishly give up, or even sacrifice, their self-interests to show love for nature, this is probably in the long run, a treacherous basis for conservation."[8]

Naess's own solution is to try to persuade people to identify with nature because, he says, it is "through identification, [that] they may come to see that their own interests are served by conservation,

---

[7] "One can indeed seek to ensure the human disinterestedness by starting with the supreme efficacy of God; one can seek to seat the religious on a philosophy of the unity and totality of being called Spirit, and to this unity which ensures the efficacy of God in the world, sacrifice transcendence, despite the inversions of the totality in to totalitarianism. All that is possible! The diachronic ambiguity of transcendence lends itself to this choice, to this option for the ultimacy of being. But is this choice the only philosophical one? One can contest the thesis that being signifies behind the one-for-the-other, and put forth the Platonic word, Good beyond being. It excludes being from the Good, for how could one understand the *conatus* of being in the goodness of the Good? How, in Plotinus would the One overflow with plenitude and be a source of emanation, if the One persevered in being, if it did not signify from before or beyond being, out of proximity, that is, out of disinterestedness . . .?" Levinas, *Otherwise than Being*, ([1998] 2004) Lingus, A., (trans.) Duquesne University Press, pp 94-5; Levinas, (1978) *Autrement qu'être*, Kluwer Academic, livredepoche, pp 151-2.

[8] Naess, *Ecology of Wisdom*, p. 85

through genuine self-love, the love of a widened and deepened self".[9] He argues that the challenge is to find a way to get people to decide to identify with nature and he suggests using the idea of Kant's "beautiful act" and reconnecting to joy as a paradigm for ecological ethics.

But by relying on Kant, Naess remains within the rational, instrumental philosophical framework. His solution would be to persuade the ones who see the heart of the forest as the geometric centre to change their perspective and see things from his point of view. This is a political aspiration and an ethics based on Kant's categorical imperative: "act only in accordance with that maxim through which you can at the same time will that it become a universal law". The key word in the categorical imperative is "will". Naess's thinking is that if we can persuade people to identify with nature, they will decide to value it. But if we are speaking here in terms of "deciding" and "valuing" in the way that Kant does, then we are still banking on the idea that man is ethical because it is rational to choose goodness. Kant places man, as thinking being, at the centre.

Levinas – we are always already response-able before we start to think

The French philosopher Emmanuel Levinas offers a radical alternative to Kantian ethics. For Levinas we do not choose the good at all, rather the good chooses us[10]. We are always already responsible

---

[9] Ibid.

[10] "Ethics slips into me before freedom. Before the bipolarity of Good and Evil, the I as 'me' has thrown its lot in with the Good in the passivity of bearing. The 'me' has thrown its lot in with the Good before having chosen it." Levinas, 'Freedom and Responsibility' in *God, Death and Time*, p.176; 'Liberté et responsabilité' in *Dieu, la mort et le temps*, p. 206. Also: "This antecedence of responsibility to freedom would signify the Goodness of the Good: the necessity that the Good choose me first before I can be in a position to choose, that is, welcome its choice. That is my pre-originary susceptiveness. It is a passivity prior to all receptivity, it is transcendent. It is an antecedence prior to all representable antecedence: immemorial. The Good is before being. There is diachrony: an unbridgeable difference between the Good and me, without simultaneity, odd terms. But also a non-indifference in this difference." Levinas, *Otherwise than Being*, p. 122; *Autrement qu'être*, p. 195

or, as it has been neatly characterised, we are the ones who are "response-able"[11] even before we start to think.

Levinas argues that human beings function in two diachronic milieus: "totality" and "infinity". Totality represents the calculating, rational, instrumental thinking of politics and, ultimately, self-interest. This is the register in which the Kantian idea of making a rational choice to do good because it is in our own best interests applies. Desmond Manderson, a philosopher of law who we will be returning to later, explains why this is a problem in ethics, writing:

> Totality cannot explain what it means to relate to others in a society, because by reducing everything to a great calculation, we find ourselves ever more alone. Other people, in short cannot be consumed, distributed, calculated or assimilated.[12]

We saw this earlier, when we wondered if there was not something ethically dubious in talking about people as "human shields", "human resources" or "collateral damage".

Separate to the totality of being, Levinas says, is infinity. This way of being functions on a completely different logic to the "totality" of being. Here the thinking, reasoning "I" is not the centre of being. Before all the hubris and politics of totality, the human being finds himself already caught up with, and bound to, the other human being who faces him[13]. Here, Levinas argues, ethics precedes ontology; I am ethical first, before being political. So that I recognise myself as human being when I recognise myself being called to respond to the needs of another. On this view, the human being is infinitely responsible, and it is this, not his ability to reason or calculate, that describes the essence of his being.

---

[11] This breaking up of the word "responsible" into "response-able" is Manderson's. It is a neat and clever characterisation of Levinas's ethics.

[12] Manderson, D. (2006) *Levinas, and the Soul of Law*, McGill University Press, p. 35

[13] "The presence before a face, my orientation toward the Other . . . this relationship of conversation. The way in which the other presents himself, exceeding the idea of the other in me, we here name face. This mode does not consist in figuring as a theme under my gaze, in spreading itself forth as a set of qualities forming an image. The face of the Other at each moment destroys and overflows the plastic image it leaves me, the idea existing to my own measure and to the measure of its *ideatum* – the adequate idea. It does not manifest itself by these qualities but καθ αὐτο. It expresses itself." Levinas ([1961] 2000) *Totality and Infinity*, Lingus, A., (trans.) Duquesne University Press, pp 50-1; Levinas (1971) *Totalité et infini*, Kluwer Academic, livredepoche, pp 42-3

Note that Levinas does not deny the reality of political, Kantian, ethics and ontology but he insists that alongside our "totalising" way of being in the world, we also exist in an "infinite" one. For Levinas, ethics has two registers: a coded, political one and an empathic, human one in which I am able to recognise that justice is served by putting the demands of the other who stands in crisis before me before my own will to power.

So, Emmanuel Levinas, like Arne Naess, recognises that ontology gets stuck if we begin from a calculative and evaluative approach to being. But Levinas goes further than Naess and argues that the very idea of a rational or "totalising" ethics is suspect. Because, as Manderson says, the phrases, " 'You are like me' and 'you are unlike me' are both just ways of talking about me."[14] Manderson continues by saying: "If philosophy is an 'egology' - just a way of talking about the self - our relationship to others becomes a crisis, a problem to be solved, for how is this something outside this closed circle of knowledge and experience possible?"[15] This is the same problem that Naess articulated in his story of the conservationist, the developer and the heart of the forest.

Naess wanted us to recognise that "part of the joy stems from the consciousness of our intimate relation to something bigger than our ego, something that has endured for millions of years . . ." so that what he suggests "is the supremacy of environmental ontology and

---

[14] Manderson, *Levinas, and the Soul of Law*, pp 27-8

[15] Manderson continues, writing: 'The two answers would appear to be either "to totalise the other at an adequate distance" and thus to institute a discourse of separation and difference or "to engulf the Other in a communion" and thus to introduce a discourse of union and sameness. Either their difference condemns this to remain forever outside my comprehension, or their sameness reduces them to a factor in my equation. The former, for example can be recognised in deontological liberalism or the philosophy of rights since it preserves the integrity of others just because their interests cannot be measured against mine. The latter may be recognised in teleological liberalism, or the philosophy of utilitarianism, since it preserves the equality of others just because their interests *can* be weighed up and summed across society as a whole. In either discourse, our ability to comprehend another person *as* other is, and must be fatally compromised: since the totality of difference (conjugated in the first person singular) rejects the possibility of any comprehension by me and since the totality of sameness (conjugated in the first person plural) rejects the possibility of otherness from me. Once the self is taken as the natural starting point from which we build our understanding of the world, it is inevitable that one will succumb to one or other of these psychoses.' pp 26-7

realism over environmental ethics."[16] But we can achieve an even more constructive re-envisioning of ontology and ethics by doing the exact opposite. Rather than choosing joyful identification with nature, we can retain a sense of wonder that is proper in the face of the majesty of the natural world by recognising our difference from it and replicating Levinas's trick of inverting ontology and ethics. In this way we can recognise our unique relationship with nature not simply such that I am a small and insignificant part of a greater cosmos but instead by recognizing that my identity as a human being is that of being the one who is uniquely response-able. Levinas teaches us to see our ethical response as the condition for the possibility of our being human.

There is an important caveat to the use of Levinas in this context however. Levinas himself is not interested in nature. His interest is in the ethical response to the other human being. This application of a Levinasian move to an ecological question requires a creative leap. In making this leap, Desmond Manderson's interpretation of Levinas's ethics in the context of the law of torts, and common law can function as a useful stepping stone.

What is common law?

We can apply the reading of Levinas that the philosopher of law, Desmond Manderson makes in his book *Levinas, and the Soul of Law* to argue that the law of torts is an indigenous and constructive way of thinking which minds the gap between ontology and ecology. This would leave space for us to retain an ancient attitude of wonder in the face of the mystery and majesty of the world. So, what is significant about "common law" or "the law of torts"?

Common law is not a coded approach to justice but an existential one. It is the law governing implicit civil responsibilities that people have to one another, as opposed to those responsibilities laid out in contracts. It is less about dogma and more about lived ethics. The common law approach is to seek to respond to the specific ethical problem facing me rather than to adapt the formulas of a lawbook. It rests on the idea of response-ability and the idea of a way of being, an ethos, which is understood in terms of face to face community. Writing about our modern law, Manderson explains:

---

[16] Naess, *Ecology of Wisdom*, p. 93

The common law is not a statutory code that we might imagine as defining people's obligations well in advance of their interactions: on the contrary, judge-made law responds to events and casts judgment on people's actions post, if not ad, hoc. So we may not even know our obligations before the law deems us to have failed to perform them.[17]

Modern common law developed from Anglo-Saxon and Anglo-Norman law. At that time, the basic building block of society and of justice was the Anglo-Saxon *"friborg"*, which became the Anglo-Norman *"frankpledge"*. J.G.H. Hudson explains the "tithing" that was the basis of the system in his book *The Formation of the English Common Law*, describing:

> A group of ten or twelve men, or sometimes of all the men of the village, acting as mutual sureties that they would not commit offences and bound to produce the guilty party if an offence were committed . . . all over twelve years of age took an oath not to be a thief or a thief's accomplice . . . Each tithing had a head man, but the general regulation of frankpledge was the business of the sheriff in the hundred court.[18]

The justice system included various courts - hundred courts, county courts, seigniorial and royal courts as well as ecclesiastical ones. Justice was delivered by the judge's ruling. Each case was heard on its own merits and evaluated according to a concept of justice that had an organic, dynamic relationship to the society that it represented.

---

[17] Manderson, *Levinas, and the Soul of Law*, p. 6

[18] "A group of ten or twelve men, or sometimes of all the men of the village, acting as mutual sureties that they would not commit offences and bound to produce the guilty party if an offence were committed. If they failed to do so, they were amerced that is they made a payment for the king's mercy. The group was referred to as a tithing, reflecting its basic number of ten members . . . all over twelve years of age took an oath not to be a thief or a thief's accomplice . . . The tithings' duties were various: to maintain a general watch on local affairs; to raise the hue and cry and make arrests; to keep captured offenders in custody; to act as surety that their members would appear in court to answer charges; and perhaps to make good damage that was done . . . It was prevention through peer pressure backed by financial interest. Each tithing had a head man but the general regulation of frankpledge was the business of the sheriff in the hundred court." Hudson, J.G.H., (1996) *The Formation of the English Common Law: Law and society in England from the Norman Conquest to Magna Carta*, Routledge, pp 64-65

The justice that persists in the modern law of torts originates here. The fact that we retain the law of torts within our legal lexicon means that we have at our disposal an alternative, equally legitimate, one could say "diachronic", form of justice to codified law. Common law reverses the thrust of technological thinking by seeing human beings as human individuals rather than resources or tokens.[19]

If Naess argues that we should choose a joyful identification with nature, celebrating "our intimate relationship to something bigger", common law already finds us bound to our responsibilities and to something bigger even before our own will to choose this position is made manifest.

Common law and Levinas's ethics

In Manderson we see a lawyer finding a kindred spirit in a philosopher. He sees that Levinas offers a coherent and consistent argument for the necessity of having two simultaneous but radically alternative articulations of justice, that is to say a justification for the situation that prevails in our legal system today. Manderson writes:

> For Levinas, and for those who have been influenced by him . . . the demand of ethics comes from the intimacy of an experienced encounter, and its contours cannot therefore be codified or predicted in advance. At least as opposed to the Kantian paradigm of morality as "a system of rules", ethics therefore speaks about interpersonal relationships and not about abstract principles. Although it has a normative

---

[19] "Justice is not a legality regulating human masses, from which a technique of social equilibrium is drawn, harmonising antagonistic forces. That would be a justification of the State delivered over to its own necessities. Justice is impossible without the one that renders it finding himself in proximity. His function is not limited to the "function of judgment", the subsuming of particular cases under a general rule. The judge is not outside the conflict, but the law is in the midst of proximity. Justice, society, the State and its institutions, exchanges and work are comprehensible out of proximity. This means that nothing is outside of the control of the responsibility of the one for the other. It is important to recover all these forms beginning with proximity, in which being, totality, the State, politics, techniques, work are at every moment on the point of having their centre of gravitation in themselves and weighing on their own account." Levinas, *Otherwise than Being,* p. 159; *Autrement qu'être,* p. 248

component, ethics explores who we are, and not who we ought to be.[20]

This is ethics with an ontological force that is robust enough to stand opposed to the idea of technology as the ground of ontology. It is ethics *as* ontology. When he writes in defence of tort law, Manderson explains the significance of duty, of distance, and of response. Of particular significance is his point with regard to duty of care under the system of corrective justice, that is under the other, Kantian system that exists alongside common law. He notes that:

> "Rescue cases" have been so often considered outside the ambit of corrective justice. I have no duty of care to save a drowning child, even in circumstances in which the rescue throws no burden of risk on me, because this would impose a responsibility in relation to an other that violates my autonomy when I have not violated theirs.[21]

Recognising the significance of seeing ethics first in an alternative idea of "duty to care" rather than a "charge of violation", and of "distance" rather than "identity", allows us, I think, to establish a more secure grasp of our ontological and ethical position with respect to the ecological demands facing us now. If we were to follow Naess's prescription and seek to identify with nature, the danger would be that we lose ourselves and become unable to respond to an ethical call because we are merely insignificant parts of the technological gestalt. Far better, I think, to recognise that as human beings we are response-able. Arguing against too hasty an identification of self and other, Manderson says:

> The concept of responsibility is incoherent without some distance between me and you. We are not the same as each other; we are not absorbed into some collective utility. *And this is just what makes responsibility possible, since otherwise I would be responsible only for me or for us.* But responsibility implies a response to you at the very point at which and only inasmuch as our needs differ . . . Our respect for this distance, not its elimination, allows us to be responsible.[22]

---

[20] Manderson, *Levinas, and the Soul of Law*, p. 8

[21] Ibid. p. 39

[22] Ibid. p. 37 (my emphasis)

As a response-able human I can work to achieve ecological justice from this position, a position that acknowledges that complexities, imperfections and *aporia* are endemic to the relationships I have[23]. On this reckoning, Levinas is right. We do not choose to be good because it is in our own interests but rather the good chooses us as the animals who are uniquely able to affect a just response to crisis.

Conclusion

Levinas is not a philosopher of deep ecology. In so far as Levinas's philosophy prioritises the human other he is at odds with the fundamental principles of deep ecology as articulated by Arne Naess. And yet, he does offer a constructive way forward for ecological ethics.

In his contrast between conservationists and developers mentioned at the beginning of this paper, Naess refers to the two groups as "antagonists" and identifies a difference in ontology between them. A common law approach to the dilemma, or a Levinasian ethics of infinity places the ontological in parentheses and starting by celebrating their differences, works to find a justice between them which allows them to keep their distance and their separate identities whilst simultaneously recognising that since they are both human their primary ability is response-ability. Responsibility that is, both to each other and to the environment.

The ancient law of torts, and Levinas's ethics of infinity both place care rather than self-interest at the heart of justice. They indicate an ethics that retains and celebrates a sense of wonder, an ethics which evaluates each call for justice on its own terms. Both common law

---

[23] It is important to note that for Levinas this ethics is one that each person recognises for himself so that it is illegitimate to roll this out across society as a normative claim made on mankind as a whole. He writes: "It is in the course of the individuation of the ego in me that is realised the elevation in which the ego is for the neighbour, summoned to answer for him . . . But to say that the other has to sacrifice himself to the others would be to preach human sacrifice! 'Me' is not an inimitable nuance of *Jemeinigkeit* that would be added on to a being belonging to the genus 'soul' or 'man' or 'individual', and would thus be common to several souls, men and individuals, making reciprocity possible among them from the first . . . It is I, I and no one else, who am a hostage for the others. In substitution my being that belongs to me and not to another is undone, and it is through this substitution that I am not 'another' but me." Levinas, *Otherwise than Being*, pp 126-7; *Autrement qu'être*, p. 201

and Levinasian ethics see ethics as ontology, ethics as first philosophy, so that it is our ability to respond ethically that is the essence of human being.

Bibliography

Drengson, A. & Inoue, Y. (1995) *The Deep Ecology Movement: an introductory anthology,* Berkeley: North Atlantic Books

Dreyfus, H. (2006) 'Heidegger on the connection between nihilism, art, technology and politics' in *Cambridge Companion to Heidegger,* Cambridge: Cambridge University Press, pp 345-372

Guth, J. H. (2009) 'A law to protect the earth: the tort of ecological degradation' in *Science and Environmental Health Network* http://www.sehn.org/lawpdf/ALawToProtectTheEarth.pdf (accessed 20/6/17)

Hand, S. (ed.) (1989) *The Levinas Reader,* Oxford: Blackwell

Heidegger, M. (2013) *The Question concerning Technology and other Essays,* Lovitt, W., (trans.) Harper Perennial Modern Thought

Holt, J. G. (1992) *Magna Carta,* Cambridge: Cambridge University Press,

Hudson, J. G. H. (1996) *The Formation of the English Common Law: Law and society in England from the Norman Conquest to Magna Carta,* London: Routledge

Levinas, E. ([1969], 2000) *Totality and Infinity,* Lingus, A., (trans.) Pittsburgh: Duquesne University Press

— ([1988] 2004) *Otherwise than Being,* Lingus, A., (trans.) Pittsburgh: Duquesne University Press

Manderson, D. (2006) *Levinas, and the Soul of Law,* Kingston: McGill University Press

Naess, A. (2008) *Ecology of Wisdom,* London: Penguin

Pattison, G. (2000) 'Technology' and 'Seeing Things' in *The Later Heidegger,* London: Routledge

Published in Australian Academy of the Humanities (2016) *Learning from the Other: Australian and Chinese Perspectives on Philosophy.* Papers from symposia held in 2014 and 2015, co-sponsored by the Australian Academy of the Humanities and the Chinese Academy of Social Sciences (Canberra: Australian Academy of the Humanities).

Do the Deepest Roots of a Future Ecological Civilization Lie in Chinese Soil?

Freya Mathews

1. Can philosophy help us to negotiate the Anthropocene?

Civilization is the product of a happy geological accident – a ten to twelve thousand year period of climate stability, known as the Holocene. With climate stability came seasonality and predictable weather, where these conditions made it possible to grow crops, store food and hence accumulate wealth. Agriculture provided the material basis for the sedentary societies that gradually evolved the stratified, literate, artisanal, administratively centralized forms of social organization known as civilization.[1] It was climate stability that also provided the conditions for the urbanism and eventually the industrialism of such societies, since stability enabled people to establish large, permanent built environments without fear of flooding or destruction of infrastructure by the elements. Climatic fluctuations in this period, leading to extended droughts or freezes, often resulted in the collapse of local instances of civilization.[2]

Prior to the advent of agriculture, when people lived in small, nomadic, hunter-gatherer societies, in dangerous and uncertain

---

[1] Prentice, Richard (2009) 'Cultural Responses to Climate Change in the Holocene' in *Anthos*, 1.1.

[2] Jarad, Diamond (2005) *Collapse: How Societies Choose to Fail or Succeed,* New York, Penguin

environmental conditions, they were dependent on the contingent affordances of nature. Without technical means of transforming the world to suit their own purposes, they had no alternative but to accommodate and adapt to the natural environment. With the onset of the Holocene and the new conditions of climate stability that allowed for the emergence of agriculture and hence for the birth of civilization however, humans began to develop the technical means for transforming nature. This transition was inevitably accompanied by a psychological re-orientation to reality - a change of mindset. Where pre-civilizational peoples had been psychologically oriented to "the given", cultivating accommodation, attunement and adaptation to the world as they found it in all its actuality and particularity, civilizational societies were built on the discovery that the given was not immutable. The natural order of things could be altered to suit human convenience. At a certain stage of civilization, some societies accordingly began to cultivate a new mindset of abstraction from the merely present and particular, allowing for the construction of conceptual alternatives to the contingently actual. This emerging way of thinking, aided of course by literacy but also in its turn productive of literacy, emphasized reflexivity and involved a shift from a pre-reflexive focus on the world in the concreteness of its inexhaustible detail to a reflexive focus on concepts and categories as abstract entities in their own right.[3]

With this new focus on concepts in their own right in addition to the original focus on the concrete things which conceptualization enables us to describe, came an interest in the nature of the cognitive processes by which abstraction is achieved: the rules of composition and coherence by which such cognitive processes are governed. A whole new, highly recursive level of awareness came into view: observation of the laws of abstraction enabled concepts to become more sharply defined, while sharply defined concepts proved increasingly amenable to the "laws of thought". Without clearly delineated concepts, basic presumed laws of thought, such as those of excluded middle and non-contradiction, do not apply. For example, if identity is conceived in a diffuse fashion, such that the identity of a

---

[3] See Walter J. Ong (1982) *Orality and Literacy: the Technologizing of the Word*, London, Methuen for a classic study of the profound changes in consciousness that accompanied the transition from orality to literacy. For an environmental perspective on these changes, see David Abram (1996) *Spell of the Sensuous*, New York, Vintage.

particular thing is understood to be context dependent, then a statement such as that a particular individual is either human or not may not be true. Whether or not a particular individual counts as human may vary according to the context of consideration. In other words, logic – in this case, the law of excluded middle - depends for its applicability on well defined concepts, while concepts in turn may be honed by the application of logic: if it is accepted that a particular individual must either be or not be human, then human-ness itself must be defined in terms that exclude other categories of the same logical type.

For hunter gatherer societies, attuned to the diffuse, context-dependent and relational modes of existence and identity that characterized the still fully ecological environments on which they depended, conceptual precision, or the sharp definition of concepts, was not adaptive. Diffuse and relational categories were essential for negotiating a life-world in which the identities of all things were still inextricably and densely ecologically intertwined. In relation to such categories, the so-called "laws of thought", first codified by Aristotle as principles of logic, did not apply.[4] As people started to disentangle their life-worlds from nature however, in the transition to civilization, they created around themselves a built or artefactual context in which the identities of objects – such as houses and chairs - were genuinely discrete and unambiguously instrumental in significance. In other words, as people replaced nature with fixed, built, human-designed environments, a whole new horizon of concepts and categories amenable to sharper delineation and hence to manipulation in accordance with the rules of what came to be known as logic, opened up. Once the rudiments of logic were available, reason emerged, paving the way for philosophy.

With the aid of reason, philosophers – notably the presocratics - were able to construct abstract and schematic representations of reality. Culturally enshrined as a revered (and indeed civilizing) epistemic end in itself, such philosophical activity can however also be seen indirectly - historically and functionally - as a prelude, a necessary condition, for the manipulation and transformation of

---

[4] The early anthropologist, Lucien Levy Bruhl, pointed out in a series of books how the thought of indigenous people follows a different "logic" from the patterns of thought discernable in the history of Western thought. See, for example, *How Natives Think* (1926), London, George Allen and Unwin and *The Soul of the Primitive* (1928) London, George Allen and Unwin.

reality. By performing logical operations on abstract representations, philosophers were able to construct new blueprints for reality, thereby motivating and enabling a new ethos of substitution, imposition and control in place of the old ethos of adaptation to nature.

Philosophy – which emerged in the so-called Axial era, 800-200 BCE, when civilization had reached maturity[5] – might thus be seen as a product of the reflexive faculty that accompanied the shift from a hunter-gatherer way of life to life under the conditions of civilization, an offshoot of the distinctive *praxis* of civilization. It was in this sense both a definitive expression of the civilizational mind-set enabled by the climatic stability of the Holocene and a powerful tool for the further development of that mind-set, a further development that would in due course see the wholesale subjugation of nature by civilization.

In the 21st century climate stability will, it seems, no longer be assured. Anthropogenic climate change seems set to disrupt weather patterns and increase the severity of extreme weather events, leading to catastrophic droughts, floods and storms. The new era of anthropogenic environmental upheaval has recently been labelled the Anthropocene. According to this new idea, Earth has "exited the current geological epoch, the 12,000 year old Holocene, and entered a new epoch, the Anthropocene" in which "the human species is now the dominant Earth-shaping force."[6] This new Earth-shaping impact on the planet "includes altering biogeochemical cycles (carbon, nitrogen, phosphorus, etc), modifying terrestrial water cycles through changing river flows, land-use changes, etc, and driving extinction rates which are unprecedented since the dinosaurs."[7]

In the Anthropocene then, the environmental context of civilization is likely to change. Philosophy, as the study of the ultimate existential questions facing humankind, must surely address such a change, and help, if possible, to navigate humanity through it. But as a product of the very consciousness that arguably enabled civilization to subjugate and hence unbalance nature in the first place, it is uncertain whether philosophy is in fact an appropriate or useful tool

---

[5] Armstrong, Karen (2006), *The Great Transformation: the Beginning of our Religious Traditions*, New York: Knopf, 2006)

[6] Baskin, Jeremy (2015) 'Paradigm Dressed as Epoch: the Ideology of the Anthropocene', *Environmental Values* 24 pp 9-29. Quote from pp 9-10.

[7] Ibid p. 10

for this task. This is the question I wish to explore in the present paper.

2. *Theoria* versus *strategia*: contrasting modes of thought

In order to pursue this question, let us return to the origins of philosophy and consider in a little more detail the phenomenology of this new method of thinking. The earliest origins of philosophy in the West were of course in ancient Greece. Philosophy emerged as a distinctive tradition in the 6th century BCE. To grasp the distinctive phenomenology of this tradition I would like to compare it with a wisdom tradition that prevailed at the same time in China. Although these two traditions nominally shared the goal of wisdom, their approaches were very different. (I shall return below to the question why philosophy did not gain as strong a foothold in ancient China as it did in ancient Greece despite the fact that civilization in China long antedated civilization in Greece.)

My starting point for this comparison was an article by French sinologist and philosopher, Francois Jullien, "Did Philosophers have to Become Fixated on Truth?".[8] Contrasting the figure of the ancient Greek philosopher with that of the ancient Chinese sage, Jullien pointed out that where the philosopher set out to *explain* the world, the sage set out to *adapt* or *accommodate* himself to it. Where the philosopher sought *truth* i.e. an abstract schema that accurately represented reality, the sage aimed at *congruence* i.e. he sought to identify tendencies or dispositions at work in particular situations that could be harnessed to his or others' best advantage. The thinking of the sage remained explicitly inextricable from agency rather than becoming, like the thinking of the Greeks, an epistemic end in itself.

I would like to suggest that Jullien's contrast between the Greek philosopher and the Chinese sage opens up a further contrast between what might be called *theory*, on the one hand, and *strategy*, on the other.[9]

---

[8] Jullien, Francois (2002) 'Did Philosophers Have to Become Fixated on Truth?', *Critical Inquiry*, 28, 4, pp 803-824

[9] See Freya Mathews, 'Why has the West Failed to Embrace Panpsychism?' in *Mind That Abides: Panpsychism in the New Millennium*, ed. by David Skrbina (Advances in Consciousness Research Series) (Amsterdam and Philadelphia: John Benjamins, (2009) 341-260. Several passages in the following pages are adapted from this chapter.

The theorist engages in a particular form of abstractive thought. He picks out concepts from the psycho-cognitive mesh of his thinking and, by further abstraction, sharpens them into well-defined abstract categories. In the process he shifts his focus from the world itself as the object of his cognition to these reified categories i.e. categories treated by him as (ideal) entities in their own right. By manipulating and combining these categories in accordance with abstract principles of inference and evidence, the theorist may eventually produce a schema that is considered accurately to reflect or represent some aspect of reality. Such a representational schema is then judged to be *true*.

The truth about reality, or some aspect of reality, is permanent. It is in fact eternal: the world changes, but the truth about the world does not change. Things arise and pass away, moment by moment, but the truth about things is timeless. The goal of thought, from the theorist's perspective, is to grasp truth, and the grasping of truth is an end in itself.[10] But in allowing his attention to become thus deflected from the "external" world to this timeless, abstract, inner realm of categories and conceptual constructs, the theorist's own position in relation to the object of his cognition changes. Unlike the "external" world, theoretical constructs are the theorist's own creation, assembled and scrutinized within the theatre of his own intellect. In grasping reality indirectly through the lens of an abstract map or model then, the theorist is engaging with something which is, in the last analysis, his own creation. Since he routinely conflates theoretical model with world itself, his status as architect or author of the model

---

10   Heidegger offered a famous analysis of *theoria*, where *theoria* was more or less equated by him with metaphysics. I am not a student of Heidegger, and do not owe the analysis I am offering here to him, so I am not particularly well placed to comment on the overlap between the two accounts. So far as I can tell however, Heidegger was aiming to bring out the distinction between things experienced discursively - as fully discursively mediated - and things experienced immediately, as instances of being, where being is an aspect of reality that cannot be captured by discursive schemas. To "remember" being was to be brought back into the actual presence of the world rather than remaining trapped within the unreal and literally lifeless world of human discourse. I am sympathetic to this project, but my own analysis is explicitly focused on overcoming dualism and does not need recourse to Heideggerian language to explain either its aims or its findings. Any overlap between the two accounts can, I think, be attributed to the fact that both bear evidence of Daoist influences, in my own case, avowedly; in Heidegger's case, unavowedly.

subliminally inflects his relationship with reality. As a result of this rarely scrutinized phenomenology of theorizing, the theorist tends subconsciously to see himself as author or active subject in relation to a world experienced as construct or passive object.

Let me explain this point in a little more detail. In the process of perceiving the world through the lens of theory – which is to say, via the inner theatre of the intellect - the ancient philosopher became subconsciously removed from the world. As the architect of the schema, he could not be included amongst its contents. This architect who could not be included in his own abstract schema was, I am suggesting, the original *subject*, and the world as abstract construct, viewed from within the theatre of the subject's intellect, was the original *object*. It was, in other words, via the subtle duplication involved in *theoria*, the introjective act of specular knowing, that the world first became a mere *object* for the human mind, ideal and hence inert and untouchable and completely devoid of real presence or agency of its own. This separation of active, world-constructing subject from the merely acted-upon, constructed object, was presumably the origin of the famous mind/body or mind/matter *dualism* that has systematically inflected Western thought. This dualism is a function of the subject-object bifurcation that inevitably accompanies the act of theorizing itself. It will implicitly block any outlook which attributes subjectivity, agency, mentality, purpose or presence to the world at large. The mode of relationship with reality encouraged by the dualist outlook will accordingly be one of presumption: the world is perceived as a mere object for the theorist to use as he sees fit.

The *strategist*, by contrast, focuses not on abstract schemas at an inner remove from reality but on the immediate field of actual, outer influences and concrete particulars in which he is immersed. He examines these concretely and corporeally in order to discern how that field is impacting on his agency. His interest is not in abstract architectonics but rather in his own immediate situation and how the influences at play in it are tangibly impinging on him in the present moment. He does not need a theory about the nature of reality in order to respond strategically to this field of influences: he can directly feel environmental pressures increasing and decreasing as he responds now this way, now that. Nor does he address this field as a completed totality; it extends just as far as the range of his own sensitivity, and, as he moves around, this range is constantly changing. Accordingly, to train the strategic faculty, one does not teach reason, which is to say, rules for the articulation and organization of thought in the abstract key, but rather sets mindfulness exercises or practices which cultivate sensitivity and responsiveness. This is why Chinese sages typically received their training in martial and other Daoist arts rather than in discursive inquiry.

In understanding the contrast between theory and strategy, etymology is helpful. The word, "theory" derives from the Greek, *theoria*, a looking at, thing looked at; *theoros*, spectator; and *thea*, spectacle. "Strategy" is derived from the Greek *strategia*, "office or command or art of a general", from *stratos*, "multitude, army, expedition" and *agein*, "to lead, guide, drive, carry off", from Sanskrit *ajirah*, "moving, active". In light of this, strategy may be understood as concerned with the coordination of collective or individual agency. Cognition is required for such coordination, but this is not the kind of cognition involved in *theoria*, which abstracts from the empirical agency of the subject in order to attain a more detached representation of the world. In *strategia*, cognition remains in the service of agency.

Strategic consciousness, in other words, is inherently nondualist. Rather than enacting an inner subject/object bifurcation and engaging with reality as a passive construct of his own devising, the strategist remains immersed in a fluxing field of concrete particulars and pressures which are registered not as part of an abstract totality at an epistemic remove from the subject, but in terms of their immediate impact or influence on the agency of the embedded, nondual self.

Through strategic experimentation the strategist quickly discovers that the best way of negotiating a field of influences in which one is immersed – where this field includes the cross-cutting wills or conativities of others - is generally to adapt to them. That is to say, the best way of negotiating such a field is to make one's own ends as consistent as possible with surrounding influences and conativities, rather than seeking to impose one's will upon them. This is self-evident inasmuch as she who achieves her goals in ways best calculated to conserve her own energy will be most fit to continue to preserve and increase her own existence. Strategy then, the province of the Chinese sage, points to *wu wei*, the way of least resistance, which can be understood not simply as the giving up of one's own ends in deference to the ends of others but rather as tailoring one's ends to theirs and using the energies already at play in one's environment to further one's goals.

The strategist thus discovers *wu wei* for himself via a process of strategic experimentation. By reflecting on this process, he also discovers that *wu wei* is the natural modality of all beings: what works for him as an agent responsively and spontaneously negotiating a field of environmental forces will work for any being strategically negotiating such a field. Hence it is the strategy that will be naturally selected for all beings. In experientially discovering *wu wei* for himself, then, the strategist reflectively, though without the aid of theory, also discovers the way of all nature. In China this way is called *Dao*.

It is arguably the dualist outlook bequeathed to the West by the theoretic orientation of philosophy which has led in our own era to environmental crisis. For when the theoretic objectification of reality inaugurated by philosophy for contemplative purposes gave rise, many centuries later, to a more accurate, detailed and comprehensive form of theorization—the body of knowledge known to us as science—humanity was empowered to exercise its agency on an unprecedented scale. This form of agency, rooted in theory, was very different from the strategic agency of the ancient sage. It was no longer the agency of a self negotiating reality from a point of immersion within it but rather that of a subject premeditating its action by reference to a once-removed abstract schema. This calculated form of agency turned out to entrain undreamed-of efficacy. However, the dualism that is built into the very process of theorizing ensures, I have suggested, that agency rooted in theory will be unaccommodating. It will be innately instrumentalist.

Such instrumentalism is indeed what may be observed in the history of the West. Science, the offshoot of Western philosophy, has given birth to modernity, the instrumentalist form of civilization par excellence that has spread industrialization throughout the world - to great human advantage but at deadly cost to the natural environment.

In the late 20th century it was philosophy itself that hunted down – and critiqued - the dualist or binary roots of Western thought. The role of binary oppositions was intensively explored by deconstructionists, notably Jacques Derrida. [11] The influence of deconstruction was in turn key across a range of critical discourses, including feminism and postcolonialism. Environmental philosophers also bemoaned the entrenched dualism of the Western tradition that has systematically elevated the human, as subject, locus of mind, agency, purpose and meaning, over nature rendered as brute object, realm of mere matter, devoid of mind and hence of meaning, purpose and intrinsic value. [12] It was this dualism, environmental philosophers pointed out, that underpinned the endemic anthropocentrism and instrumentalism of Western attitudes to the natural world. In place of dualist theories of nature, such philosophers offered theories that sought to represent nature as subject, locus of mind, agency or intentionality, and the moral values that accompany mind. [13] It was expected that when nature was reinvested with mind in this way, a more respectful and considerate attitude to the natural environment would follow. But such revised theories of nature have proved to have little traction in Western cultures. If my present analysis is correct, and it is theory itself that underwrites dualism and phenomenologically re-inscribes it in every act of theorizing, then it is not surprising that theoretical remedies for a problem which, at the deepest level, springs from theory itself, will be unavailing.

So this is a dilemma for the West. But what of China? There were of course theoretical as well as strategic tendencies in the thought of ancient China. (Scholars such as the Moists, Legalists and followers of the School of Names, as well as Confucius and Mencius, displayed theoretical tendencies in their thought.) But Francois Jullien seems right in suggesting that these theoretical tendencies never became the defining perspective of Chinese civilization. Throughout its long history, the defining perspective of Chinese civilization remained the strategic one of accommodation and adaptation, elegantly codified in the normative principle of *wu wei*. Even China's departure from

---

[11] The locus classicus of this work is Jacques Derrida, 'Structure, Sign and Play in the Discourse of the Human Sciences' in Richard Macksey and Eugenio Donato (eds.) (1970) *The Languages of Criticism and the Sciences of Man* Baltimore: Johns Hopkins Press, pp 247-265

[12] Plumwood, Val (1993) *Feminism and the Mastery of Nature,* London and New York: Routledge

[13] The entire field of ecophilosophy may be seen as the attempt, firstly, to break down dualism as it pertains to nature and thereby, secondly, to recover the moral significance of nature.

tradition in the 20th century, its embrace of modern forms of civilization dictated by Western science, may be seen, at the deepest level, as an instance of its traditional disposition to accommodate and adapt.

3. Alternative foundations for civilization: China and the West

China may have owed this difference from the West to the continuity of its civilization with its own indigenous roots. The form of civilization that evolved so gradually in China was deeply informed with, and organized around, the fundamental principle of *Dao*, a principle inherited from its pre-civilizational past. This was a principle that explicitly resisted theorization. As Laozi puts it in the opening line of the *Daodejing*, "the Dao that can be told of is not the eternal Dao".[14] As a principle, *Dao* suggests instead the strategic approach to reality that is still today characteristic of many indigenous societies. In China, theorization was kept in check by the pervasive influence of this principle. At the same time, deference to *Dao* enabled a robust syncretism that refused any exclusive bids for truth to flourish, binding together disparate traditions, such as Confucianism and Buddhism and latterly Marxism, as well as Daoism itself, to create an open yet distinctively Chinese outlook.

The continuity of Chinese civilization with its indigenous roots is evident in the prominent role that shamanism played in the early history of China. Historians of civilization note this as a distinctive factor in the development of civilization in China by comparison with the West.[15] Shamanism, a feature widely shared by a great variety of hunter gatherer societies around the globe, consists of a set of spiritual practices whereby socially ordained individuals – shamans - communicate with a spirit-world assumed to co-exist with nature. The purpose of such communication is to gain transcendent knowledge, guidance, magic or healing energy; this is then channeled back to the shaman's community. Shamans work closely with animal powers,

---

[14] Chan, Wing-Tsit (1963) *A Source Book in Chinese Philosophy*, Princeton: Princeton University Press, p. 139

[15] Chang, Kwang-Chih 'Ancient China and its Anthropological Significance' in *The Breakout: the Origins of Civilization* ed. by Martha Lamberg-Karlovsky (2004) Harvard: Harvard University Press, pp 1-11; also *The Formation of Chinese Civilization: An Archaeological Perspective* (2005) Kwang-chih Chang, Pingfang Xu, Sarah Allan, Liancheng Lu (eds.) New Haven: Yale University Press

totemic animals generally serving as spirit guides on shamanic flights between the everyday world and the spirit world. Such reverence for animals and trust in their spiritual power, rooted in totemism, is characteristic of hunter gatherer outlooks that have not yet demoted animals to the wrong side of culture-nature dualism.

In the formative stages of Chinese civilization, shamans continued to hold their earlier high status as societies transitioned from hunting and gathering to pastoralism and agriculture. By the second millennium BCE, emerging social elites were appropriating the knowledge and prestige of shamans to lend spiritual direction and legitimacy to their political intent. Shamans were co-opted to mediate between the spirit world, now figured as Heaven, and the secular world, now figured as Earth, in order to obtain a "mandate of Heaven" for the will of imperial rulers.[16]

This absorption of a pre-civilizational form of spirituality, normally associated with hunter gatherer societies, into the civilizational structure of China, might be explainable by the relative absence of rupture in the transition from pre-history to history in China. Though ethnically diverse, the cultures and languages of the Yellow River and Yangtze River basins evolved gradually and continuously over millennia – they were not subject to outright conquest or colonization by alien cultures. (Even during later imperial periods of "barbarian" (Manchu and Mongol) dominance, Chinese language was maintained as the language of governance; Manchus and Mongols themselves were significantly sinicized rather than subsuming the Chinese under their own foreign cultures.)[17]

Whatever the reason for the persistence of shamanism in the evolution of a distinctively Chinese form of civilization however, its pivotal role in turn ensured the persistence of basic elements of hunter gatherer consciousness in the Chinese outlook, where this militated against the dualizing tendencies, noted above, of civilization per se.

---

[16] Ibid. Kwang-Chih Chang.

[17] Of course, the influence of the Chinese upon their foreign rulers was not entirely one-way. Manchu and Mongolian rulers also retained and disseminated aspects of their own culture while governing China. See Standen, Naomi (2013) 'Foreign Conquerors of China' in *Demystifying China: New Understandings of Chinese History* Naomi Standen (ed.) Lanham Maryland: Rowman and Littlefield, pp 33-40

A different unfolding of civilization is evident in the West. Ancient Greek civilization, in the form described, for example, by Francois Jullien, emerged in the centuries following waves of invasion by alien Indo-European peoples, such as the Dorians, Aeolians and Ionians, from the Danube basin in the second millennium BCE. These peoples are thought to have hailed originally from the steppelands of southern Russia.[18] Their arrival in those parts of the Mediterranean which would come to be known as Greece represented a profound rupture in the evolution of civilization in the area. The prior, pre-Greek cultures of the indigenous (non-Indo-European) peoples – named by the Greeks themselves as the Pelagsians – were relatively obliterated. Although these peoples were already civilized, there is evidence that their cultures retained a spiritual orientation to nature that may well have represented a certain continuity with earlier, hunter gatherer ways of life. In any case, with the sharp cultural break that the Indo-European invasions represented, little continuity would remain between post-Homeric Greek civilization and an indigenous past.[19] The stage was accordingly set for the emergence, in the classical period, of a fully post-indigenous, dualized, theoretic consciousness.

4. Philosophy in a strategic mode as foundation for a new ecological civilization

In the 20th century China sought, for pragmatic reasons, to weave science, with its Western philosophical underpinnings, into the open texture of its outlook. However, by virtue of the spectacular material success of science - its capacity to co-opt nature for human purposes – this theoretic outlook is currently perhaps threatening to displace the notion of *Dao* as the generous well-spring of Chinese civility. It is threatening to replace *Dao* with a dogmatic materialism that hides an underlying dualism that in turn inevitably subjects the larger earth-community to human despotism.

From the perspective of the argument presented here, it would be a tragic error for China to abandon *Dao* as its guiding principle.

---

[18] Nicholson, Adam (2014) *The Mighty Dead: Why Homer Matters*, London: William Collins, ch 9.

[19] Haarmann, Harald (2014) *Roots of Ancient Greek Civilization: the Influence of Old Europe,* Jefferson, NC: McFarlane & Co, pp 9-40

Theory, with its offshoot, science, is of course of enormous developmental significance in the cultural evolution of humankind. It cannot be ignored or set aside. But unless theory is subsumed under a *strategic* orientation which leaves all ultimate questions open, and seeks only to respond to the actual promptings of the world, then it will trap China as it has the West in a dualism that will continue to play itself out in the instrumentalization of nature.

In the West, we have, I think, ceased genuinely to relate to reality itself because we have ceased to experience it directly – we apprehend it only through the dualizing lenses of theory. In the twenty-first century we exist increasingly inside a discursive bubble, a world both materially made over to suit human convenience and interpreted exclusively in terms of our own ever-intensifying self-preoccupation. We have ceased to experience what it is like to exist, to act, in synchrony with the larger community of life and hence in accord with *Dao*. Theory cannot convey this re-animating experience; on the contrary, it alienates us from it. Only through *cultivation*, defined in relation to certain kinds of arts or practices, can we engage with reality in this spontaneous and responsive way. Daoism is a repository of such arts and practices – martial arts, taiji, calligraphy, internal alchemy – but many other fields of human endeavor offer potential others.

If philosophy is to help us repair our relationship with nature in the 21st century, in the face of ecological upheaval on a planetary scale, then it may need to integrate theory with a strategic orientation that is sensitive to environmental cues and capable of responding spontaneously to them, without discursive pre-conception. Such an orientation can be achieved only through practices that enable us to immerse ourselves psychophysically in nature, thereby enabling us to experience nature immediately as the psychoactive directive and responsive matrix of our own being. If theory could in this way be subsumed under a strategic orientation, the result would surely indeed be a form of wisdom.

However, it is hard to know how such wisdom could be described, since any name would tend to co-opt it exclusively to theory. If one adopted terms such as "cosmological wisdom" or "ecological wisdom", one might be tempted to unpack them in exclusively theoretical terms, as ways of life dictated by the cosmological or ecological sciences. Laozi of course had similar difficulties working out how to refer to the wisdom of following *Dao*, since Dao itself cannot be named. "The Dao that can be told of is not the eternal Dao." But the root meaning of the term, *philosophy*, namely *love of wisdom*, is surely apposite in this connection, as it implies a form of understanding that includes an experiential, even spiritual, certainly extra-discursive dimension. To reconceive philosophy along non-dualist lines may in fact take us back to certain strands of the original philosophical enterprise. For while ancient philosophy seems indeed to have become fixated on truth, as Francois Jullien argues, and in this sense allowed theory to shape the Western tradition, counter-tendencies also existed in the Hellenistic world.

Historian of ancient philosophy, Pierre Hadot, has detailed how philosophy was understood by certain schools, notably the Stoics and Epicureans, precisely as a way of life, pursued not merely through discourse but also via spiritual exercises and meditational practices aimed at opening out the narrow perspective of the individual to the perspective of the cosmos as a whole.[20] For Stoics and Epicureans, according to Hadot, this expansion of consciousness, this capacity to perceive one's interests and assumptions in the context of a larger field of inter-relations and hence to recognize the ego-distortedness of one's habitual outlook, was a definitive key to wisdom. In the light of this consciousness, the imperative always to serve one's own interests would give way to a more generous, accommodating tendency, with a felt sense of the rightfulness of the claims of other beings. As the product of direct experience, such an expanded perspective, with its attendant moral values, would be grasped by the practitioner as self-evident rather than entertained, as it would be were it merely a posit of reason, as a contingent theoretical position open to contestation by competing theories.

In an epoch – the Anthropocene – in which humanity is rapidly destroying the ecological integrity of the biosphere, new moral values, particularly in the form of an environmental ethic, are urgently needed. Contemporary philosophers, heir to the tradition of philosophy as *theoria*, can and do offer theoretical arguments in favour of environmental ethics. But these values have so far exerted little influence on society. The reason for this is perhaps that, as an instance of theorizing, environmental ethics, like philosophy generally,

---

[20] Hadot, Pierre (2002) *What is Ancient Philosophy?* Michael Chase (trans.) Cambridge MA: Belknap Press of Harvard University Press

phenomenologically re-enacts the subject-object split that underpins anthropocentrism, thereby reinforcing anthropocentrism psychologically even as it attempts to refute it rationally. Moreover, as a mere theoretical posit, environmental ethics remains contestable and hence optional, subject to rational demurral by those for whom it is inconvenient. For modern civilization, based on an ethos of industrialism and hence subjugation of nature, any ethos of moral consideration for the interests of nature is not merely an inconvenience but a direct threat. If environmental ethics is to acquire the force of self-evidence and hence the authority it needs in order to supplant the anthropocentrism so core to modern civilization, it may need to be explored and imparted by way of more immediate, experiential methods than have so far been the province of philosophy. In other words, *cultivation* of consciousness may be required in addition to discourse.

In the West we can look back to traditions such as those of the Stoics and Epicureans in the search for clues to transforming philosophy into a discipline dedicated not merely to discourse but to the cultivation of an attitude of attunement to the interests of all beings. But Stoic and Epicurean methods pale in comparison to the methodological resources offered by China, with its long and highly evolved tradition of adaptation and accommodation, codified as the Great *Dao* and cultivated via a vast array of dedicated practices. China thus seems well placed to lead the way towards a discipline that subsumes theory under a larger strategic perspective. The figure of the Chinese sage, beckoning us down the path of *wu wei*, perhaps offers a new point of departure for thinking about appropriate cognitive modalities for the Anthropocene outside the compromised parameters of the Western tradition. Just as ancient Greek philosophy laid the foundations for the civilization, rooted in *theoria*, which would eventually manifest as modernity, so such a new cognitive modality, theoretically literate but responsive in its larger orientation to nature, might help to lay foundations for a future, ecological civilization

Bibliography

Abram, David (1996) *Spell of the Sensuous,* New York: Vintage.

Armstrong, Karen (2006) *The Great Transformation: the Beginning of our Religious Traditions,* New York: Knopf

Baskin, Jeremy (2015) 'Paradigm Dressed as Epoch: the Ideology of the Anthropocene' in *Environmental Values* 24

Bruhl, Lucien Levy (1926) *How Natives Think,* London: George Allen and Unwin

— (1928) *The Soul of the Primitive,* London: George Allen and Unwin

Chan, Wing-Tsit (1963) *A Source Book in Chinese Philosophy,* Princeton: Princeton University Press

Chang, Kwang-Chih (2004) 'Ancient China and its Anthropological Significance' in *The Breakout: the Origins of Civilization,* Martha Lamberg-Karlovsky, M., (ed.) Harvard: Harvard University Press

Derrida, Jacques (1970) 'Structure, Sign and Play in the Discourse of the Human Sciences' in Macksey, R., and Donato, E., (eds.) *The Languages of Criticism and the Sciences of Man,* Baltimore: Johns Hopkins Press

Haarmann, Harald (2014) *Roots of Ancient Greek Civilization: the Influence of Old Europe,* Jefferson North Carolina: McFarlane & Co

Hadot, Pierre (2002) *What is Ancient Philosophy?,* Michael Chase (trans.) Cambridge MA., Belknap Press of Harvard University Press

Jullien, Francois (2002) 'Did Philosophers Have to Become Fixated on Truth?' in *Critical Inquiry,* 28, 4

Kwang-chih Chang, Pingfang Xu, Sarah Allan, Liancheng Lu (eds.) (2005) *The Formation of Chinese Civilization: An Archaeological Perspective,* New Haven: Yale University Press

Jarad, Diamond (2005) *Collapse: How Societies Choose to Fail or Succeed,* New York: Penguin

Nicholson, Adam (2014) *The Mighty Dead: Why Homer Matters,* London: William Collins

Mathews, Freya (2009) 'Why has the West Failed to Embrace Panpsychism?' in *Mind That Abides: Panpsychism in the New Millennium*, Skrbina, D. (ed.), Amsterdam and Philadelphia: John Benjamins

Ong, Walter J. (1982) *Orality and Literacy: the Technologizing of the Word*, London: Methuen

Plumwood, Val (1993) *Feminism and the Mastery of Nature*, London and New York: Routledge

Prentice, Richard (2009) 'Cultural Responses to Climate Change in the Holocene' in *Anthos*, 1.1.

Standen, Naomi (2013) 'Foreign Conquerors of China' in *Demystifying China: New Understandings of Chinese History* Naomi Standen (ed.) Lanham Maryland: Rowman and Littlefield

The Relation of Crisis to Constant Order

Robert Bolton

The Competence of Philosophy

The association of "deep philosophy", with "deep ecology" reflects the fact that ecological problems have assumed an importance great enough for them to come within the scope of philosophy, although there must be doubts as to whether philosophy is of any use for understanding historically unique or unprecedented events. Philosophy's focus on universals seems to identify it with knowledge of what is true at all times, and both Platonic and Aristotelian thought explain the world according to a conception of immutable realities which are manifested in a permanent material substratum. But there the resemblance ends, because the Aristotelian kind of thought, and its derivatives, really is concerned only with constant processes. Because of its empirical tendency, it is focused on changes of a kind which most people are capable of observing most of the time, so that the material world in Aristotle can appear to be as stable in its own way as the realm of Forms in Plato.

If it were asked why an ancient philosophy should give the best means of understanding modern crises, it must be said that Platonism is the only philosophy which engages with the whole spectrum of reality. Nearly all other philosophies, starting from Aristotle's, artificially restrict the content of reality, and so exclude things their authors dislike, or fear, or do not wish to understand. Accordingly, Plato's philosophy incorporates both creation and cosmic catastrophes within its system of Forms and matter, and that was something which Aristotle would not accept. This appears from the passage in the *Timaeus* where time is created along with the world: "Time came into being together with the Heaven, in order that, as they were brought into being together, so they may be dissolved together, if ever their dissolution should come to pass;" (38B). This excludes any "empty time" in which a world could have evolved into being.

For Plato, the manifestation of Forms in matter was not simply automatic, but was subject to Divine power and choice, firstly in regard to the number of Forms instantiated at a given time, secondly in the different durations for which they appear, and thirdly in the order in which they do so. Fourthly, beyond the other three, creation is involved in the question as to how many highly-placed, and how many lowly-placed, members of the system of Forms are instantiated in a certain period. If these factors are taken into account, it will be clear that this conception of Forms and matter can cope with radical cosmic change, within its overriding focus on universals. On this basis, the world could possibly deteriorate simply by a progressive reduction in the numbers of Forms instantiated in it, even if the three other modes of change were not in operation. But we need to see why the world's in-forming principles should be withdrawn like this, and not kept numerically constant.

I shall therefore say something first about the order of cosmic change, and then about the corresponding changes in the human mind. Those are the changes which have led to an identity crisis; no longer understanding ourselves, we fail to understand our role in the world.

Cosmic Decline

An example of overall and pervasive cosmic change is to be seen in the myth which Plato presents in the *Statesman* dialogue, where we are told: "At certain times God himself guides the progress of this world and presides over its revolution. At other times, when the periods assigned to it have run their course, he leaves it alone; and then, of its own accord, it begins to travel on its circular course *in the opposite direction. . .*" (*Statesman* 269c) In the same passage it is clear that this myth does refer to God, and not just to mythical divinities, since He is referred to as "the supreme divinity" or "the greatest god." (ibid. 272 e)

Once the world is released from direct Divine control, then, an increasing disorder results from the initial reversal of its processes until the world is in danger of dissolution, at which point we are told that God resumes control of it. The issues which this conception clearly raises are those of cyclic time and of cosmic pessimism. Apparently, the world as a whole appears bound to keep on getting worse, even though no one individual is bound to become part of that. Elsewhere, this view appears in myths of a Golden Age, followed by ages of Silver, Bronze, and Iron. Here again, it seems that a downward path is somehow necessary, so that this sequence must draw mankind further and further away from an original perfection or fullness of being.

At this point I want show what is involved in this idea and will try to show that it comes from something more universal than an inclination to pessimism.

Something of a supra-human nature is at work in the pattern of change, and attention was drawn to this by René Guénon in his work on cyclic time. The determining reality in question is the Great Chain of Being, the total non-temporal structure of being, extending down from the highest divinity to the most peripheral and short-lived modifications of existence. The further down the chain one goes, the more quantity dominates quality; that is to say, the lower the level, the greater the expansion in the numbers of existences, even though they may not manifest any larger variety of Forms. At the top, there is a simplicity of fullness, while at the bottom, there is a simplicity of emptiness, and a maximum of complexity between them.

This is the order in the Chain of Being which is manifested in the succession of the ages, inasmuch as every passage from one part of time to the next corresponds to a descent from one level in the Great Chain to the next lower. The determinism involved in this is part of the cosmic order as a whole.

A pattern of cosmic descent can also be seen from the working of causality, where every cause produces first of all effects most like itself, and then effects which are progressively less and less like it. This is explained in Proclus's account of causality in the *Elements of Theology*, especially in (Propositions 28 and 29), in terms of the superiority of the cause over the effect it produces, where each part of time is the effect of the one before and the cause of the next. A loud noise sounds less and less loud the further away one is; and this can also be seen in manufactured things, which do best what they were made for when new, but gradually do less well, until they have to be replaced. This kind of change is paralleled by the irreversibility of entropy, where natural causes operate by expending and dissipating energy which can never be recaptured.

It remains to consider the reasons as to why the course taken by time is always cyclic. This idea appears to be drawn from analogies with the cycles of the seasons and the lunar cycle, along with the life-cycles of all living things, vegetable or sentient. Besides, rotation pervades the universe, as nearly all the bodies in the universe rotate about their axes, and move in closed orbits. All such examples do not amount to theoretical proof; there must still be a cyclic property essential to time itself.

For Platonists, the cyclic pattern results from the relation between the eternal causes of things, or Forms, and the world of time and change produced by them. This world cannot be separated from the Forms, or it would cease to exist, but conversely, it cannot be fully united with them without losing its temporal nature. Consequently, the world of time can only retain its own nature and at the same time remain affiliated to its formal cause by uniting in itself a pair of opposites. This is a union of motion with fixity, and the only kind of motion which does that is circular motion. In motion which keeps traversing the same path around a fixed point, the conflict between them is overcome.

Circle and cycle are clearly not identical, but they are closely related. For change in time to form a cycle, it is only necessary that the changes should repeat the same general pattern, and not repeat identical events. That is enough for them to be cycles rather than circles.

The descending property of cycles, referred to already, results from time's manifesting the initial separation of temporal being from the eternal. In this way, time-cycles fully reflect their descent from their causes.

Where this descending process involves the Forms, the passage of time appears in the realization of possibilities, beginning with the most far-reaching of them, (i.e. manifesting the more highly-placed Forms in the Chain of Being), and then subsequently more and more limited possibilities. That kind of change is the one which is expressed poetically by the descent of a world from a golden age to an iron age, but it is always the pattern of events which is repeated, not particular events or beings.

The Roots of False Consciousness

If all changes on the cosmic level happen by physical necessity, there remains the question as to how much or how little we ourselves must be involved in them. Entities which participate in just one level of being are necessarily ruled by necessity, but this is not the case for those who participate in all levels of being. The human soul is created so as to mediate between nature and the supernatural, between the changing and the unchanging, and to relate equally naturally to both. For this reason, we are a composite of everything from the Divine down to the inertia of matter. That includes our share of Plato's universal interaction of Reason and Necessity, a combination over which neither nature nor the conditions of a world-cycle have any *necessary* power since they are produced by it. Such forces cannot comprehend our whole being, therefore, and so they can rule only those who are willing to accept them, or those who just don't care.

All that is very far from what is taken to be the truth about our cosmic position today, because the ideas involved in it have been increasingly sidelined by those whom society regards as experts. We are nearly all aware that modern minds do not work in the same way as the minds of our ancestors, because the changes in the way in which we think of ourselves and the world have moved in a consistently materialistic direction for the past four hundred years. The ideas involved in this were not part of any science, but they became associated with the successes achieved by science in the same period, and thereby they were irrationally allowed to share in the prestige of science, so that most people were unaware of any difference, with the result that modern forms of speculation came under the umbrella of "new discoveries".

To shed light on the ecological crisis we need to find out what has driven this modern mindset, and why it was so susceptible to materialism. This involves the prospect of a steady deterioration of human consciousness, and that possibility needs to be accounted for, particularly where it means that a false philosophy could spread so far and so deep as to create a false consciousness, along with its failure to understand our place in the natural world.

The Rise of Empiricism

There has long been a major change in the accepted ideas of knowledge and truth, and this in turn has determined the way in which the mind thinks of itself; one's theory of knowledge becomes a theory of oneself. This change has been continually in the direction of Empiricism, the idea that knowledge comes from sense-perception, with the mind passive to the input, like blank paper being printed on. It all began with the "elevation" of Aristotle in the 13th Century.

Thanks to the work of Aquinas, Aristotle's philosophy was incorporated into the highest received wisdom. There was in the wake of this an adage that there was "nothing in the intellect except what was first in the senses." This went with a denial of the Forms or innate ideas, supported by a supposed argument that there could be no innate ideas, because a person born blind could have no idea of colours. That was accepted despite the fact that that could only be true if the senses were indeed the only source of knowledge.

To confirm the idea of Aristotle as the principal source of Empiricism in Western tradition, we need only bear in mind his rejection of the transcendental nature of the Forms and of the soul, and his reduction of the mind to the sensory level: "That part of the soul, then, which we call mind. . . *has no actual existence* until it thinks." (*De Anima* III, iv. 429a). This statement is repeated in the same text. When the mind does not think, it cannot cause any signs detectable by sight or hearing, of course, and the absence of such phenomena is taken for a guarantee of non-existence. That is the empiricist position precisely.

Besides this, the implicit idea that the non-existent can decide to start doing something is obviously self-contradictory. Whatever can start to do something must first exist; that applies to physical activity as much as to mental. During sleep, however, sense perception ceases as well as thought. Did Aristotle never ask himself whether he still existed while he was asleep? Be that as it may, this view of mind has been respectfully accepted by innumerable generations of instinctive materialists, who thought that the existence of objective and subsistent Forms was not believable. In the same passage Aristotle also says: "Hence the mind, too, can have no characteristic except its capacity to receive." (ibid.)

Even where the mind is allowed to exist, then, it could only be as a receptacle for sensory inputs, such that it must be on a level with them. Knowledge would be ready-made "out there," and would need only to find a lodging-place, and the mind would be simply a collection of images of things brought in by sense-perception. In this case, the mind could not have any independent existence in relation to the external world, let alone any innate ideas; that, incidentally, is a theory which has been made familiar in modern times by advocates of anti-dualism.

A further consequence of this is that one could have no innate personality either, but only a blank tablet to be inscribed by others. One's personality would then consist only of all the inputs received from parents, teachers and contemporaries. In this case, one could not have even second-hand personality, because those who formed us would themselves be only so many collections of inputs from yet other empirical agents. Thus personality would recede to infinity, and be reduced to nothing, while the world would consist of objects without subjects, if that were not as self-contradictory like saying there were only odd numbers, and no even.

Plotinus clearly regards this position as self-refuting: "For certainly we cannot think of the soul as a thing whose nature is just a sum of impressions from outside – as if it, *alone of all that exists*, had no native character." (*Ennead* II, 3, 15)

The Empiricist mind is gripped by a conviction that reality must be in principle *simple*, which ironically cannot be supported by empirical evidence. And then an anti-metaphysical position gives rise to a pseudo-metaphysics.

All such thinking contradicts what Plato argued for in two of his major works, the *Theaetetus* and *the Sophist,* where the idea that knowledge might be sense-perception is refuted in detail, and knowledge is shown to result from the powers of judgement and recognition of Forms. Consequently, all empiricist philosophers from the earliest times must logically have been bound to begin by refuting those arguments of Plato, but in fact they have not attempted to do so. Their kind of thought necessarily excludes God, since the attributes of the Divine can only be metaphysical, and that is why their philosophy never needs to set up explicit arguments against religious belief.

From the 17th Century, empiricism became our national philosophical tradition, in the works of Bacon, Locke, Hume, and Mill, and they ignore Plato as though he had nothing relevant to say on the subject. Instead, we are offered a way of thinking which feels comfortably close to common sense, although it is not hard to show that it cannot meet its own criteria. Firstly, the idea that knowledge comes from sense-perception is not to be found in any kind of sense-perception. It is in fact a typical mental construct. And then it gets worse: we cannot perceive our own perceiving, so we can't see our seeing, hear our hearing, and so on, in which case we could not even know that we had sense-perception, if knowledge is from the senses; knowledge would then be attributed to something whose very existence was not knowable. That has not prevented some of those who believe in perception alone from denying the very existence of minds, and to them the best answer is to ask that they prove the existence of sense-perception. As Plato has pointed out, a statement that "X exists" is not the same thing as a simple perception of X, because existence is always an inference following from consciousness, no matter how often we make it.

Empiricism gives rise to an optimistic popular belief that knowledge is ready-made out there, (as in the words of Aristotle just quoted), so that we need only open our windows and it will fly in. In this case, to hear would be the same thing as to understand, and one could master the most difficult books by staring at their pages. In reality, however, experience is turned into knowledge by subtle mental operations involving the judgement, which one can make for oneself, but not for others. That is why we can easily share beliefs or opinions, because that need only require imitation, but there is no direct sharing of items of knowledge as such; they must first be made one's own.

These facts are usually ignored today, because they are outside imagination, and can only be conceived and understood by reason. There is a clear one-to-one relation between things perceived and things imagined, and this combination of thought and sense creates a false completeness, which makes most people unwilling to think beyond imagination. But if knowledge is taken to be solely on this level, the transcendental property of knowing is lost, and the knower is brought down to the level of the known, thus making ourselves part of the flow of phenomena, and therefore one more part of the natural order.

False philosophy also comes from a misunderstanding about the external world. We agree that it is full of independently-existing material objects, but these things are not literally grasped empirically, though they may appear to be so. That is because we grasp only our *experiences* of those objects, not the things as such. This can be seen from the fact that these sense-experiences have nothing either independent or material about them. They are in fact dependent on our interests, our needs, our attention span, and things which compete for our attention. Simply by being experiences, they are psychical, not material, and they do not occupy any public space, being spatial only in form.

Knowledge of the external world thus has to be representational, in which case we cannot directly identify our perceptions with the things which cause them. However, if knowledge is really from sense-perception, empiricists must have to close this gap between perceptions and material things, which needless to say, has never been done, except by denying the existence of material reality.

Empiricism could also be said to attack the difference between being asleep and being awake, because, when dreaming, the mind really is passive to uninvited incoming phenomena, and the self-reflective principle is inactive. The dream-world is one of objects with no effective subject, (as the waking world should be for empiricists), therefore, and the mind could be said to have everything except itself. This state of mind, continued into the waking state, is one Plato attributed to the Tyrant and the Tyrannical man. (*Republic* IX 571-572, 576b).

This naturalizing of our higher faculties has been accompanied by a down-grading of man's idea of his cosmic status, which has long been regarded as progress, so much so that Copernicus, Darwin, and Freud have been called "the disillusioners of mankind," as though centrality in the universe, and in the natural order, and in the realm of intelligence, could only be illusions. It would be different if we knew who really did have centrality in these ways, but in fact we do not, unless it is ourselves.

In contrast to this sensory idea of knowledge, the metaphysical kinds of knowledge result from recognition of Forms and their relations, both in the world and in oneself, and in this case knowledge is characterized by such properties as Exactitude, Necessity, Immutability, and Universality. These result from the transcendental natures of the soul and the Forms. But when we perceive a material object, it cannot be exact, because it is always incomplete, and it cannot be identically the same in different observers. Secondly, it cannot be necessary either, because such an object is a contingency by definition; thirdly, it is always mutable; and fourthly, it cannot be universal, because it is purely individual. Thus empirical knowledge can really only amount to more or less probable belief, so that for it there can be no such thing as truth, but only approximation. No such thing as truth, however, means no such thing as spirituality.

Power in Exchange for Truth

Such considerations do not disturb the prime movers of modernity, because the whole force of the culture they believe in is aimed at replacing knowledge with factual information. Information occupies an intermediate zone between knowledge and opinion, and usually contains both, as though it resulted from an "entropic collapse" of the boundary between them. It is nearly always received as opinion, and then its truth content has to be judged according to its usefulness. Unlike knowledge, information can be, and is, multiplied almost without limit, making it ideal for a mindset which equates value with quantity.

Empiricism is at home in this context, because here "true" really does mean "supported by the most up-to-date findings". Information evades the grasp of theories of knowledge, because it involves only relations between already-perceived objects, not relations between minds and objective realities. Nevertheless, it is highly valued because of an all-pervasive pursuit of power. It has the strategic function of enabling one to define one's position in relation to various parts of the world upon which one can take action.

On this basis, a vast amount of practical power has been gained over the natural world without its becoming any less incomplete, and that means that the power we have is vulnerable to all the forces which we do not control. Power is used to create changes in the natural world, regardless of whether they might be the causes of changes elsewhere of a kind we do not want, and discover only when new problems arise. (Iatrogenic illness would be the equivalent of this in the personal sphere). This situation is becoming increasingly well-known, but without making the pursuit of power any less compulsive.

No one asks why other species do not acquire power over nature likewise, if mankind is just one species among others. In reality, this means that the more we deny our relative divinity in relation to nature, the more we commit ourselves to a materialistic travesty of it. There is no agreement as to what we ought to do with our technical power, and that indicates that it is not natural to us. Do we use it for our own benefit or not? And what exactly *does* benefit us?

Answers to such questions are lacking because modern thought will not address the question as to what mankind exists for. A passion for power is closely related to religious unbelief, because unbelieving materialism makes it impossible to find the security that comes from acting according to the will of God. Instead, mankind is trying to prove it can save itself, and so make God unnecessary.

The over-exploitation of nature will most likely continue because power over nature is very popular with the general public. The religious ideal of changing oneself so as to measure up to one's place in the world has long been replaced by the Marxist "ideal" of changing the world so that it obeys us and comes down to our measure. Consequently, the exploitation of nature is politically driven, especially as nearly all governments in the developed world keep themselves in power by promising their voters that they will get rid of poverty, and go on providing more and more of everything for everyone. No one dares object publicly that poverty is inevitable, because it is mostly owing to differing uses made of free will, and that it is not necessarily an evil, as for some it is voluntary.

The rejection of mankind's cosmic centrality and the abuse of the environment are closely related because special status in the universe implies special responsibilities as well, so the morally-undemanding option is chosen instead. When the status of individuals is lowered, the effect is usually a lowered sense of personal responsibility and a belief that "If I don't matter, my sins won't matter either." This applies to the collective as much as to the individual.

This negative self-image extends itself to a disbelief in the immortality of the soul. The consequence of that, that our bodies are all we have and all we are, is precisely calculated to intensify the fears and vulnerabilities which underlie the constant pursuit of material power. At the same time, it also intensifies the hedonistic desire to get all the good one can from material sources during the uncertain span of one's mortal life. This shows that the political and economic consequences of popular beliefs are hardly ever thought of by those who govern, since they enact equality for all beliefs, even the most unauthorized or self-destructive, or delusional.

The Golden Verses of Pythagoras have a saying that God could open everyone's eyes, but will not. I think that the meaning of this is that we are all born with the faculties necessary for the freedom of the spirit; but if we were pressured into using them, many of our previous uses of free will would thereby be annulled, and we would be forced to be free; that would imply a self-contradiction, and even omnipotence is not capable of that.

There is a purist objection that the truth of spiritual religion does not depend on or result from its ability to defuse material problems. Certainly a faith taken up for reasons of that kind would not be faith at all. But if all else fails, this can be reduced to a question of probability, namely, which is the more probable: that God and the immortal soul are realities - or that the human race is turning itself into God? The present world situation should make the choice easy, since no amount of material power makes any difference to our mortal condition. In that case, there need be nothing to exclude the conclusion that life in this world is most truly to be understood as a prelude to an eternal and more real one. The responsibility for understanding that is for every individual, and it is no more than what is contained in the precept "Know Thyself."

Bibliography

Aristotle, (1722) *On the Soul, Parva Naturalia, On Breath* Harvard University Press: The Loeb Classical Library

Cornford, F. M. (1948) 'Plato's Cosmology', R.K.P. Cornford (trans.), London: Routledge & Kegan Paul

Dacier, A. & Rowe, N. (1971) *Commentaries of Hierocles on the Golden Verses of the Pythagoreans*, Wheaton, IL: Theosophical Publishing House.

Guénon, R. (1953) *The Reign of Quantity and Signs of the Times* London: Luzak & Co.

Plato (1961) *The Statesman*, John Warrington (trans.) London: J. M. Dent & Sons

—   (1961) *The Statesman*, J. B. Skemp (trans.) in *The Collected Dialogues of Plato*, Edith Hamilton & Huntington Cairns (eds.) Bollingen Series LXXI, Princeton: Princeton University Press.

—   (1961) *The Republic*, Paul Shorey (trans.) in *The Collected Dialogues of Plato*, Edith Hamilton & Huntington Cairns (eds.) Bollingen Series LXXI, Princeton: Princeton University Press.

Plotinus (1962) *The Enneads*, Stephen MacKenna (trans.) London: Faber & Faber

Proclus (1963) *Elements of Theology* Props. XXVIII & XXIX, Thomas Taylor and E. R. Dodds (trans.) Oxford: Oxford University Press

Graveyard, incubator or something much stranger? Blind World or Multiworlds versus Deep Ecology and Neoplatonism

Kevin Corrigan

1. Introduction

Deep ecology (after Arne Naess—1973)[1] suggests that we need to rethink and to repurpose, right down to our supposed roots, all of our environmental systems on the basis of values and methods that truly preserve the ecological and cultural diversity of natural systems. Yet, at the same time, we live in a profoundly paradoxical world, full of competing narratives. Instead of a living, breathing, purposeful universe, we appear to inhabit a gigantic intergalactic graveyard, shaped by colliding black holes whose gravitational waves reach us— meaninglessly [to us, though not for quantum physicists]—1.5 billion years after their collision, a graveyard ruled by chance, randomness and the spontaneous, mechanical events that have apparently given rise to our own planetary emergence. In the process of our development, we seem to have lost touch with our broader animality, for at one point we wanted to be angels, but more recently we have forsaken both angels and other animals. Despite deep ecology, enticing tales of Gaia and all the paraphernalia of our legal and police systems that *do* hold people accountable, we seem to be caught in the maws of necessity and indeterminacy. We can prove the mathematical formulae that govern black holes but we can never be sure that our equations actually represent anything at all.

The aim of this work is not to tell scientists or philosophers how to do science or philosophy, but to trace certain connections that have been virtually lost between the ancient and modern worlds and to build a bridge between two forms of practice and thought that can sometimes seem light-years apart: contemporary science, specifically,

---

[1] Naess, Arne (1973) 'The Shallow and the Deep, Long-Range Ecology Movement: A Summary' in *Inquiry: An Interdisciplinary Journal of Philosophy and the Social Sciences*, 16: 95–100; and for overview and criticism, Nelson (2008) 206-211.

ecology and environmental philosophy, and Neoplatonism, specifically the thought of Plotinus (204/5-270 CE), Porphyry (c. 232-305 CE), Iamblichus (c. 240-326 CE), Proclus (412-85 CE) and others.[2]

Why are these connections important? They are important for two major reasons: First, because they remain hidden parts of our history. "Neoplatonism" has had a profound effect, largely unknown, upon the development of human civilization: it preserves the closest links between East and West; it helped to produce a troubled but genuine *convivencia* among Christians, Jews and Muslims from the 7th well into the 14th Centuries;[3] and it also led to the development of Western Science through the work of Robert Grosseteste, Nicholas of Cusa, Giordano Bruno, Copernicus, Kepler and Newton, among others.[4] But, second, these connections are important because they provide what some modern science lacks, namely, ways of looking at the world or worlds not as shards of blind necessity, but rather as diverse living ecosystems with their own layers of possibility that have to be recognized for their own sakes and not just from one standard or system of rationality. I shall argue here that Neoplatonism (and the Platonic-Pythagorean tradition of which it is a marker)[5] has much in common with deep ecology and that we need to rediscover some of its fundamental thinking on the interconnected implications of matter, bodies, souls, minds and the Good. After presenting two initial difficulties about such a project, I shall examine these issues under three principal headings: the Soul and Nature, then Intellect, and, finally, the Good or the One, although these three realities or 'hypostases,' as Porphyry calls them in his title for *Ennead* V I [10],

---

[2] Among recent works on this subject related to antiquity, see the many works of S. Clark (especially (2011) pp 35–60); Dillon and Clark (2013); Robinson and Westra (2002); Sorabji (1993); among other recent works are the following: Cassin & Labarrière (2000); Heath (2005); Steiner (2005); Gilhus (2006), especially the chapter on soul and reason; Newmyer (2006); Nussbaum (2006); Osborne (2007); and Beauchamp & Frey (2011); cf. also *Porphyry: On Abstinence from Killing Animals*, Clark (2000).

[3] On this see Adamson (2015); (2016); Marenbon (2007) especially 85-113, 172-2-4.

[4] I know of no comprehensive treatment of this integral connection between Neoplatonism and the birth of empirical science. For the general topic with a different focus see Ben-Chaim (2004).

[5] I take this as a marker of the entire legacy of the ancient world, Stoicism, the hermetic writings and medicine included (especially the works of Galen).

cannot be artificially separated. Because of time constraints, I shall concentrate principally on Plotinus and more on Soul, Nature and Intellect than on the Good, despite the fact that the Good is, of course, crucial.

Two initial problems are pressing at the outset: First, Neoplatonism privileges a spiritual universe, while modern thinking emphasizes the causal efficacy of science, utility, wealth, etc., in order to make for ourselves a flourishing world from what appears to be a graveyard of chance, mechanistic forces. They therefore inhabit totally different universes of discourse. Second, Neoplatonism is a top-down hierarchical way of thinking. How then can it take account of other life forms for their own sakes, of observation of the world of nature as primary, and of the richness, diversity and newness of evolutionary forms? If we adopt the principles of deep ecology as sketched out by Arne Naess and George Sessions,[6] we have to be able to learn from nature, to recognize the inherent value of non-human life, and to restrict our own proliferation in order to preserve the richness of other life forms.

2. The Soul-Dimension. Soul/body. World Soul.

In starting to give an answer, let me take the Soul-dimension first, which looks so different from our materialist, money-driven and scientific fact-laden universe. Did the ancients live in a universe anything like ours? Yes, they did. [Heraclitus famously proclaimed: "the most fair universe is like a rubbish-heap of things thrown anyhow" (Theophrastus, Metaphysics, 7a14-15, Ross-Fobes)] Plotinus, for instance, can call matter an "adorned corpse"[7] and

---

[6] I refer to the eight-point platform of deep ecology: Naess (1986) 14. See Appendix.

[7] *Ennead* II 4 [12] 5, 15-19: "The divine matter when it receives that which defines it has a defined and intelligent life, but the matter of this world becomes something defined, but not alive or thinking, a decorated corpse (νεκρὸν κεκοσμημένον). Shape here is only an image (εἴδωλον); so that which underlies it is also only an image." I use Armstrong's translation for convenience throughout, but occasionally adapted. Each *Ennead* is referred to by Roman numerals, followed by the number of the treatise, then in square brackets the chronological number of the treatise according to Porphyry's account in the Life of Plotinus, then, after the square brackets, the chapter of the treatise, and, finally, separated by a comma, the line number or numbers.

sensible substance "not true substance"[8]. Proclus can identify seven different kinds of non-being in a short paragraph of his *Parmenides Commentary*;[9] there is, then, a sophisticated diagnosis of "graveyards" in bygone ages. [Theophrastus puts the problem well in a discussion of problems with teleology in some fragments from his *Metaphysics* (Ross and Fobes): On the one hand, "what is animate is a small part of the universe, and what is inanimate is infinite; and of animate things themselves there is only a minute part whose existence is actually better than its non-existence would be." On the other hand, "to say in general the good is something rare and found only in few things, while the evil is a great multitude... is the act of a most ignorant person" (11a16-22, R-F)] But this is not their only view, for body is also a logos, that is, an intelligible entity in principle, and, in fact, although this rarely gets attention, body for Plotinus stretches from anything that can be related to logos right into full-blown Intelligible Being itself.[10] So it becomes difficult to determine where soul stops and body begins (and vice versa)—all the more so since as a single *energeia*, soul-body is a single activity from different perspectives. We are, in fact, not dealing here with a soul-body "relation" as such since a relation presupposes two distinct things and

---

[8] VI 3 [44] 8, 30-37: "And there is no need to object if we make sensible substance out of non-substances; for even the whole is not true substance but imitates the true substance, which has its being without the others which attend on it, and the others come into being from it, because it truly is; but here what underlies is sterile and inadequate to be being, because the others do not come from it, but it is a shadow, and upon what is itself a shadow, a picture and a seeming" (σκιὰ δὲ καὶ ἐπὶ σκιᾷ αὐτῇ οὔσῃ ζωγραφία καὶ τὸ φαίνεσθαι).

[9] Morrow and Dillon (1987) 349-350 (999-1000): that which is not can mean 1) that which is absolutely non-existent; 2) the negation of something; 3) matter; 4) all that is material; 5) the whole world of sense as phenomenal; 6) the element of non-existence in souls; 6) and in the intelligibles, the primary otherness in things; 7) non-Being prior to Being, cause of all beings.

[10] *Ennead* VI 2 [43] 21, 30-34, 49-53: "For in general everywhere, whatever one might apprehend by reasoning as being in nature one will find existing without reasoning in Intellect ... for it was not possible or lawful for anything to be left out; for the intelligible All is complete, or it would not be the All—and since life is running over it, or rather everywhere accompanying it, all things necessarily become living beings, and there are bodies there also since there is matter and quality" (οὐ γὰρ ἦν οὐδὲ θεμιτὸν ἦν παραλελεῖφθαι οὐδέν· τέλειον γὰρ ἐκεῖ τὸ πᾶν ἢ οὐκ ἂν ἦν πᾶν—καὶ ζωῆς ἐπιθεούσης, μᾶλλον δὲ συνούσης πανταχοῦ, πάντα ἐξ ἀνάγκης ζῷα ἐγίνετο, καὶ ἦν καὶ σώματα ὕλης καὶ ποιότητος ὄντων).

soul and body are not two things that can be added together.[11] These obvious, if puzzling features of Neoplatonism need more emphasis, I suggest.

More broadly, Plotinus sees bodily organization and matter as merely the tip of a much vaster picture: soul is not in body so much as body is *in* soul (as Plato observes, in *Timaeus* 36d-37c).[12] Bodies, nature and the entire physical world are rooted in three much larger oceans or originative principles: All Soul, All Intellect and the ultimate principle that Plotinus calls simply, the One or the Good (see for the Good VI 7 [38] 42, 21-24; and for both see the title of VI 9 [9]: *On the Good or the One*).

Everything in the physical world, composed of form and matter, is a reflection or outflow of the content of soul, organized by soul's generative power, ranging from more complex organisms such as the heavenly bodies—or "the gods who are in heaven", as Plotinus calls

---

[11] A 'relational' account in an aggregative sense is certainly the wrong way to frame the question since it implies a connection from one thing to another and the immaterial is not a thing. Indeed too, there can be no "between" - since there is nothing in between (compare Aristotle *Physics* 202b7-8 and Plotinus I 1[53] 2, 9-14; V 9 [5] 9, 8-15). Moreover, if the physical is ultimately the outward appearance or the extension of the spiritual into different material modalities, there is equally no connection between two things, for in looking only at a physical object we are, in fact, seeing the spiritual from a single perspective, not everything that it actually is. Mind/soul-body is at root a single activity seen from two different perspectives; what is an *energeia* from one viewpoint is a *kinesis* from another; this allows psychic activity from one perspective, to be physical motion from another; the movement and the activity may be distinguished ontologically, just as teacher and pupil are different beings, and guitar player, melody and string obviously distinct, but in operation a single activity; as in Aristotle's *Physics*, Book 3, chapter 3, teaching and learning constitute a single activity in two different subjects: "teaching is the activity of the teacher, but in some patient and it is not cut off, but of this in this" (202b6-8). On this and double act theory, see Rutten (1956) 100-106; Lloyd (1990) 98-106; Emilsson (2007) 22-68.

[12] *Timaeus* 36e-37a: "And when the construction of the Soul had all been completed to the satisfaction of its constructor, then He fabricated within it (ἐντὸς αὐτῆς) all the corporeal, and uniting them center to center He made them fit together. And the Soul, being woven throughout the Heaven every way from the center to the extremity, and enveloping it in a circle from without (πάντη διαπλακεῖσα κύκλῳ τε αὐτὸν ἔξωθεν περικαλύψασα), and herself revolving within herself, began a divine beginning of unceasing and intelligent life lasting throughout all time."

them,[13] and other living creatures, including all animals and plants, all the way down to rocks and the elements that we think are inanimate, but are in fact still saturated by the power of soul from different perspectives: first, All Soul from the top down includes every soul-perspective; second, the World Soul is responsible for the world's physical structure (that includes our human organic structures); third, the Souls of the stars, planets, the earth, and so on; of course, as soon as one mentions demons and star-souls in modern company, even polite interest seems no longer possible, but for Plotinus, Porphyry, Iamblichus and Proclus, nothing is entirely without soul or life, even apparently non-living things. As Plotinus argues, we don't normally characterize anything that doesn't perceptibly move itself as living, but in fact "each thing of this sort has a hidden life" (IV 4 [27], 36, 17-19). He famously describes the World Soul in different ways: As giver of the gift, the World Soul makes a "preliminary outline" whose illuminating traces the creative or productive soul articulates, and each soul becomes a trace by shaping itself 'as the dancer in relation to the dramatic part given to him' (VI 7 [38] 7).[14] Here we find something deeply relevant to any ecological concern: a mutual developmental responsibility in which different agents collaborate to produce: a) a genetic outline or blueprint; b) a specific differentiation; and c) an individual schematization. The whole process is genetically collaborative and non-rational, that is, nobody plans or thinks about

---

[13] V 8 [31] 3, 27-28; 20-21: "For all the gods are majestic and beautiful and their beauty is overwhelming: but what is it which makes them like this? It is Intellect, and it is because Intellect is more intensely active in them, so as to be visible (ἢ νοῦς, καὶ ὅτι μᾶλλον νοῦς ἐνεργῶν ἐν αὐτοῖς, ὥστε ὁρᾶσθαι)."

[14] VI 7 [38] 7, 8-16: "For what is there to prevent the power of the Soul of the All from drawing a preliminary outline, since it is the universal forming principle, even before the soul-powers come from it, and this preliminary outline being like illuminations running on before into matter, and the soul which carries out the work following traces of this kind and making by articulating the traces part by part, and each individual soul becoming this to which it came by figuring itself, as the dancer does to the dramatic part given him?" (τί γὰρ κωλύει τὴν μὲν δύναμιν τῆς τοῦ 10παντὸς ψυχῆς προϋπογράφειν, ἄτε λόγον πάντα οὖσαν, πρὶν καὶ παρ' αὐτῆς ἥκειν τὰς ψυχικὰς δυνάμεις, καὶ τὴν προϋπογραφὴν οἶον προδρόμους ἐλλάμψεις εἰς τὴν ὕλην εἶναι, ἤδη δὲ τοῖς τοιούτοις ἴχνεσιν ἐπακολουθοῦσαν τὴν ἐξεργαζομένην ψυχὴν κατὰ μέρη 15τὰ ἴχνη διαρθροῦσαν ποιῆσαι καὶ γενέσθαι ἑκάστην τοῦτο, ᾧ προσῆλθε σχηματίσασα ἑαυτήν, ὥσπερ τὸν ἐν ὀρχήσει πρὸς τὸ δοθὲν αὐτῷ δρᾶμα;)

it,[15] yet it manifests order, inherent meaningfulness, and the possibility of freedom since the dancer has the free artistic expression of her dance. Necessity and freedom spring together out of the psychic genetic cooperation between All Soul, World Soul, Nature, and individual souls. Two other images of the World Soul require mention. Plotinus calls the World Soul a "sister soul": she remains rooted in the whole Soul, whereas partial souls "have received their allotted parts" (IV 3 [27] 6, 10-15).[16] This may seem an unduly anthropomorphic image, like Francis and Clare's brother sun, sister moon, but Plotinus' purpose is not to anthropomorphize, but to indicate kinship and creative engagement. Finally, in another powerful image, this creative relationship is seen from the viewpoint of the world's body:

---

[15] Compare the arguments of V 8 [31] 5-7 and especially VI 7, 1-2; 1, 28-39: "Therefore neither forethought for a living thing nor forethought for this universe in general derived from a plan (οὔτ᾽ οὖν ζῴου πρόνοια οὔθ᾽ ὅλως τοῦδε τοῦ παντὸς ἐκ λογισμοῦ ἐγένετο); since there is no planning there at all, but it is called planning to show that all things there are as they would be as a result of planning at a later stage, and foresight (προόρασις) because it is as a wise man would foresee it. For in things which did not come to be before planning, planning is useful because of the lack of the power before planning, and foresight, because the one who foresees did not have the power by which there would be no need of foresight. For foresight is in order that there should not be this but that, and there is in it a kind of fear of what is not just so. But where there is only this, there is not foresight. And planning is "this instead of that". But when there is only one of them, why should there be a plan?"

[16] IV 3 [27] 6, 6-15: "this however requires a special discussion to itself—how then and why the Soul of the All has made the universe, but the particular souls direct [each] a part of it. There is of course nothing remarkable in some of those who have the same knowledge being in control of more, and some of less. But one could ask the reason why. But there is, one might answer, a difference between souls, and all the more in that *the Soul of the All has not separated itself from soul as a whole but remained there and put on the body, but the individual souls, since body exists already, received their allotted parts when their sister soul, as we may say, was already ruling, as if it had already prepared their dwellings for them* (καθὸ ἡ μὲν οὐκ ἀπέστη τῆς ὅλης, ἀλλ᾽ ἔσχεν ἐκεῖ οὖσα περὶ αὐτὴν τὸ σῶμα, αἱ δὲ ἤδη ὄντος οἷον ἀδελφῆς ψυχῆς ἀρχούσης μοίρας διέλαχον, οἷον προπαρασκευασάσης ταύτης αὐταῖς οἰκήσεις). There is a difference too, in that the soul of the All looks towards Intellect as a whole, but the individual souls rather to their own partial intellects. But perhaps these too would have been able to make [a world], but as the soul of the All had done so already they were unable to do so as well, since it had begun first." See now translation, notes and commentary by Dillon and Blumenthal (2015).

The universe lies in soul which bears it up, and nothing is without a share of soul. It is as if a net immersed in the waters was alive, but unable to make its own that in which it is. The sea is already spread out and the net spreads with it, as far as it can; for no one of its parts can be anywhere else than where it lies. And soul's nature is so great, just because it has no size, as to contain the whole of body in one and the same grasp; wherever body extends, there soul is (IV 3 [27] 9).[17]

3. Nature and Wisdom

The specific case of Nature is more difficult since Plotinus says different things at different times.[18] IV 4 [28] 13 represents Nature as

---

[17] I cite the larger passage from IV 3 [27] 9, 29-44: "There came into being something like a beautiful and richly various house which was not cut off from its builder, but he did not give it a share in himself either; he considered it all, everywhere, worth a care which conduces to its very being and excellence (as far as it can participate in being) but does him no harm in his presiding over it, for he rules it while abiding above. It is in this sort of way that it is ensouled; it has a soul which does not belong to it, but is present to it; it is mastered, not the master, possessed, not possessor. The universe lies in soul which bears it up, and nothing is without a share of soul. It is as if a net immersed in the waters was alive, but unable to make its own that in which it is. The sea is already spread out and the net spreads with it, as far as it can; for no one of its parts can be anywhere else than where it lies. And soul's nature is so great, just because it has no size, as to contain the whole of body in one and the same grasp; wherever body extends, there soul is (γενόμενος δὴ οἷον οἶκός τις καλὸς καὶ ποικίλος οὐκ ἀπετμήθη τοῦ πεποιηκότος, οὐδ' αὖ ἐκοίνωσεν αὐτὸν αὐτῇ, ἀλλὰ πανταχοῦ πᾶς ἄξιος ἐπιμελείας νομισθεὶς ὠφελίμου μὲν ἑαυτῷ τῷ εἶναι καὶ τῷ καλῷ, ὅσον δὴ τοῦ εἶναι δυνατὸν ἦν αὐτῷ μεταλαμβάνειν, ἀβλαβοῦς δὲ τῷ ἐφεστηκότι· ἄνω γὰρ μένων ἐπιστατεῖ· ἔμψυχος τῷ τοιούτῳ τρόπῳ, ἔχων ψυχὴν οὐχ αὑτοῦ, ἀλλ' αὑτῷ, κρατούμενος οὐ κρατῶν, καὶ ἐχόμενος ἀλλ' οὐκ ἔχων. κεῖται γὰρ ἐν τῇ ψυχῇ ἀνεχούσῃ αὐτὸν καὶ οὐδὲν ἄμοιρόν ἐστιν αὐτῆς, ὡς ἂν ἐν ὕδασι δίκτυον τεγγόμενον ζῴη, οὐ δυνάμενον δὲ αὐτοῦ ποιεῖσθαι ἐν ᾧ ἐστιν· ἀλλὰ τὸ μὲν δίκτυον ἐκτεινομένης ἤδη τῆς θαλάσσης συνεκτέταται, ὅσον αὐτὸ δύναται· οὐ γὰρ δύναται ἀλλαχόθι ἕκαστον τῶν μορίων ἢ ὅπου κεῖται εἶναι. ἡ δὲ τοσαύτη ἐστὶ τὴν φύσιν, ὅτι μὴ τοσήδε, ὥστε πᾶν τὸ σῶμα καταλαμβάνειν τῷ αὐτῷ, καὶ ὅπου ἂν ἐκταθῇ ἐκεῖνο, ἐκεῖ ἐστι)."

[18] Pierre Hadot (2004) has traced the rich and varied history of the idea of nature from antiquity up to the contemporary world. Hadot starts from Heraclitus' cryptic fragment "Nature loves to hide" (which Hadot thinks is mistranslated by later thinkers, like Philo, and means instead something like "what causes things to appear tends to make them disappear", or "form (or appearance) tends to disappear").

below reason, imagination and understanding: it is "an image of practical intelligence … the last and lowest part of soul … it does not know but only makes; for since it gives what it has without willed purpose, it has its gift to the corporeal and the material as a making … as a heated body gives its own form to what is next in contact with it" (13, 3-11).[19] By contrast, in III 8 [30], Nature possesses a

---

Thus begins the tradition of a veiled Nature and her secrets, depicted as Artemis of Ephesus and later identified with the Egyptian goddess Isis and Roman Diana, an image that reappears in the veiled Isis of late 18th Century and early 19th Century thought (233ff.). We can adopt several attitudes to Nature so depicted. We can think her secrets are impenetrable and so the study of nature will be useless. Or if we decide to unveil Nature, we can, according to Hadot's historical account, take either a Promethean or an Orphic attitude, that will often in practice spill over into each other. The Promethean approach through magic, technology or mechanics forces Nature to reveal her secrets or, at least, commands nature by obeying her laws. Among the proponents of this approach are Hippocrates, Philo, Roger Bacon, Francis Bacon, Descartes and Kant (101ff.). The Orphic approach, by contrast, tries to understand Nature by contemplative insight and aesthetic perception. The study of nature is a spiritual exercise that enlarges the soul. Among the proponents of this approach, Hadot identifies Plato's *Timaeus*, Aristotle, Cicero, Seneca, Philo-again, the German mystic, Jacob Boehme, many of the German Romantics-Schiller, Novalis, Baader, and some great modern painters such as Klee, Van Gogh and Cezanne (155ff.). What happens, according to Hadot's analysis, is that at the end of the 19th Century and in the 20th Century the unveiling of nature as a phenomenon in its own right loses its meaning and the secret of nature becomes instead the mystery of being. In my view, the illusory quality of veiling or unveiling is hinted at in the birth of the philosophy of being, when the young man – in the introduction to Parmenides' poem – on his journey to "the goddess" is borne by "very intelligent horses" and is directed by maidens, daughters of the Sun, who "having left the Palace of Night, hastened their driving towards the light, *having pushed back their veils* from their heads with their hands" (DK B1 1). The daughters of the Sun are veiled in the Palace of Night, but not in the "well-rounded truth" (fr.1) of Parmenides' whole reality or Being. In other words, I think 'nature' and 'being' go together, which is to say that they cannot be separated historically or scientifically. And the best example of this in the Western tradition is the Neoplatonic approach to nature that draws inextricably with it not only soul but the mystery of being and non-being. The Neoplatonist viewpoint, on Hadot's terms, is predominantly "Orphic", that is, it does not seek to manipulate or tame nature, but to *see and act with* her.

[19] IV 4 [28] 13, 2-11: "For nature is an image of practical wisdom, and since it is the last and lowest part of soul has the last ray of the rational forming principle which shines in it, just as in a thick piece of wax a seal-stamp penetrates right through to the surface on the other side, and is clear on the upper side, but a faint trace on the lower. *For this reason it does not know, but only makes* (ὅθεν οὐδὲ οἶδε, μόνον δὲ ποιεῖ); for since it gives what it has spontaneously (ἀπροαιρέτως) to what comes after it, it

contemplation that is a reflexive self-presence, a sort of trance-like contemplation, dimmer than the "clearer" contemplation of the higher soul, but a contemplation that includes everything, together with "understanding" and "intimate perception"[20] just as the World

---

has its giving to the corporeal and material as a making, just as a heated body gives its own form to that which is next in contact to it and makes it hot in a lesser degree. For this reason nature does not have an imaging faculty either (φαντασίαν); but intellect is higher than the power of imaging: the imaging faculty is between the impression of nature and intellect. Nature has no grasp or consciousness of anything (ἡ μέν γε οὐθενὸς ἀντίληψιν οὐδὲ σύνεσιν ἔχει...)."

[20] For the famous speech of Nature and Plotinus' interpretation see III 8 [31] 4, 1-29: "And if anyone were to ask nature why it makes, if it cared to hear and answer the questioner it would say: "You ought not to ask, but to understand in silence, you, too, just as I am silent and not in the habit of talking. Understand what, then? That what comes into being is what I see in my silence, an object of contemplation which comes to be naturally, and that I, originating from this sort of contemplation have a contemplative nature (Ἐχρῆν μὲν μὴ ἐρωτᾶν, ἀλλὰ συνιέναι καὶ αὐτὸν σιωπῇ, ὥσπερ ἐγὼ σιωπῶ καὶ οὐκ εἴθισμαι λέγειν. Τί οὖν συνιέναι; Ὅτι τὸ γενόμενόν ἐστι θέαμα ἐμόν, σιωπώσης, καὶ φύσει γενόμενον θεώρημα, καί μοι γενομένη ἐκ θεωρίας τῆς ὡδὶ τὴν φύσιν ἔχειν φιλοθεάμονα ὑπάρχειν). And my act of contemplation makes what it contemplates, as the geometers draw their figures while they contemplate. But I do not draw, but as I contemplate, the lines which bound bodies come to be as if they fell from my contemplation (ὥσπερ ἐκπίπτουσαι). What happens to me is what happens to my mother and the beings that generated me, for they, too, derive from contemplation, and it is no action of theirs which brings about my birth; they are greater rational principles, and as they contemplate themselves I come to be. What does this mean? That what is called nature is a soul, the offspring of a prior soul with a stronger life; that it quietly holds contemplation in itself, not directed upwards or even downwards, but at rest in what it is, in its own repose and a kind of self-perception, and in this consciousness and self-perception it sees what comes after it (ἡσυχῇ ἐν ἑαυτῇ θεωρίαν ἔχουσα οὐ πρὸς τὸ ἄνω οὐδ' αὖ ἔτι πρὸς τὸ κάτω, στᾶσα δὲ ἐν ᾧ ἔστιν, ἐν τῇ αὐτῆς στάσει καὶ οἷον συναισθήσει, τῇ συνέσει ταύτῃ καὶ συναισθήσει τὸ μετ' αὐτὴν εἶδεν ὡς οἷόν τε αὐτῇ), as far as it can, and seeks other things no longer, having accomplished a vision of splendour and delight. If anyone wants to attribute to it understanding or perception, it will not be the understanding or perception we speak of in other beings; it will be like comparing the consciousness of someone fast asleep to the consciousness of someone awake (Καὶ εἴτε τις βούλεται σύνεσίν τινα ἢ αἴσθησιν αὐτῇ διδόναι, οὐχ οἵαν λέγομεν ἐπὶ τῶν ἄλλων τὴν αἴσθησιν ἢ τὴν σύνεσιν, ἀλλ' οἷον εἴ τις τὴν καθύπνου τῇ ἐγρηγορότος προσεικάσειε). Nature is at rest in contemplation of the vision of itself, a vision which comes to it from its abiding in and with itself and being itself a vision; and its contemplation is silent but somewhat blurred. For there is another, clearer for sight, and nature is the image of another contemplation."

Soul is said perhaps to have such awareness in III 4 [15] 4, 10-11[21] and everything in the earth's body in IV 4 [28] 45, 8.[22] Perhaps, the difference may lie between a more material and a more formal conception of nature (such as we find in Aristotle[23]), but whatever the case, a few chapters later in IV 4 [28] 13, in a discussion of the origin of bodily desires, Plotinus makes it clear that Nature is an intelligent agent that feels in and through material things: she is "like a mother, trying to make out the wishes of the sufferer, and trying to set it right and bring it back to her, and searching for the remedy, she attaches herself by her search to the desire of the sufferer ..." (IV 4 [28] 20, 28-36).[24] In short, nature appears to be a dynamic principle on many different levels that works in and with living creatures—and even in rocks that grow if attached to the earth, according to Plotinus.[25] For our purposes here, nature is not an object or something abstract, but an intelligent form different from Intellect and from human rationalities, a form that requires not only our active engagement but

---

[21] III 4 [15] 4, 10-11: συναίσθησιν.

[22] If this is what Plotinus means here: καὶ οἷον συναίσθησις παντὸς πρὸς πᾶν.

[23] See *Physics* Book 2, 1-2.

[24] IV 4 [28] 20, 28-36: "nature is like a mother, trying to make out the wishes of the sufferer, and attempting to set it right and bring it back to herself; and, searching for the remedy, she attaches herself by her search to the desire of the sufferer, and the consummation of the desire passes from the body to nature (ζήτησιν τοῦ ἀκεσομένου ποιουμένην συνάψασθαι τῇ ζητήσει τῇ τοῦ πεπονθότος ἐπιθυμίᾳ καὶ τὴν περάτωσιν ἀπ᾽ ἐκείνου πρὸς αὐτὴν ἥκειν). So one might say, perhaps, that the desiring comes from the body itself—one might call it preliminary desiring and eagerness—but that nature desires from and through something else...(ὥστε τὸ μὲν ἐπιθυμεῖν ἐξ αὐτοῦ—εἴποι ἄν τις προεπιθυμίαν ἴσως καὶ προθυμίαν—τὴν δὲ ἐξ ἄλλου καὶ δι᾽ ἄλλου ἐπιθυμεῖν)."

[25] Cf. VI 7 [38] 11, 24-32: "Does [the forming principle] then so live in the earth here? Now, if we were to take the most earthly things generated and shaped in it, we should find here below too the nature of earth. The growth, then, and shaping of stones and the inner patterning of mountains as they grow one must most certainly suppose take place because an ensouled forming principle is working within them and giving them form; and this is the active form of the earth, like what is called the growth-nature in trees, and what we call earth corresponds to the wood of the tree, and when the stone is cut out it is in the same state as if something is chopped from a tree, but if this does not happen to it and it is still joined on it is like what has not been chopped off from a living plant."

a kindred contemplation (in III 8 [30])[26] in order to recognize living insight operative in the cosmos and also in us—not simply as physical organisms, but as agents for better or worse. I shall return to this below, but for the present we should note that Nature and the World Soul, whatever Plotinus may say in different passages, are intimately connected to primary Intelligible Wisdom from which the wisdom that pervades nature immediately springs. Plotinus calls this "physical wisdom". The artist has access to such wisdom, but this wisdom is broader and generative throughout nature "no longer composed of theorems, but one whole something ...unfolded into many from one" (V 8 [31] 4, 1-5, 10). I have argued elsewhere that it is reasonable to see this perspective as directed against the Gnostic view of a kind of fallen or bastardized physical "wisdom" that generates sicknesses, monstrosities, etc. (Notice to V 8 in the forthcoming new Budé volume on the Grossschrift, edited by J.M. Narbonne). Whatever the case, the idea that nature needs to be protected from forces and ideologies that would, without real engagement, dominate, cramp or destroy her vitality is an important part of Plotinus' aim and noteworthy for our purposes.

5. Deep Ecology and Neoplatonism

How can this strange other-worldly view fit the needs of deep ecology that is focused on the here-and-now, the networks of different eco-systems, and the irreducible values of things other than human beings? There are many compelling reasons for seeing a profound connection between the needs of ecology and Neoplatonism. First, our modern emphasis on individuality and autonomous subjectivity doesn't even fit some current scientific models. We are permeated by shards of our dead (and living) brothers and sisters; we are unconscious hosts of all sorts of organisms; and we are made of stardust, which sounds clichéd, but is literally true. By contrast, Neoplatonism cannot yet even use the later Latinate term "individual"—namely, something that is "uncuttable"; it talks instead of particulars or "eaches",[27] but argues that everything is so deeply porous or interconnected that what any thing really is can only be

---

[26] See especially III 8 [30] 6, 19-21: "The logos must not be from outside but must be united with the soul of the learner until it finds it as its own (δεῖ μὴ ἔξωθεν τὸν λόγον εἶναι, ἀλλ' ἑνωθῆναι τῇ ψυχῇ τοῦ μανθάνοντος, ἕως ἂν οἰκεῖον εὕρῃ)."

[27] That is, *hekasta, ta kath hekasta, ta en merei* etc.

seen in its living connection to the whole. We are, like all organisms, the meeting place of other dimensions of being that make us who we are, on the one hand, and make what we take ourselves to be, on the other hand, that is, a "compound" material being, a businessman, scientist etc., sometimes pretty trivial in the bigger scheme of things. Thus, one of the great values of Neoplatonism is that by virtue of the Soul-dimension it recognizes the inherent values and interconnectedness of all things. The human being is not the centre of the cosmos; and yet at the same time, there is a special urgency in being human that drives us to become aware of the whole animate universe and to care for everything, that is, everything that we human beings are too—as we will see below with Intellect.

Second, deep ecology really wants to re-sacralize the world in a post-sacred epoch. But one cannot make the world sacred by modern fiat. Roger Scruton has recently argued that a sense of the sacred is essential to human life; he calls his book "The Soul of the World" and its final sentence states, out of the blue, that "[t]he life of prayer … prepares us for a death that … unites us with the soul of the world" (2014, 198); but he never mentions the soul throughout the book except to call it mythical, and to stress instead that our interpersonal relations of self-consciousness make the world sacred: "without transcendent bonds", he insists, we have a "completely different world, and one in which we humans are not truly at home" (2014, 94-55).[28] He is right to see our interpersonal relations and our experience of art, music, and divinity as central to what is sacred, but he is surely wrong to eviscerate the "soul" of any content beyond its empty occurrence in his title and final sentence, for whatever we call it—soul, creation, expansion or gravitational waves—*something* animates things so that on a trivial level, soul-language can easily be translated into current scientific terms (DNA—unmoved movers, etc.); more importantly, however, the soul-language of Neoplatonism extends naturally in two different directions: it includes the joyful intimacy of interpersonal relations and points to the greater intimacy of Intellect: "For here below … we can know many things by the look in people's eyes when they are silent; but there all their body is clear and pure and each is like an eye, and nothing is hidden or feigned, but before one speaks to another that other has seen and understood" (IV 3 [27]18,

---

[28] For a very different approach see Fideler (2014) on which below.

19-22).[29] But it is inclusive of everything, human beings, other animals, plants and so-called inanimate things—with the result that, while allowing for differences in complexity between human beings and other animals, it does not perpetuate the Cartesian divide between introspective self-consciousness and other forms of consciousness or apparently unconscious being, but rather sees them as different life-forms along a continuum of being, as does Plotinus, or as manifesting *logos* in their own ways that makes them valuable "for themselves" and not just "for us", as does Porphyry.[30]

So Plotinus writes about the outpouring of life-forms and their diversity even in the intelligible:

> Now, there in the intelligible, intelligence is different in man and the other living beings, and reasoning is also different; for there are present somehow also in the other living beings many works of deliberate thought. But one must consider that the many lives, which are like movements, and the many thoughts should not have been the same, but different ... in brilliance and clarity ... For just as any particular life does not cease to be life, so neither does an intellect of a particular kind cease to be intellect ... since the intellect appropriate to any particular living being does not on the other hand cease to be the intellect of all, of man also, for instance, granted that each part, whichever one you take, is actually all things, but perhaps in different ways" (VI 7 [38] 9, 1-44).[31]

---

[29] A remarkable passage, IV 3 [27] 18, 19-22: "Nor do I think that we should suppose that they use speech in the intelligible world, and altogether, even if they have bodies in heaven, there would be none of that talk there which they engage in here because of needs or over doubtful and disputed points; but as they do everything they do in order and according to nature they would not give orders or advice and would know by intuition what passes from one to another (γινώσκοιεν δ' ἂν καὶ τὰ παρ' ἀλλήλων ἐν συνέσει). For here below, too, we can know many things by the look in people's eyes when they are silent; but there all their body is clear and pure and each is like an eye, and nothing is hidden or feigned, but before one speaks to another that other has seen and understood (ἐπεὶ καὶ ἐνταῦθα πολλὰ σιωπώντων γινώσκομεν δι' ὀμμάτων· ἐκεῖ δὲ καθαρὸν πᾶν τὸ σῶμα καὶ οἷον ὀφθαλμὸς ἕκαστος καὶ οὐδὲν δὲ κρυπτὸν οὐδὲ πεπλασμένον, ἀλλὰ πρὶν εἰπεῖν ἄλλῳ ἰδὼν ἐκεῖνος ἔγνω)."

[30] Generally on this see Corrigan (2014) 371-390.

[31] Another remarkable passage on the sheer diversity of forms and their 'genetic' adaptability—VI 7 [38] 9: "Now, there in the intelligible, intelligence is different in man and the other living beings, and reasoning is also different; for there are present somehow also in the other living beings many works of deliberate thought

And Porphyry in the *De Abstinentia* argues not only that justice should be extended to include other animals (contrary to the view of the Stoics) but that we should not frame this from the perspective of our own understanding of rationality: "let us not say that if beasts think (*phronein*) more sluggishly and are worse at reflection (*dianoeisthai*), they do not reflect or think at all, or even have a logos; but let us say that they have weak and turbid logos, like blurred and disturbed vision" (*Abst.* 3.23–24, trans. Clark; cf. *Enn.* VI 7 [38] 7, 29–31).[32] Further-

---

(πολλὰ διανοίας ἔργα). Why then are they not equally rational? And why are men not equally so in comparison to each other? But one must consider that the many lives, which are like movements, and the many thoughts should not have been the same, but different lives and in the same way different thoughts; and the differences are, somehow, in brilliance and clarity (ὡς τὰς πολλὰς ζωὰς οἷον κινήσεις οὔσας καὶ τὰς πολλὰς νοήσεις οὐκ ἐχρῆν τὰς αὐτὰς εἶναι, ἀλλὰ καὶ ζωὰς διαφόρους καὶ νοήσεις ὡσαύτως· τὰς δὲ διαφορὰς πως φωτεινοτέρας καὶ ἐναργεστέρας), firsts and seconds and thirds according to their nearness to the first principles ... For just as any particular life does not cease to be life, so neither does an intellect of a particular kind cease to be intellect: since the intellect appropriate to any particular living being does not on the other hand cease to be the intellect of all, of man also, for instance, granted that each part, whichever one you take, is all things, but perhaps in different ways. For it is actually one thing, but has the power to be all; but we apprehend in each what it actually is; and what it actually is, is the last and lowest, so that the last and lowest of this particular intellect is horse, and being horse is where it stopped in its continual outgoing to a lesser life, but another stops lower down. For as the powers unfold they always leave something behind on the higher level; and as they go out they lose something, and in losing different things different ones find and add on something else because of the need of the living being which appeared as a result of the deficiency; for instance, since there is not yet enough for life's purpose, nails appeared, and having claws and fangs, and the nature of horn; so that where the intellect came down to, at that very point it comes up again by the self-sufficiency of its nature and finds stored in itself the cure for the deficiency (λαμβάνομεν δὲ καθ' ἕκαστον τὸ ἐνεργείᾳ· τὸ δ' ἐνεργείᾳ ἔσχατον, ὥστε τοῦδε τοῦ νοῦ τὸ ἔσχατον ἵππον εἶναι, καὶ ᾗ ἔληξε προϊὼν ἀεὶ εἰς ἐλάττω ζωήν, ἵππον εἶναι, ἄλλον δὲ κατωτέρω λῆξαι. ἐξελιττόμεναι γὰρ αἱ δυνάμεις καταλείπουσιν ἀεὶ εἰς τὸ ἄνω· προΐασι δέ τι ἀφιεῖσαι καὶ ἐν τῷ ἀφεῖναι δὲ ἄλλα ἄλλαι διὰ τὸ ἐνδεὲς τοῦ ζῴου τοῦ φανέντος ἐκ τοῦ ἐλλείποντος ἕτερον ἐξευροῦσαι προσθεῖναι· οἷον ἐπεὶ οὐκ ἔστιν ἔτι τὸ ἱκανὸν εἰς ζωήν, ἀνεφάνη ὄνυξ καὶ τὸ γαμψώνυχον ἢ τὸ καρχαρόδον ἢ κέρατος φύσις· ὥστε, ᾗ κατῆλθεν ὁ νοῦς, ταύτῃ πάλιν αὖ τῷ αὐτάρκει τῆς φύσεως ἀνακύψαι καὶ εὑρεῖν ἐν αὐτῷ τοῦ ἐλλείποντος κειμένην ἴασιν)."

[32] *De Abstinentia* 3. 23-24: οὐκοῦν ὁμοίως μηδὲ τὰ θηρία λέγωμεν, εἰ νωθρότερον φρονεῖ καὶ κάκιον διανοεῖται, μὴ διανοεῖσθαι μηδὲ φρονεῖν ὅλως μηδὲ κεκτῆσθαι λόγον, ἀσθενῆ δὲ κεκτῆσθαι καὶ θολερόν, ὥσπερ ὀφθαλμὸν ἀμβλυώττοντα καὶ τεταραγμένον. Cf. *Enn.* VI 7 [38] 7, 29–31: "And for this reason this man here has sense-perception, because he has a lesser apprehension of lesser things, images of

more, any analogy between human justice and animal justice is more like an innate natural bond of mutual justice between all species that Porphyry argues cannot be simply "for us"; instead, other animals are naturally "like us, not for us":

> If they say that not everything came into being for us, then in addition to the great confusion and unclarity of the distinction, we still do not escape injustice, because we set upon and treat harmfully creatures which were born in accordance with nature like us, not for us. I leave aside the point that if we define what is for us in terms of our need, we should instantly have to concede that we ourselves are born for the most deadly animals, such as crocodiles, whales and snakes (*Abst.* 3.20, trans. G. Clark).[33]

So here in Neoplatonism we already have a sacred world of Soul from within many kindred traditions—pagan, Christian, Jewish, Islamic; and these hybrid traditions helped to give birth, first, to empirical science in the Middle Ages and, then, to a new cosmology and physics in the Renaissance and Modern periods. Why then should we continue the fiction or fashion of some hygienic rupture with the past when the significance of ordinary and extraordinary things was only won for modernity out of an earlier commitment to, and reverence for, Soul and Nature as dynamic forces in and beyond the cosmos?

5. Observation, natural kinds, and the emergence of new forms

Before moving to Intellect, I must make one final point about scientific observation, the diversity of natural kinds, and the emergence of new forms. Platonism, it is often urged, is hostile to modern empiricism.[34] I think that this is profoundly misguided. Let

---

those intelligible realities; so that these sense-perceptions here are dim intellections, but the intellections there are clear sense-perceptions."

[33] Ibid. 3.20, 32-39: εἰ δὲ οὐ πάντα φασὶν ἡμῖν καὶ δι' ἡμᾶς γεγονέναι, πρὸς τῷ σύγχυσιν ἔχειν πολλὴν καὶ ἀσάφειαν τὸν διορισμὸν οὐδὲ ἐκφεύγομεν τὸ ἀδικεῖν, ἐπιτιθέμενοι καὶ χρώμενοι βλαβερῶς τοῖς οὐ δι' ἡμᾶς, ἀλλ' ὥσπερ ἡμεῖς κατὰ φύσιν γεγενημένοις. ἐῶ λέγειν ὅτι τῇ χρείᾳ τὸ πρὸς ἡμᾶς ὁρίζοντες οὐκ ἂν φθάνοιμεν ἑαυτοὺς ἕνεκα τῶν ὀλεθριωτάτων ζῴων, οἷα κροκόδειλοι καὶ φάλαιναι καὶ δράκοντες, γεγονέναι συγχωροῦντες.

[34] See, for instance, the judgment of Sir Hugh Trevor-Roper, for whom the essence of Platonism is its abstract idealism, that is, "its determination to identify the universal spirit which informs matter and, having identified it, to disengage it from

me take one small example from Plato's *Phaedrus* and Plotinus' second work on "difficulties about the soul", IV 4 [28]. In his treatment of true rhetoric, Socrates emphasizes how skill and knowledge must involve experience and observation: in studying the types of soul, the orator "must observe them as they are in real life and actually being done, and be capable of following up with sharp perception" (271d7-e1).[35] This theme of observation culminates in the image of the knowledgeable farmer in the final section of the *Phaedrus* in Plato's critique of the written word that cannot help itself by comparison with the word "written in the soul" that can help and defend itself.[36] The knowledgeable farmer is more like the dialectician. He doesn't seriously sow seeds to force them to sprout eight days later as a kind of party trick, but instead "knowledgeable" means that "he would make use of the skill of farming, sow them in appropriate soil at the appropriate time, and love it if what he sowed came to term in the eighth month" (*Phaedrus* 276b1-8).[37] Two things are striking in this passage: First, in the person of the farmer, skill, observation and good practice go together; she must be able to listen to nature, not force her, in order to help nature help herself. Similarly for dialectic: the

---

the bewildering variety, the inert machinery, the practical compromises in which, in practice, it is trapped and buried". (*Renaissance Essays*, Chicago-London (1985) 24-58).

[35] *Phaedrus* 271d: δεῖ δὴ ταῦτα ἱκανῶς νοήσαντα, μετὰ ταῦτα θεώμενον αὐτὰ ἐν ταῖς πράξεσιν ὄντα τε καὶ πραττόμενα, ὀξέως τῇ αἰσθήσει δύνασθαι ἐπακολουθεῖν.

[36] *Phaedrus* 275e-276a: the written word "when ill-treated or unjustly reviled ... always needs its father to help it; for it has no power to protect or help itself... Now tell me; is there not another kind of speech, or word, which shows itself to be the legitimate brother of this bastard one, both in the manner of its begetting and in its better and more powerful nature?—What is this word and how is it begotten, as you say?—The word which is written with scientific understanding in the soul of the learner, which is able to defend itself and knows to whom it should speak, and before whom to be silent. –You mean the living and breathing word of him who knows, of which the written word may justly be called the image."

[37] *Phaedrus* 276a-b: "Now tell me this. Would the knowledgeable farmer (ὁ νοῦν ἔχων γεωργός), who has seeds which he cares for and which he wishes to bear fruit, plant them with serious purpose in the heat of summer in some garden of Adonis, and delight in seeing them appear in beauty in eight days, or would he do that sort of thing, when he did it at all, only in play and for amusement? Would he not, when he was in earnest, make use of the skill of farming, sow them in appropriate soil at the appropriate time (τῇ γεωργικῇ χρώμενος ἂν τέχνῃ, σπείρας εἰς τὸ προσῆκον), and love it if what he sowed came to term in the eighth month?"

wisdom-lover, using dialectic skill (*techne*), sows seeds pregnant "with *episteme* in an appropriate soul, which are able to help themselves and the one who planted them, and are not without fruit but contain a seed, from which others grow in different dispositional frameworks,[38] capable of rendering it forever immortal, and making the one who has it as happy as a human being can be" (*Phaedrus* 276e4-277a4).[39] Second, dialectic, or higher order thinking and practice, emerges out of nature—from a particular place, time and condition; it assists and expands nature and, like the farmer, helps to create *something new*.

We find a similar bottom up approach in Plotinus. Higher-order thinking does not supplant nature and regular causality. It grows out of it. In his treatment of the world's body in IV 4 [28] 31-36, Plotinus argues from the *Timaeus* that "this All is a single living being encompassing all the living beings in it" (32, 5-6; *Timaeus* 30d3-31a1). Does this mean that everything is prearranged in the Intelligible Living Creature or determined by physical causality? Not at all. Physical causality makes art and freedom possible (31, 1-8).[40] Some arts are designed to a specific purpose; others help nature to help itself; and still others transform us to become free, self-dependent beings, whose choice is not determined by humours or feelings (cf. 31, 17ff.; cf. 35, 23-25[41]): "As for the arts, those which produce a house ... stop in producing such a thing; but the arts of medicine and agriculture ... are ancillary and *help natural things to be in their natural state*; but rhetoric and music and all the arts that train the soul lead to

---

[38] I translate ἐν ἄλλοις ἤθεσι in this way to catch the ambiguities of the analogy.

[39] *Phaedrus* 276e4-277a4: ὅταν τις τῇ διαλεκτικῇ τέχνῃ χρώμενος, λαβὼν ψυχὴν προσήκουσαν, φυτεύῃ τε καὶ σπείρῃ μετ' ἐπιστήμης λόγους, οἳ ἑαυτοῖς τῷ τε φυτεύσαντι βοηθεῖν ἱκανοὶ καὶ οὐχὶ ἄκαρποι ἀλλὰ ἔχοντες σπέρμα, ὅθεν ἄλλοι ἐν ἄλλοις ἤθεσι φυόμενοι τοῦτ' ἀεὶ ἀθάνατον παρέχειν ἱκανοί, καὶ τὸν ἔχοντα εὐδαιμονεῖν ποιοῦντες εἰς ὅσον ἀνθρώπῳ δυνατὸν μάλιστα.

[40] IV 4 [28] 31, 1ff.: "We must, then, take a general view of all actions and experiences which occur in the whole universe, both the ones which are called natural and those which come about by art: we must say that some of the natural ones are effects of the All on its parts and [some] of the parts on the All or of the parts on the parts; and that in those which come about by art the art either ends as it began, in the products of art, or brings in natural powers to help in producing acts and experiences which belong to the works of nature."

[41] IV 4 [28] 35, 23-25: "there are other powers of the living being, which are, apart from deliberate choice, like parts of the living being, since what belongs to deliberate choice in these beings is outside [the universal organism]..."

the better or the worse *by changing us*... in each case, we must engage ourselves with the 'why'."[42] Note the phrase "helping natural things to be natural," a variant derived clearly from the *Phaedrus*. Note also the phrase "by changing us". Plotinus means nothing mysterious but simply qualitative change together with the standards of more or less healthy functioning, based on experience, that accompany it. In other words, there is no question of the so-called naturalistic fallacy, that is, of deriving "ought" from "is"; instead, ethics emerges out of nature and ordinary experience. And if there is a "better" then surely too there is a "best", which Plotinus a little later suggests arises from a consideration of the world's body: "The coming into being and destruction and alteration for worse or better of all these brings to its fullness the unhindered life according to nature of that one living creature" (32, 44-48), which "has communication of experience itself to itself" (35, 9-10); and "the Whole does these things in its parts, but itself seeks the good/Good or rather looks to it. This too is what the right choice that goes above the passions seeks and in this way contributes to the same object" (35, 32-34).[43] In fact, the goodness of the whole cosmos partly resides in its teeming diversity (36, 1: "the All is full of the richest diversity"[44]), which sometimes involves its parts hampering, even making meals of each other,[45] and sometimes

---

[42] IV 4 [28] 31, 16-24: "As for the arts, those which produce a house and the other products of art terminate in these; but the arts of medicine and agriculture and others of this kind are ancillary and help natural things to be in a natural state (ἰατρικὴ δὲ καὶ γεωργία καὶ αἱ τοιαῦται ὑπηρετικαὶ καὶ βοήθειαν εἰς τὰ φύσει εἰσφερόμεναι, ὡς κατὰ φύσιν ἔχειν); but rhetoric and music and all the class of arts which influence the soul must be said to lead men to be better or worse by changing them (ῥητορείαν δὲ καὶ μουσικὴν καὶ πᾶσαν ψυχαγωγίαν ἢ πρὸς τὸ βέλτιον ἢ πρὸς τὸ χεῖρον ἄγειν ἀλλοιούσας); in these we must enquire how many they are and what is the power they have; and in all these which are relevant to our present purpose we must, as far as is possible, concern ourselves with the reason why."

[43] IV 4 [28] 32, 44-48: πάντων δὲ τούτων ἡ γένεσις ἥ τε φθορὰ ἀλλοίωσίς τε πρὸς τὸ χεῖρον ἢ βέλτιον τὴν τοῦ ἑνὸς ζῴου ἐκείνου ἀνεμπόδιστον καὶ κατὰ φύσιν ἔχουσαν ζωὴν ἀποτελεῖ. 35, 9-10: οὕτως ἔχον συμπαθὲς αὐτὸ ἑαυτῷ. 35, 32-34: τὸ δ' ὅλον καὶ ἐν τούτοις μὲν ταῦτα ποιεῖ, αὐτὸ δὲ τὸ ἀγαθὸν ζητεῖ, μᾶλλον δὲ βλέπει. τοῦτο τοίνυν καὶ ἡ ὀρθὴ προαίρεσις ἡ ὑπὲρ τὰ πάθη ζητεῖ καὶ εἰς τὸ αὐτὸ ταύτῃ συμβάλλει.

[44] Ibid. 36, 1-2: Ποικιλώτατον γὰρ τὸ πᾶν καὶ λόγοι πάντες ἐν αὐτῷ καὶ δυνάμεις ἄπειροι καὶ ποικίλαι.

[45] Ibid. 32, 34-39: "but in so far as it is many, when the many encounter each other they often injure each other because they are different; and one injures another to

manifests remarkable interaction from afar—despite the vast distances separating things,[46] which suggests that even for Plotinus, space like time[47] is not simply linear, but a vertical, curved movement of co-feeling or sympathy. This instantaneous interaction does not necessarily mean that particles can travel faster than 186,232 miles per second, but rather that another mode of kinship, another way of being, is operative. And this kinship and sympathy of a sacred universe in this work, IV 4, is exactly what we find in a fragment of Proclus' *On the Hieratic Art*. Proclus writes: "Why do heliotropes move together with the Sun, selenotropes with the Moon...? All things pray according to their own order, intellectually, rationally, naturally or sensibly..."[48] To modern eyes, this looks silly, but unless deep ecology

---

supply its own need, and even makes a meal of another which is at the same time related to and different from it; and each one, naturally striving to do the best for itself, takes to itself that part of the other which is akin to it, and makes away with all that is alien to itself because of its self-love."

[46] Ibid. 32, 13-22: "This one universe is all bound together in shared experience and is like one living creature, and that which is far is really near, just as, in one of the individual living things, a nail or horn or finger or one of the other limbs which is not contiguous: the intermediate part leaves a gap in the experience and is not affected, but that which is not near is affected. For the like parts are not situated next to each other, but are separated by others between, but share their experiences because of their likeness, and it is necessary that something which is done by a part not situated beside it should reach the distant part; and since it is a living thing and all belongs to a unity nothing is so distant in space that it is not close enough to the nature of the one living thing to share experience."

[47] Plotinus defines time in III 7 [45] 11, 43-51 as follows: "So would it be sense to say that time is the life of soul in a movement of passage from one way of life to another (Εἰ οὖν χρόνον τις λέγοι ψυχῆς ἐν κινήσει μεταβατικῇ ἐξ ἄλλου εἰς ἄλλον βίον ζωὴν εἶναι, ἆρ' ἂν δοκοῖ τι λέγειν)? Yes, for if eternity is life at rest, unchanging and identical and already unbounded, and time must exist as an image of eternity (in the same relation as that in which this All stands to the intelligible All), then we must say that there is, instead of the life There, another life having, in a way of speaking, the same name as this power of the soul, and instead of intelligible motion that there is the motion of a part of Soul." Time therefore bears not simply a linear dimension, 'this after this,' but a vertical dimension, between two different forms of life; and if that movement is in any way like the radius of a circle meeting and yet proceeding from the center of a higher circle, then time must be expressive of different tensions along the axis of its dependence upon soul.

[48] I cite the first paragraph of this work in the translation of Brian Copenhaver ("Hermes Trismegistus, Proclus, and a Philosophy of Magic" in *Hermeticism and the Renaissance: Intellectual History and the Occult in Early Modern Europe*, Folger Books, Washington DC, I. Merkel and A. G. Debus eds., 1988, 79-110): "Just as lovers

can find some equivalent attitude, I suggest, it will just be legislation; law is necessary, but only second-best, as Plato put it. And as Aristotle so pungently recognized, "when people are friends they have no need of justice, while when they are just, they need friendship as well" (*EN* 8, 1, 1155a26-27).

Finally, on the question of the emergence of the new, I have space for only two instances out of many in the *Enneads*. *Kainotomia* or cutting edge novelty was frowned upon in the ancient world, and so I mean by "new" something not hitherto seen or suspected. If we think the One and Intellect as up there and everything else down here, then the story may seem over before we even enter upon the scene. But Plotinus doesn't think of it like that. In IV 8 [8] 5 he argues that, if the powers of soul had remained quiet in the immaterial world, they would have been useless and soul wouldn't have known her own powers had they not emerged: "Actuality everywhere reveals

---

systematically leave behind what is fair to sensation and attain the one true source of all that is fair and intelligible, in the same way priests—observing how all things are in all from the sympathy that all visible things have for one another and for the invisible powers—have also framed their priestly knowledge. For they were amazed to see the lasts in the firsts and the very firsts in the lasts; in heaven they saw earthly things acting causally and in a heavenly manner, in the earth heavenly things in an earthly manner. Why do heliotropes move together with the sun, selenotropes with the moon, moving around to the extent of their ability with the luminaries of the cosmos? All things pray according to their own order and sing hymns, either intellectually or rationally or naturally or sensibly, to heads of entire chains.[48] And since the heliotrope is also moved toward that to which it readily opens, if anyone hears it striking the air as it moves about, he perceives in the sound that it offers to the king the kind of hymn that a plant can sing (1-13). Ὥσπερ οἱ ἐρωτικοὶ ἀπὸ τῶν ἐν αἰσθήσει καλῶν ὁδῷ προϊόντες ἐπ' αὐτὴν καταντῶσι τὴν μίαν τῶν καλῶν πάντων καὶ νοητῶν ἀρχήν, οὕτως καὶ οἱ ἱερατικοὶ ἀπὸ τῆς ἐν τοῖς φαινομένοις ἅπασι συμπαθείας πρός τε ἄλληλα καὶ πρὸς τὰς ἀφανεῖς δυνάμεις, πάντα ἐν πᾶσι κατανοήσαντες, τὴν ἐπιστήμην τὴν ἱερατικὴν συνεστήσαντο, θαυμάσαντες τῷ βλέπειν ἔν τε τοῖς πρώτοις τὰ ἔσχατα καὶ ἐν τοῖς ἐσχάτοις τὰ πρώτιστα, ἐν οὐρανῷ μὲν τὰ χθόνια κατ' αἰτίαν καὶ οὐρανίως, ἔν τε γῇ τὰ οὐράνια γηΐνως. Ἢ πόθεν ἡλιοτρόπια μὲν ἡλίῳ, σεληνοτρόπια δὲ σελήνῃ συγκινεῖται συμπεριπολοῦντα ἐς δύναμιν τοῖς τοῦ κόσμου φωστῆρσιν; Εὔχεται γὰρ πάντα κατὰ τὴν οἰκείαν τάξιν καὶ ὑμνεῖ τοὺς ἡγεμόνας τῶν σειρῶν ὅλων ἢ νοερῶς ἢ λογικῶς ἢ φυσικῶς ἢ αἰσθητῶς· ἐπεὶ καὶ τὸ ἡλιοτρόπιον ᾧ ἔστιν εὔλυτον, τούτῳ κινεῖται καί, εἰ δή τις αὐτοῦ κατὰ τὴν περιστροφὴν ἀκούειν τὸν ἀέρα πλήσσοντος οἷός τε ἦν, ὕμνον ἄν τινα διὰ τοῦ ἤχου τούτου συνῄσθετο τῷ Βασιλεῖ προσάγοντος, ὃν δύναται φυτὸν ὑμνεῖν."

completely hidden potency/power, in a way obliterated and non-existent because it does not yet really exist" (5, 31-36).[49] I translate '*dunamin*' as both potency and power since there is no potency without the power of the Good. All the same, this is a remarkable statement that forces us to understand hierarchy in a new way. Another example is I 4 [46] 13 where Plotinus observes that the activities of the *spoudaios* or really good person will not be hindered by chance, but will be adapted to chance; he continues: "... they will all be fine and, perhaps, *finer for being adapted to circumstances*" (πᾶσαι δὲ ὅμως καλαὶ καλλίους ἴσως ὅσῳ περιστατικαί).[50] Adaptability and unexpected development do not have to be accidental or later additions to what things really are. They may well express something more valuable than a linear or hierarchical view of what things might, can, or should be. From this perspective, when the much-enduring and crooked-thinking Odysseus makes his free choice of the lowliest herdsman's life on the Plain of Truth,[51] the world of Plato's *Republic* changes forever with something decidedly both old and new. He completes the question "what is justice" that began with Cephalus in Book 1,[52] but turns the expectations of the world upside down. He has come through much experience to know the good and so he gladly embraces its lowliest part.[53]

---

[49] IV 8 [8] 5, 31-36: and soul "manifesting its powers, making apparent works and activities which if they had remained quiescent in the spiritual world would have been of no use because they would never have come into actuality; and the soul itself would not have known the powers it had if they had not come out and been revealed. Actuality everywhere reveals completely hidden potency, in a way obliterated and non-existent because it does not yet truly exist (εἴπερ πανταχοῦ ἡ ἐνέργεια τὴν δύναμιν ἔδειξε κρυφθεῖσαν ἂν ἀπάντη καὶ οἷον ἀφανισθεῖσαν καὶ οὐκ οὖσαν μηδέποτε ὄντως οὖσαν). As things are, everyone wonders at what is within because of the varied splendour of the outside and admires what the doer is because it does these fine things."

[50] I 4 [46] 13, 1-3: "The good man's activities will not be hindered by changes of fortune, but will vary according to what change and chance brings; but they will all be equally fine, and, perhaps, finer for being adapted to circumstances."

[51] *Republic* 10, 620c-d.

[52] *Republic* 1, 328c-331d.

[53] *Republic* 10, 620d: καὶ εἰπεῖν ἰδοῦσαν ὅτι τὰ αὐτὰ ἂν ἔπραξεν καὶ πρώτη λαχοῦσα, καὶ ἀσμένην ἑλέσθαι...

[Even more important, the emergence of the new has to be seen simultaneously from below and from above…The "above" is not really above but simultaneously "below", "sideways", "diagonal" and in multi-dimensions altogether]

6. Intellect

Let me turn but briefly to Intellect and the Good, both crucial for deep ecology, that is, crucial not for taking a "shallow" approach based on the same consumption-oriented values and methods of the industrial economy (e.g. recycling, increased automotive efficiency, export-driven monocultural organic agriculture), but for rethinking our values all the way down.[54] The physical cosmos, as we seem to experience it, is an *unfolded* world where distance and conflict separate things and where my little ego-territory can feel very lonely. Soul experiences something of this dividedness, since Soul is both undivided and divided: a "one *and* many", Plotinus calls it.[55] Intellect, by contrast, is an *enfolded* or implicate world,[56] a "one *in* many" or "one-many"[57] and with somewhat remarkable features: It is not, for Plotinus, an abstract type or some universal nature linking everything, but a different, comprehensive axis of our being. Intellect is a complete living animal—as in Plato's *Timaeus*, so pervaded by immediate living thought or insight that it contains everything not as objects but as subject-objects. For Aristotle, Al Farabi or Avicenna (Ibn Sina) we human beings have intellects that might seem disconnected from the great 48 or 55 Intellects[58] moving different celestial spheres down to the Archangel Gabriel, yet there is only one agent intellect for all humanity. Ibn Rushd goes one step further: there is only one potential or material intellect for all human beings.[59] Plotinus' thought is more daring still and more inclusive. Every bit of intellect is simultaneously a subject thinking itself and everything else,

---

[54] On this see Alan Drengson, http://www.deepecology.org/deepecology.htm, but see especially Dillon and Clark (2013).

[55] See V I [10] 8, 26.

[56] See VI 7 [38], chapter 1 and the passages cited in note 62 below.

[57] V I [10] 8, 23-26.

[58] Depending upon how one interprets Aristotle, *Metaphysics* 12, 8.

[59] On this see Adamson (2015); (2017); Adamson and Taylor (2005); and more broadly, D'Ancona (2005) 10-32; Pessin (2014) 541-558.

and so too is every other bit of intellect, even horses and wilder things too![60] Nothing is only an object. And nothing is just a "bit" or fragment, since what characterizes Intellect is "all-at-onceness,"[61] that is, complete enfoldedness or implicate being without obliteration of identity.[62] To be a successful you or me in our educational systems is to have a better brain, better marks than other people and to be distinct, different, original. To be you or me in Intellect is to be more ourselves *because of* the identities and othernesses of *everything else*—all species and things. This notion of identity contradicts virtually all of our civilization's major rites of passage. And quite naturally it makes the major religions a little queasy. Yet it is fundamental to ecology— even simply as a holistic model for understanding ecosystems.

Second, Intellect is not the cold light of reason, for Intellect is where desire and reason come into the proper focus of understanding and love.[63] Intellect is supremely alive (boiling with life, Plotinus says)[64] and alive as a whole in rather curious ways. It is whole in itself and whole in each of its parts—whether those parts are stars, earth, human beings, horses or plants— so that every part is simultaneously

---

[60] See VI 7 [38], chapters 1-11 and VI 7, 9 cited above (note 30).

[61] See III 7 [] 8, 50-51; 11, 22 and 55-57; V 5 [32] 7, 8; VI 8 [39] 14, 31.

[62] See VI 7 [38] 1, 54-58: "All things, then, existed already and existed for ever, and existed in such a way that one could say later "this after that"; for when it is extended and in a sense unfolded it is able to display this after that, but when it is all together it is entirely this (ἐκτεινόμενον μὲν γὰρ καὶ οἷον ἁπλούμενον ἔχει δεικνύναι τόδε μετὰ τόδε, ὁμοῦ δὲ ὂν πᾶν τόδε); but this means having its cause also in itself." 2, 18: "...if also you unfold each form itself to itself, you will find the reason why in it" (εἰ καὶ αὐτὸ τὸ εἶδος ἕκαστον πρὸς αὐτὸ ἀναπτύττοις, εὑρήσεις ἐν αὐτῷ τὸ "διὰ τί"). Cf. V 8 [31] 5, 4-8: "...the craftsman goes back again to the wisdom of nature, according to which he has come into existence, a wisdom which is no longer composed of theorems, but is one thing as a whole, not the wisdom made into one out of many components, but rather resolved into multiplicity from one (οὐκέτι συντεθεῖσαν ἐκ θεωρημάτων, ἀλλ᾽ ὅλην ἕν τι, οὐ τὴν συγκειμένην ἐκ πολλῶν εἰς ἕν, ἀλλὰ μᾶλλον ἀναλυομένην εἰς πλῆθος ἐξ ἑνός).

[63] Cp. III 8 (30) 11, 23-24 and VI 7 [38] 35-36.

[64] This is a remarkable synaesthetic passage altogether - VI 7 [38] 12, 22-30: "there is no poverty or lack of resource there, but all things are filled full of life, and, we may say, boiling with life. They all flow, in a way, from a single spring, not like one particular breath or one warmth, but as if there was one quality which held and kept intact all the qualities in itself, of sweetness along with fragrance, and was at once the quality of wine and the characters of all tastes, the sights of colours and all the awarenesses of touch, and all that hearings hear, all tunes and every rhythm."

the whole and each part in the whole is all the other parts too. As Plotinus puts it: "all things there are transparent...for light is transparent to light...all are everywhere and each and every one is all...the sun there is all the stars, and each sun star is the sun and all the others. A different stands out in each but in each all are manifest" (V 8, 4. trans. A. H. Armstrong, adapted).[65] Here then, before the discovery of holographic images, created by interference patterns in which every portion of a piece of the image contains all the information of the whole, and before the discovery of the curious behaviour of atomic "particles", we already have a strangely prescient model for understanding the simultaneity, non-locality and yet existential wholeness of the physical universe—not as an object, but as a living, loving, contemplative whole in which subject and object pervade each other.

The gap between my consciousness and Intellect is an abyss. We have almost lost the words "soul" and "spirit" from polite company. The social sciences wish to resurrect "quality" from the "quantity" of the hard sciences. But substance or being, it seems apparent, died some time ago—though Being is perhaps lingering in the morgue after Heidegger refused to apologize to Paul Celan.[66] Yet if we posit a flattened out world where everything is fully explained by aggregate and by Ockham's razor without anything being understood from its own threshold, then we can have no poetry, music or real religious spirit. As a 15 year-old in England reading Virgil's *Georgics* with a kindly teacher and three other students, I was mortified to make a mess of translation in one class. So we prepared meticulously for the next class and triumphantly rattled off a thousand lines. The master thanked us for our work, looked somewhat sadly at us and observed:

---

[65] V 8 [31] 4, 4-11, a passage evidently upon *Phaedo* 109dff. and *Phaedrus* 247ff.; but it also has to be read in light of its clear parallel, and obvious target, namely, *Zostrianos* 48-55, which appropriates elements from both Platonic passages: "[The self-generated Aeons] were all eternal lights and perfect, being individually complete. At each of the aeons I saw a living earth, a living water...possessing a variety of beauty, trees of many kinds...as well as plants...imperishable fruit, human beings alive with every species, immortal souls, every shape and species of intellect, gods of truth, angels dwelling in great glory with an indissoluble body..." (trans. Turner).

[66] Heidegger had the opportunity to apologize to Celan after the War for his pro-Nazi activities, but never did so.

"But always remember boys—this is *poetry.*" For a split second, I didn't understand; and then it dawned on me and my previous complacency changed abruptly to shame so that the world changed for me that day—or rather I entered a new world but from its own threshold. And this is what Plato, Plotinus and the later Neoplatonists ask their interlocutors to do: to awaken a new axis of being that does not revolve about ourselves alone, to wake up to the whole of being, not as a spectacle or supermarket, but as an experience of transformation.[67] And of course while they know that human beings cannot entirely do this, they think that the aspiration is still "a noble risk".[68]

7. The Good or the One

Finally, I noted above how the good/Good emerges out of Plotinus' consideration of the World's body in IV 4 [28]. This is faithful to the spirit of Plato's *Republic* 6, where Socrates represents the Good not simply as the theoretical ground of everything but as *the* most practical and useful good of all: without it, nothing is truly beneficial (504e–505b). It is, according to Socrates, the regulative ground of all our judgments, dimly glimpsed or "divined" in all our experience (from perplexity [*Republic* 505d11–e2; 506a6] to sex – the latter according to Aristophanes in the *Symposium* [192c–d]); and it is also what provides both the power and the means of seeing, feeling or thinking anything (*Republic* 508e–509b). In short, the Good is that by which the best state or capacity of anything is felt, seen, imagined or thought reflexively. By reflexively I mean that the Good is the principle by which we are able to conceive the best state of anything, a principle disclosed in the acts of seeing or thinking themselves, just as in seeing we see the light of the sun, according to Socrates' analogy in *Republic* books 6–7, and in thinking objects of thought we think of them as "good-form" (508d–509b). As Roger Scruton observes, "we pursue the true, the good and the beautiful, even though the false, the nasty and the messy might have been just as useful to our genes" (2014, 5). I agree wholeheartedly, but would add that while the beautiful can be misleading, and the true sometimes perfectly nasty and trivial, the good is surely always to be preferred, as Diotima

---

[67] See *Protagoras* 313a-314c.

[68] *Protagoras* 314a-b.

insists,[69] and it is also what most truly belongs to who we are, as Socrates argues in the *Republic*.[70] Michael Fideler, in his wonderful book *Restoring the Soul of the World* outlines the history of thought from the ancient to the Renaissance worlds before reconnecting this to ecological design, bio-mimicry and learning from nature's intelligence;[71] but he does not mention the Good, only the One— which is, of course, perfectly acceptable. But I want to suggest that without the Good no deep ecology is possible, for there can be no inherent values of all things without either romanticizing or managing snakes or rocks.[72] You will say, of course: Whose good? Whose rationality? And I will have to reply: the good/Good of none and the good/Good of all. Without a marker, the good goes unnoticed and other goods are quick to supplant it—all the more so, since, as Plotinus observes, possibility, potentiality, power seem in a steady state universe to be "non-existent".[73]

Why do I think the Good or the One is important for ecology? Without the possibility of what is best, we have a drab hole in which to live, not a world. Critics of deep ecology have argued that while "all biota have intrinsic value [they] are not equal in intrinsic value because the 'richness of experience' " (Fox, 1984, 198) or the intensity of sentience differs (Ferre, 1994).[74] Obviously, hard compromises have to be made but the principle of a Good that gives and yet escapes all goods is a worthy one to retain, especially since, without it, intensity of sentience is a dubious and slippery slope. Whose intensity, after all? Second, the Good is not only the source of value at every level, but *the* source of diversity, newness, and the unexpected that

---

[69] Plato, *Symposium* 205a; *Republic* 505d; and Plotinus V 5 [32] 12, 23-24.

[70] *Republic* 9, 586e: ἄτε ἀληθείᾳ ἑπομένων, καὶ τὰς ἑαυτῶν οἰκείας, εἴπερ τὸ βέλτιστον ἑκάστῳ, τοῦτο καὶ οἰκειότατον—in following the truth, all the parts of soul will reap their own truest pleasures, 'if what is best for each is that also that most belongs to each.'"

[71] Fideler (2014) 236-258.

[72] Naess has observed, "I'm not much interested in ethics or morals. I'm interested in how we experience the world. . . . " (Fox (1995) 219). In Sessions' words, "The search . . . is not for environmental ethics but for ecological consciousness" (Fox (1995) 225). See Nelson, M. P. (2008) "Deep Ecology" in *Encyclopedia of Environmental Ethics and Philosophy*, (2nd edition) 206-211.

[73] See IV 8 [8] 5 cited above.

[74] See Nelson (2008) 209.

makes the world radically open-ended. [75] Third, its presence is everywhere and immediately to everything, different from the presence of anything else: unlike Intellect and Soul which make things think and live, the Good lets them "be"; (VI 7 [38] 23); [76] it is "present even to those asleep"; [77] it is the guarantee of "oughtness" and the proper moment or *kairos* (VI 8 [39] 18, 44-47) [78] that surely guides all other forms of willing that seek the *kairos* when the need is present (IV 4 [27] 17, 7); [79] its will is the self-constituting creator of all wills

---

[75] See V 5 [32] 8, 14: "But he did not come as one expected, but came as one who did not come" (ὁ δὲ οὐκ ἦει, ὥς τις προσεδόκα, ἀλλ᾽ ἦλθεν ὡς οὐκ ἐλθών).

[76] VI 7 [38] 23, 23-25: "But what is it making now? Now as well it is keeping those things in being and making the thinking things think and the living things live, inspiring thought, inspiring life and, if something cannot live, inspiring to be."

[77] V 5 [32] 12, 10-15: "The grasp of the beautiful and the wonder and the waking of love for it come to those who, in a way, already know it and are awake to it. But the Good, since it was there long before to arouse an innate desire, is present even to those asleep and does not astonish those who at any time see it, because it is always there and there is never recollection of it; but people do not see it, because it is present to them in their sleep."

[78] VI 8 [39] 18, 44-51: "He is then in a greater degree something like the most causative and truest of causes, possessing all together the intellectual causes which are going to be from him and generative of what is not as it chanced but as he himself willed. And his willing is not irrational, or of the random, or just as it happened to occur to him, but as it ought to be, since nothing there is random. For this reason Plato speaks of "due" and "right moment", desiring to indicate as far as possible that it is far from "as it chanced", but what it is is what it ought to be. But if this is what ought to be, it is not so irrationally, and if it is the right moment it has the most authentic mastery among the things which come after it, and has priority in its own right and is not what it in a way chanced to be, but what he in a way wished to be, since he wishes what ought to be and what ought to be and the active actuality of what ought to be are one." Armstrong mentions in his note ad loc. that Plotinus refers to Plato's *Politicus* 284e6-7, a totally different context where measurement is in question and from which, as Armstrong observes, Aristotle developed his own notion of the mean. But Plotinus surely means that the Good is what constitutes *kairos* for itself and for every subsequent measurement of any kind. Therefore, any arts concerned with the right moment, whether arithmetic, geometry, music, harmonics or ethics are so constituted by the Good and, consequently, in getting something right we are sharing in the life of the Good (something, I suggest, that Plato, Aristotle, and Plotinus profoundly agree with).

[79] Why are we not self-dependent like the World Soul? Because we are in time "as a result our decisions are different and relevant to the occasion when the need arises (ὅθεν ἄλλο τὸ βούλευμα καὶ πρὸς καιρόν), and now this and now that external incident occurs".

(VI 8 [39])[80] even to the extent that the Good's presence is immediately and democratically in our willed power: "The Good is gentle and kindly and gracious, and present to anyone when *anyone wishes or wills* it" (V 5 [32] 12).[81] Its pure unity, Plotinus says, is what people proclaim *naturally of themselves* or *from their own nature* (*autophuōs*) when they say that "the god that is in each one of us is one and the same" (VI 5 [23] 1).[82] Of the immensity of the One, nothing can be thought or said, and yet its intensive and extensive unity is greater than that of Intellect or Soul; "when you think him as intellect or soul, he is more," Plotinus insists (VI 9 [9] 6, 12).[83] Such a unity is therefore enough for one or many universes. Multiverse theory, it should be noted, is as old as Anaximander, for whom the *apeiron* (whatever he meant by it) was enough for many *kosmoi*.[84] Most important perhaps is that such Unity is not some blind or automatic principle but something stranger and yet more familiar still: the source and refuge of all things, living and non-living, that is, animals, plants, the simplest existences, and even the barest possibilities in which no rational analysis could reasonably discern any genuine potential or dream anything other than hope.[85] As Pindar sang long before Plato or Plotinus in Epode 5 of *Pythian* 8: "Creatures of a day! What is someone? What is no one? A dream of a shadow is man. But whenever god given radiance comes, a shining light rests upon human beings and a gentle life."[86]

---

[80] VI 8 [39], chapters 13-21.

[81] V 5 [32] 12, 34-35: καὶ ἔστι δὲ τὸ μὲν ἤπιον καὶ προσηνὲς καὶ ἁβρότερον καί, ὡς ἐθέλει τις, παρὸν αὐτῷ.

[82] VI 5 [] 1, 1ff: "A general opinion affirms that what is one and the same in number is everywhere present as a whole, when all men are naturally and spontaneously moved to speak of the god who is in each one of us one and the same (Τὸ ἓν καὶ ταὐτὸν ἀριθμῷ πανταχοῦ ἅμα ὅλον εἶναι κοινὴ μέν τις ἔννοιά φησιν εἶναι, ὅταν πάντες κινούμενοι αὐτοφυῶς λέγωσι τὸν ἐν ἑκάστῳ ἡμῶν θεὸν ὡς ἕνα καὶ τὸν αὐτόν)."

[83] VI 9 [9] 6, 12: ὅταν γὰρ ἂν αὐτὸν νοήσῃς οἷον ἢ νοῦν ἢ θεόν, πλέον ἐστί.

[84] DK A14 (Aëtius, *de plac.* 1.3,3).

[85] For a variant on this theme see Corrigan (2014) 387-388.

[86] Pindar, *Pythian* 8, Epode 5, 95-98: ἐπάμερον τί δέ τις; τί δ᾽ οὔ τις; σκιᾶς ὄναρ ἄνθρωπος. ἀλλ᾽ ὅταν αἴγλα διόσδοτος ἔλθῃ, λαμπρὸν φέγγος ἔπεστιν ἀνδρῶν καὶ μείλιχος αἰών.

Appendix: Eight-point Platform of deep ecology

1. The well-being and flourishing of human and non-human life on Earth have value in themselves (synonyms: intrinsic value, inherent worth). These values are independent of the usefulness of the non-human world for human purposes.

2. Richness and diversity of life forms contribute to the realization of these values and are also values in themselves.

3. Humans have no right to reduce this richness and diversity except to satisfy vital needs.

4. The flourishing of human life and cultures is compatible with a substantially smaller human population. The flourishing of non-human life *requires* a smaller human population.

5. Present human interference with the non-human world is excessive, and the situation is rapidly worsening.

6. Policies must therefore be changed. These policies affect basic economic, technological, and ideological structures. The resulting state of affairs will be deeply different from the present.

7. The ideological change will be mainly that of appreciating life quality (dwelling in situations of inherent value) rather than adhering to an increasingly higher standard of living. There will be a profound awareness of the difference between bigness and greatness.

8. Those who subscribe to the foregoing points have an obligation directly or indirectly to try to implement the necessary changes.

Bibliography

Adamson P. and R. C. Taylor (eds.) (2005) *The Cambridge Companion to Arabic Philosophy. Cambridge.*

Adamson, P. (2015) *Philosophy in the Islamic World. A Very Short Introduction,* Oxford.

—— (2016) *Philosophy in the Islamic World,* Oxford.

Armstrong, A. H. (1966-1988) *Plotinus,* Volumes 1-7, Loeb Classical Library, Cambridge, Mass. and London.

Beauchamp, T. L. and Frey, R. G. (2011) *The Oxford Handbook of Animal Ethics,* Oxford.

Ben-Chaim, M. (2004) *Experimental Philosophy and the Birth of Empirical Science: Boyle, Locke, and Newton,* Ashgate, UK.

Cassin, B. and Labarrière, J.-L. (2000) *L'animal dans l'antiquité,* Paris: Vrin.

Clark, G., *Porphyry. On Abstinence from Killing Animals,* Ithaca, NY: Cornell University Press.

Clark, S. (2011) "Animals in Classical and Late Antique Philosophy," in Beauchamp & Frey *The Oxford Handbook of Animal Ethics,* Oxford, 35-60.

Copenhaver, B. (1988) "Hermes Trismegistus, Proclus, and a Philosophy of Magic" in *Hermeticism and the Renaissance: Intellectual History and the Occult in Early Modern Europe,* Folger Books, Washington DC, I. Merkel and A. G. Debus (eds.) pp 79-110)

Corrigan, K. (2014) "Humans, other animals, plants and the question of the Good: the Platonic and the Neoplatonic traditions," in Remes, P. and S. Slaveva-Griffin (eds.) *The Routledge Handbook of Neoplatonism,* London and New York, pp 372-390.

—— (2015) "Divine and human freedom: Plotinus' new understanding of creative agency," in A. Marmadoro and B. D. Prince (eds.) *Causation and Creation in Late Antiquity,* Cambridge.

D'Ancona, C. (2005) 'Greek into Arabic: Neoplatonism in Translation', in P. Adamson and R. C. Taylor (eds.), *The Cambridge Companion to Arabic Philosophy. Cambridge,* 10–32.

Dillon, J. M, and Blumenthal, H. J. (2015) *Ennead IV.3—4.29, Problems Concerning the Soul*, translation, introduction, commentary, Las Vegas, Zurich, Athens, Parmenides Publishing.

Dillon, J. M. and Clark, S. R. (2013) *Towards the Noosphere: Futures Singular and Plural*, foreword by Tim Addey, Prometheus Trust.

Dillon, J. M. and Morrow, G. R. (1987) *Proclus' Commentary on Plato's Parmenides*, Princeton.

Drengson, A. (2017) http://www.deepecology.org/deepecology.htm

Emilsson, E. K. (2007) *Plotinus on Intellect*, Oxford.

Ferre, F. (1994) "Personalistic Organicism: Paradox or Paradigm?" in *Philosophy and the Natural Environment*: Royal Institute of Philosophy Supplement 36, Robin Attfield and Andrew Belsey (eds.) New York: Cambridge University Press.

Fideler, M. (2014) *Restoring the Soul of the World*, Rochester, Vermont/Toronto, Canada: Inner Traditions.

Fox, W. (1984) "Deep Ecology: A New Philosophy of Our Time?" *The Ecologist* 14 (5,6), pp 94-200.

— (1995) *Toward a Transpersonal Ecology: Developing New Foundations for Environmentalism*, Albany: State University of New York Press.

Gilhus, I. S. (2006) *Animals, Gods and Humans: Changing Attitudes to Animals in Greek, Roman and Early Christian Ideas*, London: Routledge.

Gutas, D. (1998) *Greek Thought, Arabic Culture*, London: Routledge.

Hadot, P. (2008) *The Veil of Isis: An Essay on the History of the Idea of Nature*, Michael Chase (trans.) (*Le Voile d'Isis*), Harvard University Press.

Heath, J. (2005) *The Talking Greeks: Speech, Animals, and the Other in Homer, Aeschylus, and Plato*, Cambridge University Press.

Lloyd, A. C. (1990) *The Anatomy of Neoplatonism*, Oxford.

Marenbon, J. (2007) *Medieval Philosophy. An Historical and Philosophical Introduction*, London and New York: Routledge.

Marenbon, J. (2016) *Medieval Philosophy. A Very Short Introduction*, Oxford.

Marmadoro, A. and Prince, B. (eds.) (2015) *Causation and Creation in Late Antiquity*, Cambridge.

Naess, A. (1973) "The Shallow and the Deep, Long-Range Ecology Movement: A Summary." *Inquiry: An Interdisciplinary Journal of Philosophy and the Social Sciences*, 16. pp 95–100. And for overview and criticism, Nelson (2008) pp 206-211. See also Naess, A. and Sessions (1984)

— (1986) "The Deep Ecology Movement: Some Philosophical Aspects," *Philosophical Inquiry*, 8, pp 10-31.

Nelson, M. P. (2008) "Deep Ecology," *Encyclopedia of Environmental Ethics and Philosophy*, 2nd Edition, pp 206-211.

Newmyer, S. (2006) *Animals, Rights and Reason in Plutarch and Modern Ethics*, London: Routledge.

Nussbaum, M. (2006) *Frontiers of Justice: Disability, Nationality, Species Membership*, Cambridge, MA: Harvard University Press.

Osborne, C. (2007) *Dumb Beasts and Dead Philosophers: Humanity and the Humane in Ancient Philosophy and Literature*, Oxford: Clarendon Press.

Pessin, S. (2014) "Islamic and Jewish Neoplatonisms," in Remes, P. and S. Slaveva-Griffin (eds.) *The Routledge Handbook of Neoplatonism*, London and New York, pp 541-558.

Remes, P. and S. Slaveva-Griffin, eds. (2014) *The Routledge Handbook of Neoplatonism*, London and New York.

Robinson, T. M. and Westra, L. (2002) *Thinking about the Environment. Our Debt to the Classical and Medieval Past*, Lanham/Boulder/New York/Oxford, Lexington Books.

Rowe, C. J. (1986) *Plato. Phaedrus*, Aris & Philips, England.

Rutten, C. (1956) "La Doctrine des Deux Actes dans la Philosophie de Plotin," *Revue Philosophique* 146, pp 100-106.

Scruton, R. (2014) *The Soul of the World*, Princeton.

Sorabji, R. (1993) *Animal Minds and Human Morals: The Origins of the Western Debate*, Ithaca, NY: Cornell University Press.

Steiner, G. (2005) *Anthropocentrism and its Discontents: The Moral Status of Animals in the History of Western Philosophy*, Pittsburgh: University of Pittsburgh Press.

Tress, D. M. (2002) "Reuniting Science and Value in the Natural Environment," in Robinson, T. M. and Westra, L., *Thinking about the Environment. Our Debt to the Classical and Medieval Past*, Lanham/Boulder/New York/Oxford, Lexington Books, pp 213-222.

Turner, J. D. (2001) *Sethian Gnosticism and the Platonic Tradition*, Laval, Quebec.

Wagner, M. F. (2001) *Neoplatonism and Nature: Studies in Plotinus' Enneads*, SUNY: New York.

Wallis, R. T. (revised and edited by L. P. Gerson) (1995) *Neoplatonism*, Duckworth: London.

Contributors

Etain Addey moved to Rome at the age of twenty and worked for a decade in a Dutch multinational pharmaceutical company until the lack of ethics pushed her to look for some kind of right livelihood. She ended up on a small sheep farm in the Umbrian hills and has lived there for forty years with her partner Martin, gradually learning how to live in the old way. The milking and wine-making and olive-picking were a way in, but the hard work slowly revealed the voices of place and over the years following the 1984 earthquake and the rebuilding, the small group of people who live at Pratale and the people who come and go have been the recipients of many epiphanies.

Tim Addey is Chairman of the Prometheus Trust and the author of *The Seven Myths of the Soul, The Unfolding Wings* and *Beyond the Shadows*.

Robert Bolton's education was originally scientific, in chemistry and physics, but he studied Plato's philosophy in his spare time. He went to the University of Exeter and took postgraduate degrees in philosophy, and subsequently was the author of several books, including *The Order of the Ages, Self and Spirt, Keys of Gnosis, Person, Soul and Identity: philosophy and the real Self*, and *Foundations of Free Will*. He has also been a regular contributor to *Sacred Web*.

Kevin Corrigan graduated in Classics from Oxford in 1963 and gained a PhD from the University of California at Berkeley in 1969, after which he joined the faculty of the Department of Classics at Berkeley, where he remained until 1980, serving as Chairman of the Department from 1977-80. He then returned to Ireland, to assume the Regius Professorship of Greek at Trinity College, Dublin, where he remained until his retirement in 2006. He is the author or editor of a series of books in the area of Greek Philosophy, in particular the history of the Platonic tradition, including *The Middle Platonists*, 1977, 2nd ed. 1996, Alcinous; *The Handbook of Platonism*, trans., with a commentary (Clarendon Later Ancient Philosophers Series), Oxford, 1993; Iamblichus, *De Anima* , ed. with introduction, translation and commentary (with John Finamore), Leiden: Brill, 2002; *The Heirs of Plato: a study of the Old Academy, 347-274 BC*, Oxford, 2003, and three collections of essays, *The Golden Chain: Studies in the Development of Platonism and Christianity* (1991), *The Great Tradition: Further Studies in the Development of Platonism and Christianity* (1997), and *The Platonic Heritage* (2012), all with Variorum: Aldershot or Farnham.

Mary-Ann Crumplin is a member of the philosophy tutor panel at Oxford University's Department of Continuing Education. She received her PhD in Philosophy from the University of London and has published research in ethics, psychology and phenomenology. Her primary interest is in ethics and ontology of difference.

Stuart Dunbar received his Bachelor's degree from Yale University in 1985 with a concentration in philosophy. He has pursued his interest in philosophy privately and through participation in various courses of study, seminars, and live discussion forums, including courses at the University of Colorado in Boulder, Williams College in Massachusetts, University of California in Berkeley and more recently with the Prometheus Trust in the UK. His interests are in the philosophy of mind, developmental psychology, systems theory and ancient and medieval philosophy. He moved to the UK in 2015 from the United States to advance his career in the technology industry. He designs software systems for healthcare organisations.

Paul Fagan is a panel member for *Ask a Philosopher* and his interests include any areas where philosophy may be applied to solving problems we experience in the present. He graduated from the University of Hull with a PhD entitled *Who Owns Renewable Energy? – An Argument for Independent Ownership*.

Sally Jeanrenaud is an Honorary Senior Research Fellow in Sustainability, Business School, University of Exeter. She has worked in Nepal, Rwanda, Cameroon and Europe, in field based and international leadership positions. She led IUCN's Future of Sustainability Initiative, co-founded the Green Economy Coalition, helped establish Exeter's One Planet MBA, and

OPEN for Business. She researches innovation in sustainability philosophies and practices, teaches on Masters programmes and is a Visiting Professor in Audencia School of Management in France. She is a Trustee of the Fintry Trust which is dedicated to Integral Wisdom and a qualified Mindfulness (MBSR) teacher.

Jean-Paul Jeanrenaud MSc (Oxon) is Senior Advisor to WWF Switzerland. During his career he worked as a Director of Development projects in South Asia, Africa and Europe. He worked for WWF International for 26 years as Director of the International Forest Programme; Director of Corporate Relations; and Director of Business Education. He co-founded the Forest Stewardship Council (FSC); One Planet Leaders; the award winning One Planet MBA; and OPEN for Business (One Planet Education Networks). He is Visiting Professor at Audencia School of Management, Nantes, France. He has been a student of universal and integral wisdom for 40 years and is a qualified Mindfulness (MBSR) teacher.

Eccy de Jonge, a former Lecturer in Philosophy at the University of Middlesex and a Tutor in Research Ethics at University College, London, is a freelance writer and researcher. An expert in deep ecology she has published two books *Spinoza and Deep Ecology* (London: Routledge, 2004) and *Reinstating the Infinite* (Delft: Eburaon, 2003) and a number of journal articles. In 2016 she was a guest speaker on BBC Radio 3's programme 'Free Thinking' talking on Arne Naess, the founder of Deep Ecology. She has recently completed a book on the nature of grief entitled *On St Ninian's Isle* and is currently working on a book on Policing. She lives in Central London.

Marilynn Lawrence teaches philosophy at Immaculata University outside of Philadelphia and works as a user experience writer. Her primary research interests have included Neoplatonism, ecstatic naturalism and aesthetics. She is a member of the Board of Directors for the International Society for Neoplatonic Studies, and her work on Neoplatonism and middle Platonism is featured in several anthologies, such as

Perspectives sur le néoplatonisme (2008) and *The Neoplatonic Socrates* (2014). She has recently co-edited a book on ecstatic naturalism called *Nature's Transcendence and Immanence* (2017), published by Lexington Books.

Freya Mathews is Adjunct Professor of Environmental Philosophy at La Trobe University, Australia. Her books include *The Ecological Self* (1991), *Ecology and Democracy* (editor) 1996, *For Love of Matter: a Contemporary Panpsychism* (2003), *Journey to the Source of the Merri* (2003), *Re-inhabiting Reality: Towards a Recovery of Culture* (2005), *Without Animals Life is not Worth Living* (2016) and *Ardea: a philosophical novella* (2016). She is the author of over seventy articles in the area of ecological philosophy. Her current special interests are in ecological civilisation; indigenous (Australian and Chinese) perspectives on sustainability and how these perspectives may be adapted to the context of contemporary global society; panpsychism and critique of the metaphysics of modernity; ecology and religion; and conservation ethics and rewilding in the context of the Anthropocene. In addition to her research activities she co-manages a private biodiversity reserve in northern Victoria. She is a fellow of the Australian Academy of the Humanities.

Ann van Ryn has a background in comparative religious studies with a keen interest and Honours Degree in the metaphysical underpinning of traditional art and symbolism, Similarly, her PhD thesis, entitled *The Noetic Unity of Nature* draws upon traditional metaphysics as the context for her enquiry into the relationship between Man and Nature.

Valeria Zanon graduated with a degree in Philosophical Sciences from the University of Padua with a thesis on *The Revisitation of the Stoic Sage in Seneca*; she has a Master's degree in Management of Local Development within Parks and Protected Areas. Valeria is also a professional Environmental Educator, trained to communicate environmental values to children and adults through direct participation. Her philosophical interests concern environmental philosophy, especially in relation to virtue ethics and psychology of motivation.

The Prometheus Trust Catalogue

Platonic Texts and Translations Series

I   Iamblichi   Chalcidensis   in   Platonis   Dialogos
Commentariorum Fragmenta

John M Dillon   978-1-898910-45-9

II The Greek Commentaries on Plato's Phaedo (I – Olympiodorus)

L G Westerink   978-1-898910-46-6

III The Greek Commentaries on Plato's Phaedo (II –
Damascius)   L *G Westerink*   978-1-898910-47-3

IV Damascius, Lectures on the Philebus

L G Westerink   978-1-898910-48-0

V The Anonymous Prolegomena to Platonic Philosophy

L G Westerink   978-1-898910-51-0

VI Proclus Commentary on the First Alcibiades

Text L G Westerink Trans. W O'Neill   978-1-898910-49-7

VII The Fragments of Numenius

R Petty   978-1-898910-52-7

VIII The Chaldean Oracles

R Majercik   978-1-898910-53-4

* Conference collections in association with the ISNS *

Metaphysical Patterns in Platonism
(ed. J Finamore and R Berchman)   978-1-898910-83-1

Platonic Traditons in American Thought
(ed. J A Bregman and M B Mineo)   978-1-898910-86-2

Platonic Inquiries
(ed. C. D'Amico, J. Finamore & N. Strok)   978-1-898910-85-5

Platonic Pathways
(ed. J. Finamore and D. Layne)   978-1-898910-87-9

The Thomas Taylor Series

1 Proclus' Elements of Theology

Proclus' Elements of Theology - 211 propositions which frame the metaphysics of the Late Athenian Academy. 978-1-898910-00-8

2 Select Works of Porphyry

Abstinence from Animal Food; Auxiliaries to the Perception of Intelligibles; Concerning Homer's Cave of the Nymphs; Taylor on the Wanderings of Ulysses. 978-1-898910-01-5

3 Collected Writings of Plotinus

Twenty-seven treatises being all the writings of Plotinus translated by Taylor. 978-1-898910-02-2

4 Writings on the Gods & the World

Sallust On the Gods & the World; Sentences of Demophilus; Ocellus on the Nature of the Universe; Taurus and Proclus on the Eternity of the World; Maternus on the Thema Mundi; The Emperor Julian's Orations to the Mother of Gods and to the Sovereign Sun; Synesius on Providence; Taylor's essays on the Mythology and the Theology of the Greeks. 978-1-898910-03-9

5 Hymns and Initiations

The Hymns of Orpheus together with all the published hymns translated or written by Taylor; Taylor's 1824 essay on Orpheus (together with the 1787 version). 978-1-898910-04-6

6 Dissertations of Maximus Tyrius

Forty-one treatises from the middle Platonist, and an essay from Taylor, The Triumph of the Wise Man over Fortune. 978-1-898910-05-3

7 Oracles and Mysteries

A Collection of Chaldean Oracles; Essays on the Eleusinian and Bacchic Mysteries; The History of the Restoration of the Platonic Theology; On the Immortality of the Soul. 978-1-898910-06-0

8 The Theology of Plato

The six books of Proclus on the Theology of Plato; to which is added a further book (by Taylor), replacing the original seventh book by Proclus, now lost. Extensive introduction and notes are also added. 978-1-898910-07-7

9 Works of Plato I

Taylor's General Introduction, Life of Plato, First Alcibiades (with much of Proclus' Commentary), Republic (with a section of Proclus' Commentary). 978-1-898910-08-4

10 Works of Plato II

Laws, Epinomis, Timæus (with notes from Proclus' Commentary), Critias. 978-1-898910-09-1

11 Works of Plato III

Parmenides (with a large part of Proclus' Commentary), Sophista, Phædrus (with notes from Hermias' Commentary), Greater Hippias, Banquet. 978-1-898910-10-7

12 Works of Plato IV

Theætetus, Politicus, Minos, Apology of Socrates, Crito, Phædo (with notes from the Commentaries of Damascius and Olympiodorus), Gorgias (with notes from the Commentary of Olympiodorus), Philebus (with notes from the Commentary of Olympiodorus), Second Alcibiades. 978-1-898910-11-4

13 Works of Plato V

Euthyphro, Meno, Protagoras, Theages, Laches, Lysis, Charmides, Lesser Hippias, Euthydemus, Hipparchus, Rivals, Menexenus, Clitopho, Io, Cratylus (together with virtually the whole of Proclus' Scholia), Epistles. An index to the extensive notes Taylor added to his five volumes of Plato. 978-1-898910-12-1

14 Apuleius' Golden Ass & Other Philosophical Writings

The Golden Ass (or Metamorphosis); On the Dæmon of Socrates; On the Philosophy of Plato. 978-1-898910-13-8

15 & 16 Proclus' Commentary on the Timæus of Plato

The Five Books of this Commentary in two volumes, with additional notes and short index. 978-1-898910-14-5 and 978-1-898910-15-2

17 Iamblichus on the Mysteries and Life of Pythagoras

Iamblichus On the Mysteries of the Egyptians, Chaldeans & Assyrians; Iamblichus' Life of Pythagoras; Fragments of the Ethical Writings of Pythagoreans; Political Fragments of Archytas, Charondas and other Pythagoreans. 978-1-898910-16-9

18 Essays and Fragments of Proclus

Providence, Fate and That Which is Within our Power; Ten Doubts concerning Providence; The Subsistence of Evil; The Life of Proclus; Fragments of Proclus' Writings. 978-1-898910-17-6

19 The Works of Aristotle I

The Physics, together with much of Simplicius' Commentary. A Glossary of Greek terms used by Aristotle. 978-1-898910-18-3

20 The Works of Aristotle II

The Organon: The Categories, On Interpretation, The Prior Analytics; The Posterior Analytics, The Topics, The Sophistical Elenchus; with extensive notes from the commentaries of Porphyry, Simplicius and Ammonius. 978-1-898910-19-0

21 The Works of Aristotle III

Great Ethics, Eudemian Ethics; Politics; Economics. 978-1-898910-20-6

22 The Works of Aristotle IV

Rhetorics; Nicomachean Ethics; Poetics. 978-1-898910-21-3

23 The Works of Aristotle V

The Metaphysics with notes from the Commentaries of Alexander Aphrodisiensis and Syrianus; Against the Dogmas of Xenophanes, Zeno and Gorgias; Mechanical Problems; On the World; On Virtues and Vices; On Audibles. 978-1-898910-22-0

24 The Works of Aristotle VI

On the Soul (with much of the Commentary of Simplicius); On Sense and Sensibles; On Memory and Reminiscence; On Sleep and Wakefulness; On Dreams; On Divination by Sleep; On the Common Motions of Animals; On the Generation of Animals; On Length and Shortness of Life; On Youth and Old Age, Life and Death; On Respiration. 978-1-898910-23-7

The Music of Philosophy Series

A Casting of Light by the Platonic Tradition 978-1-898910-57-2

The Song of Proclus   978-1-898910-62-6

The Chant of Plotinus   978-1-898910-65-7

The Music of Plato   978-1-898910-67-1

The Hymn of Thomas Taylor   978-1-898910-68-1

A Flight of Souls   978-1-891910-69-5

Students' Edition Paperbacks

The Sophist
Trans. Thomas Taylor. Includes extensive notes and introductory essays.

978-1-898910-93-0

The Symposium of Plato
Trans. Floyer Sydenham & Thomas Taylor. Includes Plotinus' *On Love* (En III, 5), and introductory essays.

978-1-898910-97-8

Know Thyself – The First Alcibiades & Commentary
Trans. Floyer Sydenham & Thomas Taylor. With introductory essays.

978-1-898910-96-1

Beyond the Shadows - The Metaphysics of the Platonic Tradition
Guy Wyndham-Jones and Tim Addey   978-1-898910-95-4

The Unfolding Wings - The Way of Perfection in the Platonic Tradition
Tim Addey   978-1-898910-94-7

The Meno
Trans. Sydenham & Taylor. With introductory essays

978-1-898910-92-3

Other titles available from
the Prometheus Trust

Philosophy as a Rite of Rebirth – From Ancient Egypt to
Neoplatonism
Algis Uždavinys   978-1-898910-35-0

The Orphic Poems
M L West   978-1-898910-84-8

Collected Works of Thomas Moore-Johnson   978-1-898910-82-4

The Philosophy of Proclus – the Final Phase of Ancient
Thought
L J Rosán   978 1 898910-44-2

Platonism and the World Crisis
John M Dillon, Brendan O'Byrne & Tim Addey   978-1-898910-55-8

Towards the Noosphere – Futures Singular and Plural
John M Dillon and Stephen R L Clark   978-1-898910-60-2

The Seven Myths of the Soul
Tim Addey   978-1-898910-37-4

Release Thyself – Three Philosophic Dialogues
Guy Wyndham-Jones   978-1-898910-56-5

Song of the Solipsistic One
Deepa Majumdar   978-1-898910-63-3

Selections from the Prometheus Trust Conferences 2006-2010
                                                978-1-898910-66-4

An Index to Plato - A Subject Index using Stephanus
pagination   978-1-898910-34-3

For further details please visit the Prometheus Trust website at:

www.prometheustrust.co.uk